# Feel Better in Five Minutes

## Amanda Hainline

Published by
Hybrid Global Publishing
301 E 57th Street
4th Floor
New York, NY 10022

Manufactured in the United States of America.

Hainline, Amanda
*Feel Better in Five Minutes: An Empowering Guide to Gain Control of Your Emotions*
  LCCN: 2021904886
  ISBN:  978-1-951943-61-5
  eBook: 978-1-951943-62-2

Cover design by: Natasha Clawson
Copyediting by: Lara Kennedy
Interior design by: Suba Murugan
Author photo by: Angela Doran Photography
Photos in Book Interior by: Tiara Baylor

amandahainline.com

# Contents

# From Hot Mess Mom to Emotional Freedom

As I approached the school, I was still groggy from my nap. I walked toward the doors with an unfamiliar heaviness. Each step brought on more anxiety. Thoughts barged into my head: "I have to take the kids to swim practice, first baseball, then I have to make dinner, what about homework? I have to finish making that costume tonight." It was like I had ten voices in my head at once. And none of them were mine. Uncontrollable waves of emotion washed over me and blurred together with each set of thoughts: stress, anger, resentment, frustration, depression, excitement. And loud. Everything was so loud. By the time I got inside the school, it was so intense that I had to back against the wall and breathe. I closed my eyes tight and patted the wall behind me. *Everything's okay. Everything's okay.* Even though I had absolutely no idea what was happening to me, all I could do was breathe. And wait.

The instant my kids rounded the corner, I grabbed their hands and got outside as quickly as I could. I wanted to just run, to get away from everyone. We somehow tumbled into the car. I was shaking and crying. My whole body felt exposed and raw. I just wanted to claw a hole in the ground and bury myself until it was all over. Whatever had happened to me the day before had to be fixed, but I had absolutely no idea how. The only choice I had was to return to where it all began.

It started with me just trying to feel better. Depression and apathy had a grip on me that I just couldn't shake. I would get frazzled at the tiniest of things, and everyday tasks felt like mountains rather than molehills. A friend had recommended an energy healer as something to try. I had no idea what that is, but why not? I had tried everything else, short of getting on medication.

When I got to the energy healer's office, I was led into a room and asked to lie on a massage table. The woman flicked my wrist around and seemed to somehow be getting information from my body. She tapped on my head and my heart, telling me that she was releasing energy that wanted to come out. I felt a little light-headed after the session, but I was more relaxed than I had been in a long time. The next day, I felt amazing. I found myself smiling and laughing. The little things didn't get to me, and I was just generally happier. This might be the answer, I thought. I might have finally found something that could help.

And I reasoned that if one session was good, two is better, right?

At my second appointment, I lay down on the table just like the first time, but after a couple of minutes, she told me that all of my chakras wanted to open at once.

I asked, "What's a chakra?"

"They're just energy centers that run down the middle of your body."

*Umm, okay.* I had no idea what she was talking about.

She started to tap on my head and heart, just like my first visit. Suddenly the most intense fear consumed me. Complete and utter terror slammed into me from every side. I started screaming. My body felt like I was burning from the inside out. Every muscle tensed. I felt like I was being electrocuted. After what seemed like an eternity, my body collapsed onto the table. I just looked at her in complete confusion.

"What happened?" I said.

She just looked at me and said, "All of your chakras opened at once."

*That* didn't really help. I didn't even know what one was, let alone understand what had just happened.

She instructed me to go outside and walk around in the grass barefoot for a few minutes before driving my car. I did as instructed, went home, and went straight to bed. I figured I would feel better in the morning. But I didn't. I was weepy, and my body felt extremely heavy. I couldn't think straight. My mind was in a complete fog. I switched on my mom-autopilot and hustled my kids to school just in time. Back home, I crawled in bed and cried myself to sleep. I set the alarm for the last possible minute before I had to head out to retrieve them again. And that's where this story starts, on that long walk into the boys' elementary school when I finally woke up to the realization my life would never be the same.

At the time, no one knew what had happened to me or what it was called, including the healers that I was going to for help. It wasn't until years later that I happened across the answer on a completely unrelated Google search. There it was: every symptom and experience I'd had, laid out in bullet points. I had experienced a spontaneous kundalini awakening. Apparently, those aren't super common in the United States but are more commonplace in India. There, they understand these experiences and how to help one navigate them. All I had was Google and a few healers that didn't understand what had happened to me either.

I didn't realize before all of this happened how much I had suppressed my emotions over the years. But when I had my spontaneous kundalini awakening, everything that I'd suppressed, buried, and stuffed way down deep came to the surface, and I had no choice but to release it. I relived the death of every pet that I ever had. Traumas from when I was two, three, four, five years old replayed in front of my eyes so vividly, instantaneously, and almost simultaneously. I was back in the pain and terror again. The memories barraged my every sense. I had no ability to control them. And they continued. The most innocuous things, like someone saying a specific phrase, a loud noise like glass breaking, or bumping my head on a cabinet, could trigger a twenty-minute uncontrollable spiral, where I had to lock myself in my room until it was over. Things went on this way intensely for six months. I was terrified. Would I ever be able to regain control?

I continued to go to healers. I didn't know what else to do. It was the only lifeline I had. Each one had small tips on how to release these emotions that were coming to the surface. The problem was, I found myself not only dealing with my own emotional states but the emotional states of anyone else that I was around. Whether that was my family or people at the grocery store or my children's school, I would soak up whatever emotions they had going on like a sponge: anxiety, fear, depression, anger, or excitement. It didn't matter. I was taking everything on involuntarily as my own. I stayed home as much as possible, and when I did have to get out in the world, I would return home and have to purge all the energy that I had picked up from other people.

It was exhausting. But something slowly started to happen. As I let go of more and more of my own emotions, I became more stable. I could focus again. My crying spirals became less and less frequent. Best of all, I could reengage with the world again without taking on the energy of everyone else around me as often, but when I did, I developed a new set of tools for releasing emotions so that they didn't weigh me down.

I learned my **emotions could be dealt with fairly easily most of the time. There were actual techniques to release them. And by addressing my emotions effectively, I felt better and better, faster and faster, each day.** Furthermore, the emotional states of others affected me less.

Over the past fifteen years, I have fine-tuned these methods and taught them to countless clients, from CEOs to preschoolers.

All of us deal with emotions. It's part of what makes us human. It is what binds our relationships and can also be what tears them apart. They define how we show up in the world and how we interact with others in personal and professional relationships and, most importantly, how we show up in the relationship with ourselves.

Unfortunately, society really doesn't teach us how to deal with emotions. We're taught to either stuff them down and not express them or take a pill and make them go away. "Be happy. Get over it. So and so has it so much worse than you…" We've all heard this said to us or someone else. But what if there was a better way? What if you could actually learn to deal with your emotions in the moment and let them go, rather than stuff them down to blow up later or get physically ill from not expressing them at all?

Hey, let's be real. We all lead very busy lives. We really don't have time to think about our emotions in a deep and perplexing way, and most of us don't want to spend a lot of time there. That's why, in this book, I'm going to show you ways to feel better, to feel happy. The way you have been dealing with your emotions is not your fault. No one taught you how or why you feel the way that you do, much less how to control or process it. So we're going to talk about that at the beginning of the book, laying a foundation for you to understand emotions in a new way: to separate who you are from your emotional states, doing away with the recurring script in your head that begins with, "What is wrong with me?" **Spoiler alert:** The answer is nothing, and I'll explain why.

As we go through each chapter, I'll share client stories (along with some of my own personal stories) with you of what they were going through at the time of their session and how these tools helped them to transform their lives, starting with the simple concept and then teaching you variations and refinements of the technique so that you can customize it to what works for you. And because I'm sort of an energetic "gearhead," I'm going to tell you WHY these techniques work on the energetic, mental, and physical levels of the body. In my opinion, it's fun to share this with you, AND if you know why something works, it becomes even more powerful and effective.

## Two Ways to Use This Book

This book is designed so that it can be used in two ways. First, it can be used for you to feel better quickly. If you just have a few minutes, flip to the end of each chapter, where you will find the "Feel Better Five," the five main ideas of the chapter, so you can get the gist of the chapter in a few seconds. This is followed by the chapter technique titled "Transform in Five," where you can get a summarized version of the technique for the chapter that takes five minutes or less. Each chapter also includes a chapter challenge to get you thinking about what you read and start relating it to your life.

Nervous before a meeting? Pull out the cool tricks you will learn in chapters 8 and 9 to go in confident and centered. Did you just open up an email that has you enraged right before you walk in the house to greet your family at the end of the day? Do a quick little bit of the skill you will pick up in chapter 7 so that you can greet them with a smiling face. We all need these types of in-the-moment life rafts. But the real magic happens if you use the book the *other* way. This requires a little more time, but the results you will have over the long term will be life-changing.

The techniques in this book are also designed for you to go deeper, to get to the really wounded things in you that you might not have been aware of. That is the reason for the assessment in chapter 3 and also the "Transform in Ten" sections at the end of some of the chapters. The assessment's purpose is to help you shed a light on areas of your life that you struggle with and help you to understand why. Then, as you gain that awareness through the assessment and "Feel Better in Ten" techniques, you can start to heal those energetic imprints in your energy system so you can be a better version of yourself than you ever thought possible. It can actually change your life. You will have fewer reactive moments, your moods will be more level, your relationships will improve, and you will be happier. For some, this takes very little time. For others, it may take longer, but this book's bigger goal is to help you really and truly shift your life for good.

So, turn the page. I can't wait to begin this journey with you. I'm going to teach you how to finally feel better, in *just five minutes*.

# CHAPTER 1

---

# Emotions Are Not Who You Are

 "Hello?" I eagerly answered the phone. Claire, a girl who I had been looking forward to working with, was on the other end of the line.

"Hello." I was met with a lackluster voice. Her energy felt heavy to me and defeated.

"How are you today?" I said, trying to pep it up a bit.

"Mmm. Okay…"

I was going to have to take a new approach, or this would be a very short session. Knowing what I knew about her, I didn't take it personally. She had been through a lot in recent years and struggled with stress, anxiety, and depression. Some of her family dynamics had aspects that were difficult for her to handle. Her personality was to take on everything around her and try to fix it herself, but she was a teen. She should be worrying about things like friends, school dances, and social media, not the family dynamics in her life she couldn't control.

I gently started to explore with her what was going on in her life, leaving her lots of room to talk and think things through. When I asked her what her biggest issue was, she simply said, "I'm stressed. All the time. I can't ever get rid of it."

She had been going to a counselor, whom she had sought out herself with her parents' support, and it was helping some, but she was still struggling to get to the bottom of things. Since her stress load was so high all the time, it made everything else difficult. She had very little patience with her family, and her advanced schoolwork could quickly overwhelm her. The cup was always full, and not in a good way. As we continued to talk, she kept coming back to the same point. "I'm just stressed," she would say. As if to say, "That's just me. That's who I AM."

There was a defeated acceptance in that response, and it was then that I realized where we needed to start.

## Emotions Are What Get Our Attention First

We needed to really start with the basics. And that is where this book begins. The basics—but in this case, that means starting in the middle. Confused?? Let me explain...

I'm sure by now, somewhere, somehow, you have heard the phrase "body, mind, spirit." Whether it's a yoga studio slogan or the adage on your favorite shampoo bottle, it's kind of everywhere. But seriously, what does it mean, anyway?

Honestly, I used to roll my eyes at this slogan. It's overused. For everything. It's been a catchall for just about every self-help book out there in the last few years, and honestly, I cringe to use it myself. So why am I, then? It's familiar to you. You have at least a vague idea of the concept, so it's the easiest place to start. But instead of the traditional way of looking at it, let's say it's a sandwich. The top bread is the body, it's what you see first; the bottom bread is the spirit. which is the foundation for everything else; and the middle? The middle of the sandwich is where the work starts. The juicy stuff. When is the last time you said, "That was the best bread I ever had on a sandwich"? Nah—you talk about what's in the middle, don't you? Who doesn't? So let's start with the mind (the middle), or in the case of this book, the emotions.

Emotions are what tend to get our attention first. We may feel anxiety, stress, depression, or anger. Sometimes it's manageable, and sometimes it's not, but emotions can't really be ignored for very long before they start to take their toll on our physical body. We lose sleep, eat too little or too much food, or withdraw or lash out. Concentration and relationships suffer, and if we let it go too far, it can lead to physical ailments and disease.

## Shifting Our Fundamental Emotional State Lies in Our Spirit

So how do we deal with shifting our undesired emotional states? Do we just let them pass? Take a couple of deep breaths and hope it blows over? Yeah, you can do that, and sometimes it's enough. For now. But what happens when those states don't change? What happens when we are experiencing the same emotions over and over again and can't get a grip on them? We have to dig deeper.

While the emotions are what get our attention, the actual key to shifting these states lies in a different layer of the sandwich altogether. The spirit, or the bottom piece of bread. It's the root, or foundation, of everything. And by this I don't mean religion or any other spiritual practice. The secret sauce to releasing and permanently shifting our fundamental emotional states lies in our spirit, or human energy system. What?

Bear with me here. This is my jam. I'm not going to go off on too deep of a tangent, but if we were having a conversation in person, I SO would. While the emotions are what call our attention to something being "amiss," the human energy system is where the heart of the issue lies.

## Disruptions in the Energy System Cause Disruptions in the Mind and Physical Body

For the last fifteen years, I have been working with my clients' energy systems, or in our sandwich analogy, the spirit, to shift their lives. During this time, I have come to understand at a deep level how all of the layers of *us* are connected and affect each other. It really was trial by fire, starting with my own experiences and building from there. Before all of that happened I didn't even have an understanding that my energy system existed, let alone how to work with it and that it was the key to healing the rest of my life.

I'm going to share a little more of my story here so you get a better picture of how I came to this work and why I am so passionate about helping others understand their energy system is the foundation for healing literally everything in their life. My story is in short, a little crazy but the extreme nature of it taught me so much about the world we can't see that affects us so deeply.

If you read the introduction to this book (if you didn't do it yet, check it out… this next part will make more sense), you know a little about me already. You know that I came to this work through dealing with my own stuff, namely, after a spontaneous kundalini awakening. That's basically a fancy spiritual term that means my human energy system (chakras and aura) opened up, in my case all at once, and left me exposed to all of the energy around me. I talk about how I dealt with my emotional states and the emotions of others I could suddenly feel. I talk about how during this time I went to healers to get a grip on it all. All of that is true. But I left something kind of *big* out of that version of the story. The kundalini awakening did something else. It left me with the ability to communicate with the spirit world, talk to angels and spirit guides, see the past and the future, and see deep into people's energy systems. Quite an instant flip of the switch into complete chaos. It took a little while to start understanding what I was seeing, feeling, and experiencing.

I didn't come to that understanding on my own, though. About six months after I had this awakening experience, I felt pretty good. I was able to deal with my new reality, and my life started functioning again. And that's when *they showed up*. Three giant angels walked into my living room and told me they were going to teach me how to heal people, and while I resisted at first (*Have you seen my life??* I thought), they have been my teachers, and I have worked on countless clients with their assistance, yielding profound results. It's been an awesome journey, and I couldn't really go any further in this book without sharing that with you. The client stories would make a lot less sense to you if you didn't know that tidbit.

## What Is a Spiritual Kundalini Awakening

We'll start off by explaining what kundalini is. Kundalini is a life-force energy that is coiled and lies dormant like a snake at the base of the spine. Everyone has it. In a normal spiritual awakening, this energy is active, helping the person to move closer to remembering who they are as a soul. This is a journey that can take a lifetime, and while it can have rough spots mentally and energetically, it smooths back out over the course of a day or two as emotions and energetic congestion are released to raise that person's vibrational state.

In the case of a kundalini awakening or rising, something different happens. That "snake" of life-force energy rises up through the main energy channel that runs up the center of the body. If a full kundalini rising or awakening occurs, that energy travels from the base of the spine until it reaches the crown chakra and wraps around to the forehead. If it gets that far, the awakening is permanent.

There are practices in yoga specifically designed for raising the kundalini, and it is cautioned that it can be very dangerous to do this without years of meditation and mindfulness practice, as well as a teacher to help facilitate the journey after it occurs. In a tiny number of people who have no knowledge or preparation, this can spontaneously occur. The spiritual awakening that other people are experiencing in a lifetime happens in a kundalini awakening in an instant and can be accompanied by psychic powers and abilities. If this happens, it can destroy the person's life because they have no understanding of what is happening to them. They have no skills for dealing with the emotional and energetic overload that occurs in their bodies. All of their "demons," or shadow side, come up at once. They relive their traumas repeatedly, and reality can get distorted. They often have mental breakdowns and are unable to control their emotions. It is not uncommon for them to end up in mental hospitals diagnosed with some type of psychosis such as schizophrenia or bipolar disorder. This is what happened to me. I was lucky enough to move through it without having to be committed or diagnosed, but I was left with psychic and healing abilities that are permanent. This is what allows me to have unique insight and do the work that I do today. It's what enabled me to write this book for you.

All of that to say, part of what I want you to get out of this chapter is that EVERYONE has a human energy system. There isn't a person on this planet without one. While many people think of this as a "woo-woo" concept, it's been a known fact of cultures such as China and India for thousands of years. The ancient medical systems of Traditional Chinese Medicine and Ayurveda are based on it. While they have their differences, their core premise is the same: disruptions in the energy system cause disruptions in the mind and physical body. That is also the big idea of this book. Along with the fact that you can change and heal your energy system with the techniques you are about to learn.

## The Human Energy System Is Invisible

Your energy system consists of mainly your aura (outer energy field), chakras (spinning discs of energy down the middle of your body), and meridians (channels of energy that run all over your body—think electric wires).

I'm not going to go too deep into their individual functions, but this system is no different than your circulatory system, your nervous system, or your digestive system. It's there, even though you can't see it. Just like your emotions, it exists. Only you don't hear anyone saying, "My chakra hurts" or "My aura is heavy today." No one really thinks about having an energy system, and they think even less about it being out of whack. But that is where the emotions come in. It's what we notice when something isn't right, but in order to shift it, we need to look in the right place. The bottom piece of bread. The spirit, or human energy system.

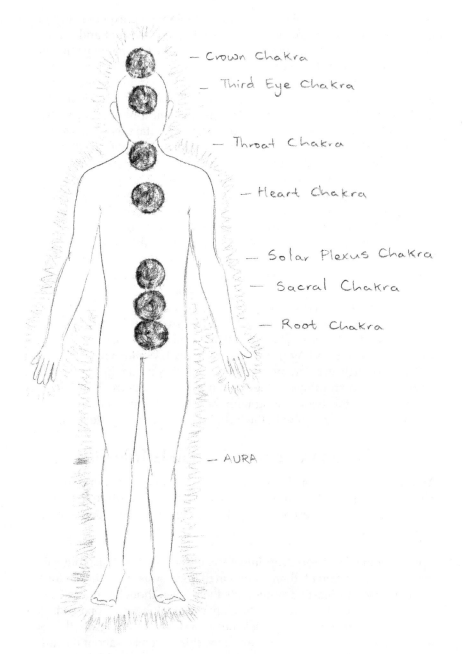

— Crown Chakra

— Third Eye Chakra

— Throat Chakra

— Heart Chakra

— Solar Plexus Chakra

— Sacral Chakra

— Root Chakra

— AURA

*Picture of Aura and Chakras*

# Emotions Are an Experience, Not Our Identity

So that is where we will revisit the beginning of our story. Claire's simple statement, "I'm stressed." What does this statement actually say? Let's break it down into two things: what we mean and what we are actually saying.

What we mean is that we are experiencing a state of stress, or we feel stressed. The problem is that that is not what we are actually saying. We are saying, "I am stressed." We are using an "I am" statement to express something that we are experiencing, meaning we are verbally identifying the emotion as WHO WE ARE versus something we are experiencing. Let me explain why this is a big deal. Our body, mind, and energy systems are very literal and are intricately intertwined. The statement *I am stressed* tells our being that we actually ARE that emotional state rather than it being separate from us. That may not seem like a big deal, but the difference is huge. If we ARE stress, how do we ever release this emotion? How is it possible to release WHO WE ARE from ourselves? It's not.

Every time we use an I AM statement to describe emotions (whether they are positive or negative), this is what happens: our energy system takes that belief and string of emotional energy and weaves that emotion deep into our being. It's like winding a string really tight around something, and the more we do it, the more tangled it gets. Have you ever tried to untangle a ball of string or a cell phone cord? How frustrating is that? Now what if you have two or three cords tangled together? What if you are regularly saying, "I'm stressed," "I'm anxious," "I'm angry," "I'm depressed," or "I'm sick"? These negatively charged emotions and beliefs get harder and harder to untangle and separate from who you are.

Now, this is not to say these emotions aren't valid. All emotions are. It's just that when we are trying to release them, if they are embedded into our energy system and mind with I AM statements, our minds say, "I can't let that go. It's who I am. If I do that, I will lose myself." **Using "I AM" statements for our emotions cause them to become our identity.** This is what makes it so hard to let go of them and to fundamentally shift the way we think and feel.

**That is why it is only when we separate our identity from our emotions that healing can begin.** When we realize that emotions are just meant for us to have an awareness of what is going on more deeply, versus it being who we are as a person, we can start to take control of the surface emotions and heal the deep places within us that are wounded, causing profound fundamental shifts to occur. Our lives change. We change.

## Technique 1.1. Your I AM Statements

1. What I AM statement(s) do you use for negatively charged emotions on a regular basis?
2. Close your eyes and say that statement now.
3. How does it feel?
4. Now, change the statement to *I am experiencing (emotion)*.
5. How does it feel to hold it separate from who you are? (If you can't tell a difference yet, that's okay!)
6. Practice doing this daily out loud when you feel it and even to yourself in your mind.
7. See how often you go to the I AM statement and have to redirect your thoughts.

## There Is Nothing Wrong with You

And that is where I started with Claire. Once I explained she was not her emotions and her emotions were a result of other deeper things that could be healed *and* there was nothing wrong with *HER*, she began to relax. We could then begin to address her emotional states as separate from her as a person.

She was able to begin releasing her emotions through some of the techniques you will find in this book. Even several weeks after her energy work session, Claire stated she had consistently been using the tools that she learned and reported that she felt more relaxed, was sleeping better, and was happier overall. Things just weren't bothering her like they did before, and when they did, now she had tools she could use to take care of emotions in the moment or dig deep when she had more time.

## Chapter Challenge

What I AM statements do you use for negatively charged emotions on a regular basis?

Do these statements always feel true to you, or only sometimes?

How do others react when you say these statements?

When you hear other people say similar statements about themselves, do they strike you as true about that person?

## Feel Better Five

- Emotions are the first place we are most likely to notice that things are amiss in our lives.
- In order to shift our fundamental emotional state, we have to look to our energy system.
- Disruptions in the energy system cause disruptions in the mind and physical body.
- Emotions are meant to be experienced, not taken on as part of who we are.
- There is nothing wrong with you. You simply have to address your emotional states to change and heal.

## Transform in Five

Technique 1.1. Your I AM Statements

1. What I AM statement(s) do you use for negatively charged emotions on a regular basis?
2. Close your eyes and say that statement now.
3. How does it feel?
4. Now, change the statement to *I am experiencing (emotion)*.
5. How does it feel to hold it separate from who you are? (If you can't tell a difference yet, that's okay!)
6. Practice doing this daily out loud when you feel it and even to yourself in your mind.
7. See how often you go to the I AM statement and have to redirect your thoughts.

Note: Don't exhaust yourself! This technique is just meant to make you aware of some of your inner and outer dialogue.

Congratulations! This technique is your first step to *feeling better in five minutes*.

In chapter 2, you'll learn to look at your emotions in a whole new way that will empower you. It helps you not be so hard on yourself. So, get excited! You are about to discover yourself for the very first time and truly be able to shift your life for the better.

# Trauma Isn't Forever

 **B**y the time Rachel came to see me, she was at her wits' end. She had a recurring nightmare that plagued her almost every night. She hardly slept. She had a customer service job that was very difficult for her. Her soft nature led to people yelling at her often when they didn't like what she had to say. Her mother and sister lived with her, and both of them refused to pay rent or get jobs but were happy to eat the food she would buy. They would borrow her car without asking.

One time when Rachel was out of town, her sister sold Rachel's chihuahua because she wouldn't give her sister money to go to a concert. Rachel had to track her dog down and retrieve it from three hundred miles away.

I asked her when the nightmares had started, and she stated it was after she was raped at the age of sixteen. She knew who had done it and so did her family, but because the boy was from a prominent family in town who were friends of her parents, it was swept under the rug. She was forbidden to talk about it, and her parents would not allow her to go to counseling.

In her early twenties, she had turned to drugs and alcohol to ease her pain. This only made the nightmares worse. She had been clean for six years when we met, but her life was still painful everywhere she turned. She looked like a shell of a person.

## Deep Healing Is Possible with a New Approach

Rachel is a classic example of what happens when we are unable to process and release traumatic events. These events take on a life of their own and start to define who we are as a person. Even though it's a false belief, over time it becomes very real. One's whole life can be based on it.

Most people do things similar to what Rachel did. They try to numb the pain somehow, or they may seek out counseling, which unfortunately she was unable to do. And counseling can help. It is one way of addressing life traumas. But what happens when talking it out doesn't work? Many people have difficulty verbally expressing what has happened to them and therefore have difficulty dealing with the emotional weight of their ordeal. They may mentally skirt the issue and are never able to address the heart of the matter and, therefore, never heal to the level that they deserve.

When we create a safe space for healing that gently moves the mental blocks aside to get to the source of the emotional turmoil, we can reach a level of healing that was never before possible.

While there are many models to explain how trauma affects the body and mind and even changes the chemical makeup of the brain, I am not going to go into this here. There is a lot of science to back up these methods and models, and many practitioners have used them, with varying levels of success.

For the sake of this book, we are going to approach this with a different perspective, an energetic perspective that will help you understand how traumas affect us long-term and how we can go about shifting the emotional states that they trigger within us to help us change our lives for good.

## Emotions Fall into Two General Categories

When we talk about emotions, it can seem like an abstract concept that is hard to nail down, but the goal is to give you a way to frame them so you can have a concept to work with. Emotions fall into two general buckets, what humans view as "good" and "bad" emotions: ones we want to experience and those we would rather not. In energetic terms, these fall into the two categories of higher-vibration and lower-vibration emotions. Higher-vibration emotions can actually make our energy system work correctly and *better*. Everything flows well when these are present in your body. They enhance who we are and bring out the best in us, our highest selves. A few examples would be joy, happiness, peace, and love. All the feel-good stuff. These form positive energetic imprints as they are experienced in our lives and enhance our energy system and quality of life.

The second bucket of emotions is the lower-vibration emotions. These are emotions that are just no fun to experience, such as fear, anger, anxiousness, and sadness. They mostly happen as a result of an external experience in our lives causing a negative effect. These emotions restrict our energy systems and our lives and, if not released, can impact our physical health. Releasing these emotions is the focus of this book.

## The Conscious Mind versus the Subconscious Mind

When we talk about the conscious versus the subconscious, it's really pretty simple. The conscious mind holds those parts of our memories, belief systems, and personality that we are aware of—the stuff we remember. The subconscious mind holds everything else. The kicker is, the conscious mind only makes up about 10 percent of your total brain function, while the subconscious mind makes up about 90 percent. That means your awareness of what drives you to make everyday decisions, what you believe about your life, your emotional states, success, and failure are largely driven by your subconscious mind.

So, why is this a big deal? Because the lack of awareness for what is driving us actually holds us back. If you don't have an awareness of why you are functioning the way you are, it's pretty hard to change those behaviors and beliefs. You are operating in the dark, so to speak. It's super frustrating when you can't get a grip on why you are experiencing anxiety, depression, or some other low-vibration emotion or belief.

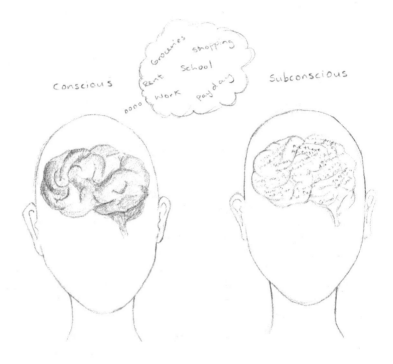

The good thing is, there is a way to change this. In order to process what is in the subconscious mind, you have to first move it to the conscious mind to be processed. It's like shining a light in the dark to see what is going bump in the night.

By working with your human energy system (and filling out the assessment in the next chapter), you can move these things from your subconscious mind to your conscious mind so that you can process and release them. The great thing is, it doesn't require you to actively remember anything, although memories can be triggered by doing this.

Be gentle with yourself in this process, especially if you know of, but don't remember, traumas in your past. These events are stored collectively in the subconscious and conscious mind, physical body, and human energy system. Processing subconscious events can induce physical and emotional reactions; cause vivid, strange, or disturbing dreams; or temporarily increase current emotional states. This does not always occur, but it's good to be aware of how your body and mind might process these events. Processing can sometimes feel like the equivalent of digesting a bad meal. It's uncomfortable, but you will have it out of your system soon.

## Traumas Freeze Parts of Us in Time

When we experience a traumatic event, our energy system does something very interesting. It takes a snapshot of the event in our energy system and arrests our development in regard to that trauma, storing that energy signature somewhere inside of us. It's what we call a *trauma imprint*. For example, let's take the simple case of Sam.

When Sam was three years old, he visited the home of a neighbor who had a large dog that was about the same size as him. The dog and Sam had never met before. When the dog saw Sam, he jumped on him, knocking him over. The dog stood over Sam and licked his face. Even though the dog had no ill intent toward Sam, Sam felt powerless to escape the dog. Sam's perception of the event was that dogs, especially large dogs, made him feel powerless and would attack him.

As a result of this encounter, Sam was understandably traumatized by the event. His energy system took a snapshot of the event from his perspective. This snapshot included the physical, emotional, and energetic components of the event, which made for a powerful memory he would not soon forget. His emotional and mental maturity at that point in his life was also frozen in time by the event.

As a result, every time after that event, when Sam would see a large dog, his energy system would pull up that snapshot and overlay it onto the possible experience he could have with this new experience, creating a stress response in his body. His mental and emotional maturity would revert back to that moment as well, so as Sam grew into adulthood, he couldn't help but react as if he were three years old when a large dog approached him.

This embarrassed Sam a great deal, and his friends teased him for it. They would say things like, "Don't be such a baby!" or "Why do you always freak out? It's not going to hurt you!" But Sam couldn't help it. His mind reverted to that of a scared little three-year-old boy in that moment, and he had no control over it. He *was* a baby at that moment.

## Traumatic Energetic Imprint Process

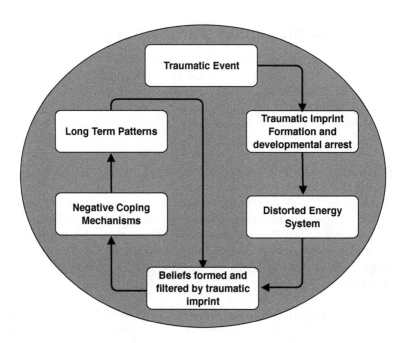

The traumatic energetic imprint process occurs rather quickly, but its effects can last a lifetime if not addressed. The imprint process begins with the occurrence of the traumatic event. The imprint contains all of the energy of the event, including any sensations from the five senses (sight, sound, smell, taste, and touch) and emotions, as well as causing a developmental arrest in regard to the trauma. The imprint changes the energy system wherever it is stored, distorting it, causing it to not function properly. As a result of the imprint, beliefs form that are filtered by the imprint. These beliefs are crafted from the mental capacity the person had at the particular age at which the trauma occurred. Negative coping mechanisms and behaviors are formed from these beliefs, manifesting, in basic terms, as either a fight or a flight response, depending on the individual. These coping mechanisms, such as withdrawing, lashing out, or becoming passive-aggressive, for example, can become elements of long-term patterns when energy or situations similar to the traumatic imprint are experienced. After these patterns form, the person is likely to experience the patterns over and over again, reinforcing these filtered beliefs and coping mechanisms.

*It is important to understand that these traumatic imprints can occur as early as in utero or before we have limited active memory of the event (0–4 years). Our subconscious stores all of it, and things can be actively affecting our lives without us realizing it.*

To address this trauma with Sam, we went through some of the techniques in this book to help Sam release the energy around this traumatic event. His energy system had to "grow up" in that particular area, being his perception of and behavior around large dogs. By releasing the highly charged emotions around this event, his energy system could let go of and discharge all of the scary feelings of that moment. The snapshot or traumatic imprint that had kept him stuck mentally as a three-year-old in that moment became merely a memory versus something that caused him to react in fear. His rational adult mind was then able to process his interaction with dogs versus reverting back to his limited three-year-old perspective.

He reported that the next time he saw a large dog, he was surprised he reacted "much better" and was even able to pet it. When he did feel some anxiety about the dog come up, he was able to let it go in the moment using tools he had learned in our session.

Sam is a great example of how traumas can be discharged using simple techniques and not only dissolve a fear but shift a fundamental perspective about dogs, something most of us take for granted.

He's even talking about getting a dog. A big one.

## Negative Coping Mechanisms

**Coping mechanisms** are the strategies people use when a traumatic imprint is activated in stressful or traumatic situations to help manage painful or difficult emotions. They can help people adjust to stressful events while helping them maintain their emotional well-being.

But what about when the coping mechanism is detrimental to the person's well-being or relationships? These are called **negative coping mechanisms**. These reactions to a situation or person as a result of an imprint being activated can take many forms, such as mental or physical withdrawal, excessive verbal expression, putting off a prickly vibe, picking a verbal or physical battle, overreaching persuasiveness, having to be "right," projecting, rejecting others, or freezing.

## Nontraumatic Events Can Cause Limitations Too

But what if you can't recall having anything traumatic happen to you and you still have recurring patterns, negative events, or emotions in your life you can't explain? Yep, that happens too.

Take the case of Lisa. She had experienced many relationships that didn't go her way. She would fall head over heels, romanticizing about this "perfect guy" she had found, only to become completely disenchanted by the smallest things, causing her to abandon the relationship. Or in contrast, she would pick men that she disliked from the beginning and try to change them.

Lisa didn't understand why this kept happening, and it caused her a great deal of emotional stress.

When we had our session, I could energetically see the pattern had something to do with her father. It wasn't an abusive pattern at all, which I often see with women. It was the contrary. She had a great relationship with her father, but he would often say something to her to try and make her feel special that created a negative belief pattern in her, causing her to revert to a young child in relationships. He would say, "No boy is ever good enough for my little girl." There was obviously no ill intent here, but it created an energetic signature in her that acted like a traumatic imprint. When no trauma is present, as in Lisa's case, we call that a **verbal inhibitory imprint**. As a result, she was unable to show up as a full adult in a relationship. The belief caused an unhealthy energetic pattern that had to be shifted in order for her to create a mature adult relationship with rational adult thinking.

# Verbal Inhibitory Imprint Process

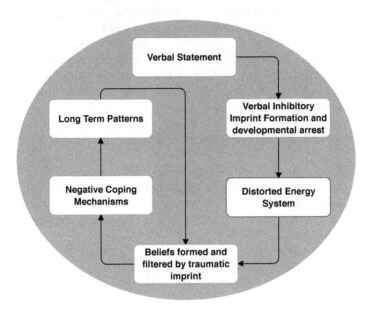

The verbal inhibitory imprint can be caused by hurtful statements or ones that are not ill-meaning. The process can occur quickly but often occurs over time, unless of course it is linked to a one-time traumatic event. Either way, its effects can last a lifetime if not addressed. The imprint process begins with the occurrence of the verbal statement. The imprint contains all of the energy of the moment, not just the verbal statement, including any sensations from the five senses (sight, sound, smell, taste, and touch) and emotions, as well as causing a developmental arrest in regard to the event. The imprint changes the energy system wherever it is stored, distorting it, causing it to not function properly. As a result of the imprint, beliefs that are filtered by the imprint form. These beliefs are crafted from the mental capacity the person has at the particular age at which the verbal statement occurred. If the statement or some semblance of the statement is made over and over again, multiple imprints can be created that are similar but contain the emotional maturity of each age when the statement was made. Often, though, by addressing the first occurrence energetically, the other imprints lessen their effectiveness or fall away altogether. This is called **addressing the root event**.

Negative coping mechanisms and behaviors are formed from the beliefs in the imprints, and the type of coping mechanism or behavior depends on the individual. These negative coping mechanisms can become elements of long-term patterns when energy or situations that activate the imprint are experienced. After these patterns form, the person is likely to experience the patterns over and over again, reinforcing these filtered beliefs and coping mechanisms.

*It is important to understand that these verbal inhibitory imprints can occur as early as in utero or before we have limited active memory of the event (0–4 years). Our subconscious stores all of it, and things can be actively affecting our lives without us realizing it.*

**Technique 2.1. Recognizing Your Tendencies and Habits**

1. Close your eyes and take some deep breaths as you think about all of the things that you might not like about your tendencies and habits.
2. Say, "I love myself and I understand I was doing the best I could at the time."
3. Open your mind up to the possibility that you can change these things, even if you have not been open to them before.
4. Allow yourself to see the links between your past and present, how things that have happened in your life have shaped you.
5. This will begin to help you make the connections to get you ready for the next chapter.

# Lisa's Recognition

Once Lisa was aware of this event being the reason for her failed relationships, she began to see the pattern. It was then that she started to shift her beliefs, using a variety of techniques from this book as well as a little energy work.

She was able to begin exploring relationships with her new adult perspective, and if she felt a glimmer of that old thought process come up, she now had tools to deal with it.

# Unlocking Emotions in Imprints Can Dramatically Shift Your Life

The approach with Lisa was straightforward and pretty easy to address. Rachel, on the other hand, was a more complicated case. Rachel had not only traumatic imprints but also traumatic verbal inhibitory imprints as well. She had varying levels of physical and verbal abuse she had endured over the years, and these imprints were weighing her down heavily. When verbal inhibitory imprints occur with malice and are accompanied by physical abuse, they can do heavy damage energetically, mentally, and psychologically, especially if they are repetitive. This was unfortunately the situation with Rachel. All of these things had to be addressed if Rachel was going to make a shift in her life.

She had used alcohol, drugs, and food to numb her pain of the root event. In addition, she had formed beliefs from her trauma that she was worthless and powerless, which allowed the recurring patterns of abuse from her mother and sister to occur. Her subconscious had formed nightmares, which was the initial reason for her visit, so that is where we started.

She told me it was always the same. A large black shadow figure was chasing her. It felt menacing and she was terrified of it. When I looked at her energy, I didn't see the disruption in her energy system I was expecting. All I saw was her. She was running from herself. Her inability to deal with her trauma and be supported by her family left her with the feeling that there was something wrong with her. She was trying to get away from herself, to separate from what she viewed was "bad" in her life. This event had created an inescapable nightmare.

We then addressed the abuse directly. We used some healing techniques and techniques to clear the traumatic imprint from her energy system. Next, we worked on the energy that her subconscious had created that was chasing her in her nightmares. We released the energy and emotions from the traumatic imprint. During the assessment, we found several traumatic imprints of abandonment that had been a theme throughout her life. We worked on healing all of the traumatic imprints that were linked to these, which in turn repaired the areas of the aura and chakras that were affected.

Rachel did require some energy work on her chakras, in addition to teaching her the techniques in this book, but giving her these tools to work on herself made her feel deeply empowered. She finally had a way to manage herself in difficult circumstances, and the techniques were a way for her to clear out any imprints she found over the long haul. After the session was over, Rachel felt relaxed and lighter. My spirit guides wanted me to see her back in a couple of weeks for another session.

When she returned, I almost didn't recognize her. She had gotten a promotion at work. She'd had a talk with her sister and told her she had to start paying rent or move out, so her sister left. Her mother was in the process of moving out as we spoke. She had lost eight pounds from not overeating anymore. Her nightmares were gone, and her skin was clearer than it had been in years. She had started meditating as well.

We did another session and released some more traumatic imprints. Her chakras were holding up pretty well, but we gave them a tune-up. I told her to just come back when she felt like she needed it. I never saw her again.

I spoke to Rachel a few months later and asked how she was doing. She told me she was doing really well. She had met someone, a great guy, and moved to New Mexico. She was getting married the following spring. Her new job paid more than she had been making, and she had room to move up.

# Chapter Challenge

Start thinking about what traumatic and verbal inhibitory imprints you might have in your energy system that are holding you back in your life. Make a couple of notes if you like.

After reading this chapter, how do you feel about yourself in regard to your tendencies and habits?

Are there things you do or say that you don't like?

Can you identify any of your negative coping mechanisms?

# Feel Better Five

- Traumatic and verbal inhibitory imprints form in our energy system from life events.
- These imprints affect how we function in life today.
- The imprints create a "snapshot" in our energy system that causes us to revert back to the age we were when the imprint occurred.
- We can learn to clear out these imprints so that the traumatic and verbal inhibitory imprints no longer limit our lives.
- Understanding how these imprints function helps us to understand ourselves better and to move from feeling powerless to feeling powerful.

# Transform in Five

Technique 2.1. Recognize Your Tendencies and Habits

1.  Close your eyes and take some deep breaths as you think about all of the things that you might not like about your tendencies and habits.
2.  Say, "I love myself and I understand I was doing the best I could at the time."
3.  Open your mind up to the possibility that you can change these things, even if you have not been open to them before.
4.  Allow yourself to see the links between your past and present, how things that have happened in your life have shaped you.
5.  This will begin to help you make the connections to get you ready for the next chapter.

In the next chapter, we dive in deep and explore what makes you tick. We do this with the Feel Better Assessment. It's important to fill it out, because it's going to give you a window into yourself that sets you up for success later in the book. The assessment is designed to help you understand where you are right now and where you want to ultimately be. This way, as you work on releasing the emotions in your traumatic and verbal inhibitory imprints, you can see how far you've come by looking back at where you started. There is nothing more motivational than that!

# CHAPTER 3

---

# Your Feel Better Assessment

 I got a frantic voicemail from my client Joseph, who I had been seeing for about a year that didn't make a whole lot of sense. It was something about him not feeling any better from the work we had been doing, and he wanted to cancel his next session. As a healer, it can be hard to not take things like this personally, because you want your clients to feel better. Over the years, I have learned to accept that everyone has their own path, and this happens from time to time. In Joseph's case, though, it was confusing. He had made so much progress over the year we had been working together, so I decided to give him a call. I honestly didn't expect him to answer the phone, but he did.

He was very ungrounded and started talking really fast. "I just don't think it's helping. I thought it was helping, but I just don't feel any better. I know you are trying to help, but I don't know…"

I got him to take a couple of deep breaths and calm down. I told him if he didn't want to come back, that was totally fine. I wanted to honor wherever he was. After he calmed down, he told me that he had a rough weekend with his wife and they had a huge argument. She had gone to stay with her sister, and he didn't know if she was coming back.

We were supposed to have a session the next day, but the whole reason he started coming to me was his relationship, and now it was over. First off, I told him I was sorry this had happened. Then I started asking him to recount what led up to it and how he handled it. As he went back through the replay, I heard him using tactics that he had learned through our year together to be more objective and compassionate toward his wife while releasing his emotions as they came up. He even talked about what he did after she left. "I tried to take the higher view, and I let myself cry. I just let it out, and then I did what we talked about. She didn't come back, though."

Then I started to ask him questions like, "Joseph, if this argument had happened a year ago, how would you have handled it?"

In order to get you on the right track, you have to know where you are right now. This assessment is designed to help you take stock of yourself so that you can understand what *now* looks like for you versus *where you want to be*. There are no right or wrong answers.

## How to Learn What Is Driving You

In the last chapter, we talked about moving things from your subconscious mind to your conscious mind. Traumas and other events are often not actively remembered, and if so, there are things we forget about events, especially if the event happened before we could talk. Having the grasp of speech allows things to more easily reside in conscious memory. Regardless of whether we actively remember something or not, everything from the event is stored in the subconscious, and this is what is driving the bus, so to speak. So in order to understand what is driving you, all of that stuff in the subconscious has to be moved to the conscious mind in order to have an awareness and process it. That doesn't mean you are reliving it, but you are able to look at it and let it go. That allows you to move through fear, anxiety, and depression and on to a happier, stable place.

This assessment is the beginning of the process of moving things from the subconscious to the conscious mind. It accesses your traumatic and verbal inhibitory imprints that are stored in your energy system and gently shuffles things so that they can break loose and leave your life.

When this happens, it doesn't mean you won't have the memory of the event anymore. It means that the event won't be emotionally charged and hold you back in your life. You will be able to view your old traumas with a new perspective, old limiting beliefs fall away, and your behavioral patterns change. You change for the better. So, where are you now?

THIS ASSESSMENT IS COMPREHENSIVE. PLEASE DON'T GET BOGGED DOWN IN IT. (And skip what doesn't apply…) If you want, do a little, read more and come back to it, or skip it altogether. But it is a good way to be able to look back and see how far you've come as you progress on the journey of feeling better. It will also help you to understand what it is you need to shift.

## Self-Assessment—Your "Before Snapshot"

The first technique is to write down what comes to mind when you think about yourself in regard to the following scenarios. It's important that you don't omit anything that comes to mind. These techniques are not about judging your thoughts. They are more effective if you don't. Even if something feels odd to consider, write it down.

The point of this technique is to understand how you view yourself now. Try to be as honest as possible, and please don't beat yourself up. It's just your "before snapshot."

1. Close your eyes and imagine you are looking at yourself in the mirror (or actually do it). What do you look like?

   - This question goes beyond physical characteristics, but you can definitely write those down. Describe yourself: your face, your expression, posture, etc. What kind of vibe do you put off? Be as detailed or as general as you want.
   - Do you describe yourself generally in a positive or negative way?
   - If you described your "perfect self," what would you say?

2. Imagine that you are having a conversation. What kinds of things do you say about yourself?

   - What are your "go-to statements"?
   - Are they positive or negative?

3. What are your relationships like?

   - If you struggle with your relationships, how do you struggle?
   - If you had perfect relationships, what would they look like?

4. Describe how you feel about your job.

   - If you struggle with your job, how do you struggle?
   - If you had the perfect job, what would that look like?

By looking at where you are now and what you would describe as perfect right now, you will be able to tell where you feel like you are falling short. That may be in one category, or it may be every category. If it's every category, don't worry. I have been there myself. It just means that when you start making changes and clearing out your imprints, your life will change that much for the better.

I find that when we describe where we are and what we think is perfect, it does a few things:

- It helps us realize where we stand in our life now and what we value.
- It gives us a perspective of what we spend time subconsciously thinking about.
- It helps us understand how much societal pressures of perfection impact us.

The interesting thing is, as you clear out the energy of traumas and verbal limitation imprints, things change. Your perception of yourself changes, as well as your values and your perception of perfection. That's why it's good to write it down. After three to six months, you can go back and look at it again. If you want, do another assessment. You will start to see how much you've changed for the better.

## The Imprint Assessment

This assessment is meant to help you figure out what types of imprints you have and where you are in regard to their effect on your life. Then, as we begin moving through the techniques in this book, you can revisit this assessment and monitor your progress.

## Traumatic Imprint

Do you recall a traumatic event in your life at any point? If you have more than one (most of us do), you can start with just one, or you can list more than one.

On a scale of 1–10, when you think about that event, how much of an emotional reaction do you have to it? 1 is the lowest, 10 is the highest.

How did you react during that event?

What were the emotions you experienced during that event?

How old were you?

What sights, smells, tastes, sounds, or physical sensations were present, if any?

When you think about your life after that event, are there types of situations or people that remind you of that event?

If so, when an event happens that reminds you of the traumatic imprint event, do you react similarly to when the trauma occurred?

Do sights, smells, tastes, sounds, or physical sensations that were present during the trauma cause you stress?

Does the traumatic imprint keep you from doing things in your life that you enjoy or keep you from having things you wish to have?

Do you have any recurring life patterns that you would attribute to that traumatic imprint?

## Verbal Inhibitory Imprint

Do you recall someone saying something to you in your life on a one-time or repeated basis (it can be negative or not ill-meaning) that has "stuck with you"? If you have more than one (most of us do), you can start with just one, or you can list more than one.

On a scale of 1–10, when you think about that statement, how much of an emotional reaction do you have to it? 1 is the lowest, 10 is the highest.

How did you react to what was said?

What were the emotions you experienced when it was said?

What sights, smells, tastes, sounds, or physical sensations were present, if any?

When you think about your life after that event, are there types of situations or people that remind you of that event or that embody that statement?

If so, when an event happens that embodies or reminds you of the statement, do you react similarly to when the statement occurred?

Do sights, smells, tastes, sounds, or physical sensations that were present during when the statement was made cause you stress?

Does the verbal inhibitory imprint keep you from doing things in your life that you enjoy or keep you from having things you wish to have?

Do you have any recurring life patterns that you would attribute to that verbal inhibitory imprint?

## The Emotions Assessment

As you start learning to work with your emotional imprints, you will be asked to call out specific emotions in some of the techniques in this book. The following list is meant to get your mind open to the possibilities of which emotions may be inside your traumatic and verbal inhibitory imprints.

Oftentimes, with traumatic events in particular, the emotions and events occur in such rapid succession that our conscious minds do not process them. They get lodged in our subconscious minds and energetic imprints, where they cause long-term issues.

This technique brings these emotions into your conscious mind by putting words to them so that they can be processed and cleared.

Simply put a little mark next to that emotion so that you can refer back to the list later if you need help in the techniques.

If you want to take it a step further, read through the list and put either a 1, 2, 3, 4, or 5 next to the emotions that you feel or have felt. With 1 being an emotion you have felt occasionally, where 5 is recurring often for you.

For emotions that rank a 4 or 5, make some notes on a sheet of paper as to when you feel these emotions the most. Refer to the assessment sections on this and previous pages for your answers there to connect some dots.

For example, if you had a trauma of being lost in a store as a child, being separated from loved ones may cause you stress at this point in your life due to the traumatic imprint that formed from that root event. You might mark the feeling of abandonment as a 5 on your list, and in your assessment, you may mention the event that caused you trauma.

*If you don't see any connections yet, don't worry. That is not a requirement for moving forward in the book. Just do the best you can to answer everything as honestly as possible, and the rest will take care of itself.*

# How to Use This List

This list is pretty extensive, but it is not all-encompassing. If you think of an emotion that is not listed that applies, by all means, use it. Each emotion listed here carries a different vibrational frequency. Some vary greatly in vibration, like *Controlling* and *Useless*, and some are very similar, such as *Anger* and *Rage*. It's important for you to be able to put words to these emotions so that you can call them out of your energy system and subconscious mind to be released. Each person has a unique dialogue they use for emotions that vary (such as *Depressed* versus *Sad*), and this list helps to encompass those differences. Seeing the word of the emotions that you are carrying will kind of "jump off the page" at you, asking you to pay attention. If you feel this, put at least a tick mark next to the word or use the scale on the previous page to rate them.

| | |
|---|---|
| Abandoned | Guilt |
| Aggressive | Hopeless |
| Anger | Hyperactive |
| Anxious | Imbalanced |
| Betrayed | Imperceptive |
| Confused | Impulsive |
| Controlling | Indecisive |
| Critical | Indulgence |
| Defensive | Ineffective |
| Depressed | Insecure |
| Detached | Jealous |
| Discomfort (not physical) | Lonely |
| Disorganized | Manipulative |
| Distrust | Materialistic |
| Dramatic | Negative (with no anger) |
| Embarrassed | Overstimulated |
| Fearful | Overbearing |
| Flawed | Overly independent |
| Frustration | Overwhelmed |
| Grief | Powerless |

Rage
Resentful
Sad
Selfish
Sleepless
Stifled
Stressed
Suicidal
Temperamental
Tired
Unable to express self
Unable to speak your truth
Unclear
Uncreative

Underwhelmed
Unforgiving
Ungrounded
Unintelligent
Unloved
Unmotivated
Unsafe
Unsuccessful
Untruthful
Unworthy
Vulnerable
Weak
Withdrawn

# Joseph's Epiphany

He thought about how he would have handled this argument with his wife a year ago and laughed. "Oh, I would have screamed at her and thrown things. And... scared her. I would have scared her." He trailed off into his sadness.

"But did you do that this time? Were you even close to that?"

He was quiet for a second. "No. It didn't even cross my mind to react that way."

We talked through each piece of the argument, recounting how he'd reacted now versus how he would have reacted before he started working on himself. As we did this, Joseph started to see the difference and how far he had come. "It's hard to remember where you were after you leave those old ways behind. I didn't even realize how much I had changed. I'm actually proud of myself for how I handled it."

It can be hard to see how much you change through an emotional healing process unless you take a baseline. Since Joseph, I started recommending that all of my clients do this so they can pat themselves on the back when things get tough by remembering how far they have come.

# Chapter Challenge

Where are you now?

What are your greatest struggles and weaknesses?

What is the biggest thing you want to change?

Even if you don't do the full assessment, answering these three questions in a notebook you keep throughout your healing process will give you a record of how far you have come.

# Feel Better Five

- Bringing memories from the subconscious to the conscious mind can help us process the emotions that are linked to them.
- Evaluating where you are right now is important for developing intention for where you are going.
- Traumatic and verbal inhibitory imprints shape your reality. Recognizing what they are helps to start the process of healing.
- Putting names to the emotions you are feeling helps you to process them out of your energy system and physical body.
- It's easy to forget how far you've come unless you write it down.

# Transform in Five

Technique 3.1. Keeping Up with Your Progress

1. Go through each portion of the assessment and fill it out the best you can.
2. Keep a record of your progress as you work through releasing your emotions to see how far you have come. It's especially helpful on those days when it feels like you are back at square one.
3. If you feel this way, ask yourself how you would have handled the situation even six months ago or a year ago. Was your thought process different now than it would have been then?
4. Write down the differences and then flip back to your original assessment. Chances are you are in a different place right now, even if it seems like the situation is the same. This means you are changing, and your outside reality will begin to reflect that, if it hasn't already.

Now that you have finished your assessments, it's time to learn how to prepare for the techniques. In chapter 4, we will talk about how to set yourself up for the best possible, long-lasting results.

# CHAPTER 4

---

# Set Your Intention = Get Phenomenal Results

When I first started doing sessions with clients, I was learning a lot and quickly. I was constantly writing things down to try out in sessions, and it all came pretty innately. I was so eager to help others and loved sharing my insights. My angels and spirit guides who were teaching me these techniques were amazing, and they taught me as fast as I could learn. Before I would use these techniques on clients, I would always try them out on myself first, so I could intimately understand the technique, its process, and what it felt like before and after it was completed. Before trying each technique, I would do some of the steps in this chapter, only I didn't have words for what I was doing yet, and they weren't actions I was told to do by my guides. I just did them. They made it easier for me to focus on the technique, and I was amazed by my results. I couldn't wait to share these insights with my clients.

However, when I started to teach these techniques during sessions, my clients weren't having quite the same results as I was. And worse yet, after they left the session and tried these techniques at home, the results were pretty minimal. I was starting to feel really discouraged. Why weren't things working for anyone else but me? Were these just techniques that my guides were teaching me to use on myself and didn't intend for me to share with my clients? That didn't make any sense. The problem was, I was focusing on the wrong thing. It wasn't the technique that was the problem.

## Preparing Your State of Mind Is Important

We are often so eager to get something done, we ignore the crucial steps that come before the task at hand. We want to accomplish something quickly, especially if it involves relieving some sort of discomfort, but this can cause us to get a lesser result than if we were a little more patient. This is especially true when it comes to working with the human energy system. **When working with emotions and energy, preparing our state of mind is as important as the technique itself.**

There are basic setup techniques that create a space in your mind and energy to make them more receptive to change. These techniques work regardless of what emotions you are trying to shift or what type of energetic imprint you are working with. They are universal in nature to simplify the process of releasing, because having some simple way of releasing and shifting emotions quickly is what this book is all about. Some of these setup techniques take a little more time than others, but I encourage you to try them all to see what works best for you.

In the following chapters, we get into the heart of the book, which is the techniques themselves. There are no strict rules here. Each chapter starts with the teaching of a main technique or general principle. It can be used "as is" and is effective on its own. This is a good place to start to gain a comfort level with the technique. It is recommended that you try a main technique at least a couple of times before you try out variations of the technique found later in the chapter. There will be recommendations that may work better for certain circumstances, such as types of emotions you are releasing or whether you are working with a traumatic or verbal inhibitory imprint. In addition, there are times we just need a quick-fix, in-the-moment type of technique if we encounter something that we need to address *right away*. Many of the concepts can be used in this way, hence the phrase *feel better in five minutes*. In reality, some of the skills you will learn take considerably less time in the moment, which is helpful if you really don't have time to think about it. However you choose to use the book, the techniques act just like physical exercise. The work is cumulative, so the more you use them, the better and more stable your emotional state will be.

## Starting to Work with Your Emotions Is the First Step

It's important to understand that working with your energy system and releasing emotions is just like anything else. When you first start doing it, you're going to be thinking, *Am I doing it right? How do I know if I got all of that emotion out? Is this working at all??* Everyone asks these questions, me included when I started this work. The key is to keep doing it. It's like starting to work out. You're not going to walk into the gym on the first day after sitting on the couch for three years, eating nachos and watching reality TV, and lift two hundred pounds. It's just not going to happen. You may be able to lift the bar with no weight, or get halfway through a work out class, before you would swear you are dying. Working with emotions and energy is the same. At first, you may wonder if anything is happening at all. And that's normal. The more you practice these techniques, the more your awareness of your energy system and emotional states will increase. You'll be more tuned in to your body than ever before, increasing your ability to manage your emotions, and better yet, they will take a lot less management because you will be healing your energetic imprints.

## Emotional Imprints Distort Our Reality

Most people walk around with very arrested energy systems. The energy is stuck in certain places due to energetic imprints from traumas and other things in their energy system. It's like plopping a big rock in the river. The water has to find a way around it. But another thing happens when a "rock," or imprint, plops down in your energy system. It not only reroutes the energy, it distorts it.

Let's think about the river again. Imagine that you are standing on the banks of a crystal-clear river. The water is flowing smoothly, and you can see all the way to the bottom. Every single fish is in clear view. So much so that you can even see the gills moving on the fish. Every scale is in focus. Now, when you keep walking down the bank of the river, you come to a place where there is a very large rock in the water. When you look at the river next to where this rock is, what do you notice? The water has to flow around the rock, and where the water is flowing around the rock, there are fish swimming around there too. Only, the fish don't look like fish. You know they are fish because you intuit this, but they look like squirmy things moving around in the water, and you probably can't even see all the way to the bottom. The view is distorted by the rock that is in the river. This is exactly what happens when we have an imprint on our energy system. Our view of our reality, our beliefs, and our emotions are distorted because of this imprint. Things are not clear. That is why it is so important to release the emotions that are present in these imprints; so that the energy can flow through them again. Having energy cut off from a part of our energy system is like cutting off the circulation to your hand. It hurts after a short while of doing this. It throbs and tingles. If you left it cut off, you would lose that hand. Cutting off the circulation of energy does the same thing.

Every ailment or disease starts in the energy system first as stuck energy, namely from an imprint. If the emotions are not cleared, over time it trickles down to the physical level, manifesting as some sort of illness. The illness manifested depends on the energy and emotions that are stuck there. This subject warrants a book of its own, but it's important to understand that releasing emotions is not just something that helps improve your emotional state, but it's vital to your physical well-being too.

The human energy system really is the basis for all health. It is the cornerstone of what everything else that is *you* is built on. When we address things just from the physical perspective, as far as diet and exercise, and forgo shifting ourselves mentally by using mindfulness and affirmations, we are not addressing the root of what everything else is built on. We're not addressing the root cause of emotions going haywire or our thoughts and feelings being difficult to manage. Taking care of our energy system is just as important as taking care of our physical body. So let's get to this, shall we?

## Your Intention Sets You Up for Success

The core idea of each technique in the following chapters is to release emotions, because as we have learned in earlier chapters, the *emotions*, or the middle of the *body, mind, spirit* sandwich, is what lets us know that something is amiss in the energy system. So the first thing we need to do is to set the body, mind, and spirit up for the emotions to be released. You do not have to do all of these (or any of these) for the techniques in the following chapters to work, but the setup amplifies their potency.

## Be Mindful of Where You Are, but Don't Judge Yourself

Part of the process of releasing emotions is having an awareness for what those emotions are. As I said earlier, this is easier for some people than others. If you have an awareness for what the emotions are that you need to release, great! The following steps will be easier for you. If you are still struggling with it, refer back to your emotions assessment in chapter 3, where you identified possibilities.

# What Emotions Are You Feeling?

If you have difficulty feeling anything at all or are overwhelmed by many emotions and are having trouble sorting them out, that's okay too. Knowing what emotions you are feeling may take a little while for you to discern. That can be due to several factors. Mainly, it is due to so many emotional imprints being in place that you have a great deal of stuck energy in your energy system. It's in a state of shutdown. For some people, they disassociated from their feelings at a young age because they were taught that it is not okay to feel or their feelings were invalid, or perhaps there was so much trauma, it was safer to shut off and not feel anything at all. This is one of the coping mechanisms that we discussed earlier. However, that is not to say that this coping mechanism is not valid for that earlier time period. Sometimes, shutting down is the only way we can function in other parts of our lives. I know this firsthand. But the good news is, you can change that now. Being shut down is not who you are, it's what you had to do at the time. Now is your moment to shift those old patterns so you can find yourself once again.

# Where Do You Feel These Emotions?

This is a little bit further step into feeling your emotions. If you can, see if you can tell where in your body they are coming from. For some people, this will be pretty easy. For others, it's really hard to tell. I will say, personally, sometimes I can tell where it is coming from and sometimes I can't. Being able to tell where you feel the emotion in your body is just another form of awareness that helps you in the releasing process, but you can release emotions without knowing this. It is, however, necessary for some of the advanced techniques in later chapters. (But there are ways to guess where they are hiding... I'll teach you how.)

The more you have an awareness of your emotions, where they are coming from, and what they are, the bigger the intention you are setting to heal. Like I said, these things can take time and practice. Be gentle with yourself. You are just learning to walk here. Don't expect yourself to run a marathon out of the gate.

# What Physical Sensations Are These Emotions Creating in Your Body?

If you have difficulty telling where the emotion is coming from in your body, it may be showing up as a physical sensation. Our physical body (the top bread of the sandwich) is closely linked to our emotions, and oftentimes we will have physical pain, tightness, muscle cramps or twitching, or illness in an area of the body that is storing the emotion. This is an indicator that the emotion has trickled down to a physical level. This happens when emotions are stored in the body for a long period of time. Fresh emotions that are similar can trigger imprints in specific areas of the body to let you know that something is up and you need to work on it.

Every symptom or ailment you have starts as energetic first. It then manifests as an emotion and later shows up in the physical body. It's kind of like someone yelling at you louder and louder to get your attention, and eventually it can stop you dead in your tracks if you don't listen. This is why releasing emotions is so important.

### Technique 4.1. Setting the Intention

Just like in the later chapters, this technique starts with a general concept that you can make more specific as you become more comfortable with it. The purpose of setting the intention is to let your body, mind, and energy systems know what you are about to do. It lets the Universe know as well, which is important as you go down this path. The more of an intention you have to feel better, the more opportunities the Universe will give you to do it. Which is the whole point of it all.

1. You can set the intention for a technique by simply saying, *"I choose to feel better"* or *"I choose to release the emotions I am feeling."*

This is a general and simple way of doing it. It doesn't require you to even specify what you want to let go of, just that by doing the technique, you expect that you will feel better as a result.

2. If you have a further awareness of what emotion you are feeling, you can call out that emotion (or emotions) by name.

This can be more effective than setting a general intention, as it directs your energy system to focus on a particular emotion, or vibrational frequency, to release.

3. You can also name more than one emotion here, something like, "I choose to release all of the anger, sadness, and grief that I am feeling right now."

The downside to calling out specific emotions is that you might miss some. Perhaps when you are calling out anger, sadness, and grief, you have some despair in there too. You can add this after the first intention as an additional statement.

4. If you are not sure what the other emotions are, you can simply say, "I choose to release anger, sadness, and grief *and any other emotions that I need to release at this time in my best and highest good.*"
5. If you are interested in diving deeper and getting out more stuck emotions a little at a time, just add this statement onto the end of your intention statement. "...and whatever it is attached to." For example: "I choose to release all of the anger and sadness that I am feeling *and whatever it is attached to.*"

Why is this so powerful? It's like this: emotions aren't just these free-floating things in our energy system, randomly causing us to feel various feelings and react to them. There is a rhyme and reason to it. They are all strung together in one way or another.

## Emotions Are Always Part of Your Energetic Network

Our energy system creates a network of energy from our energetic imprints that strings emotions together in categories. More accurately, it groups them by vibrational frequency. While that is a whole other rabbit hole we could go down, let's keep it simple. Imagine a string of beads all jumbled up. Each bead is an emotion from an imprint. Some are bigger beads than others, but these strings of beads are kind of jumbled in a big, messy ball. Now imagine that some of these beads have glue on them and they stick to some of the other beads. What does this sound like to you? I would say, a mess. We really have no concept of this until we start unraveling these strings and start to understand how seemingly unrelated things are grouped together.

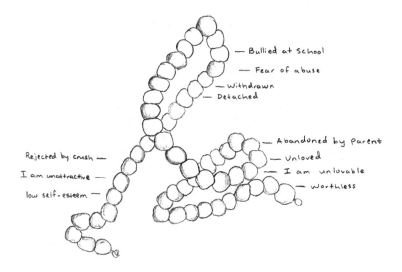

- Bullied at School
- Fear of abuse
- Withdrawn
- Detached
- Abandoned by Parent
- Unloved
- I am unlovable
- Worthless

Rejected by crush —
I am unattractive —
low self-esteem —

For instance, you can have a root event, like in the story of Sam in chapter 2. Sam got jumped on by a dog when he was three years old. Now let's say the only thing Sam was aware of when this happened is the event that was happening to him; getting knocked over by the dog. That is what is in his active memory. As a result, he is afraid of dogs. That makes sense. But what about everything else that was going on around Sam when this happened? His subconscious mind made a record of all of those things too. Let's say that when Sam was knocked over, he was wearing a red shirt and overalls. The carpet in the room where he got knocked over was green. He was holding a chocolate chip cookie in his hand, and *Sesame Street* was on TV. He doesn't remember any of those things in his conscious mind, but his subconscious mind grouped all of those things in the same bucket. His mind and energy system created the traumatic imprint with all of those things grouped into the same vibrational category. As a result, Sam is allergic to chocolate and refuses to wear red. *Sesame Street* characters give him the creeps, and sometimes he has nightmares about them chasing him. These are seemingly unrelated things that are related in his energy system because they are in the same traumatic imprint. Even more events can be on this "string of beads" as well. Anything that the energy system sees as "related" to that root event in some way can cause an emotional reaction and create yet another traumatic imprint as a result. The latter imprints are generally milder than the root imprint, and oftentimes, dealing with the root imprint will render the latter imprints that are on the same "string of beads" inactive.

You have to remember, Sam has no recollection of anything else that was going on in the room at that time. So how does he get to the root traumatic imprint? He starts with setting a simple intention and adding on the new ending, for example, *"I choose to release any fear I have regarding being jumped on by a dog **and whatever it is attached to.**"* This allows Sam to address not only the root event but any other energy or vibrations that are in his traumatic imprint. Namely, the things that he doesn't remember that are on the same string of beads. Adding the phrase "whatever it is attached to" tells your energy system to release anything in that string of vibrational emotions that is attached to the root imprint.

It's important to understand that diving deeper into these imprints is a process. It takes time. There are layers and layers of emotional strings of beads that we have to unravel at times, but if you keep going, you will start seeing a difference in your fundamental reactions and emotional states to things that once caused you to react negatively.

## Going Deeper: Emotions Are Related in Unexpected Ways

Using the technique above of adding *whatever it is attached to* on the end of your intention is the first step to going deeper. As you practice this technique, you will start to notice something. When you make an intentional statement and perform a technique of your choice from later in the book with it, you will start to have memories pop up during or after the technique that are seemingly unrelated. For example, let's say Sam makes the statement: *"I choose to release any fear I have regarding being jumped on by a dog and whatever it is attached to."* After he makes this statement and performs one of the techniques found later in the book, another memory pops into his head that seems unrelated. He remembers being at school in third grade and being served a chocolate chip cookie for a birthday party. After he ate it, he broke out in hives. The other kids laughed at him, and he had to go to the nurse. He was embarrassed. He then makes a new statement: *"I choose to release the embarrassment of getting hives at school and whatever it is attached to."* This may lead him to a memory of not wanting to go into a bathroom when he was five because there was a green bath mat in there and he was afraid it would "get him." As a result, he wet his pants and was embarrassed. This gets added as a new imprint. While these things seem unrelated to Sam, he keeps going. He makes the intention statement, "I choose to release my fear of green bath mats and the embarrassment of wetting my pants and whatever it is attached to."

Knowing what we know from his root imprint, this association makes perfect sense. All of these things are vibrationally connected on the same string of energetic emotional beads. That is why this is a process. It can take time to get to the bottom of things, but if you keep working on it, over time, you will reap huge rewards. Your life will change for good.

1.  When you have time, sit with and release memory after memory that comes up for you around your root imprint by saying, "I choose to release (emotion or event) and whatever it is attached to." Refer to the section on the previous page-Going Deeper: Emotions are Related in Unexpected ways for an example of how to do this.

## Releasing Emotions Doesn't Have to Be Complicated

If you have a lot of emotions stirring at once, it may be hard to get a handle on what you are feeling. For some people, it's hard to feel at all. Their energy system is so shut down that no energy is flowing, or very little. This makes it hard to discern one emotion from another, especially if the emotions are closely related, like sadness and despair or anger and rage.

2.  In the case of not being sure what emotion to call out, you can start with the general statement, "I choose to feel better" or "I choose to release the emotions I am feeling."

3.  Then, try calling out to release just one emotion and see if you feel any different. This way, you can start to learn what each emotion feels like.

This awareness is very helpful for several reasons. It makes it easier to express yourself to others, it allows you to release emotions more easily, and it helps to heal the energetic imprints you have in your energy system by getting the energy moving inside them. When energy is stuck and not moving, it is hard to release. It's like having a piece of hard chewing gum stuck to a wall. It's hard to pick off, but if it were soft and malleable, you could move it around, stretch it, and ultimately remove it. So, feel free to experiment with the format of setting your intentions for the techniques later in the book.

Important note: It's important to say "I choose to release an emotion" versus "I want to release an emotion." Wanting and choosing are not the same thing. If you want to do something, you are not actively doing it, you are simply wishing for it to happen. Choosing, in contrast, is taking action to remove the emotion. This seems like a subtle difference, but it's not. Your energy system, your mind, and the Universe will not act on a want, only a choice.

## Shifting How I Taught Clients to Release Emotions Changed Everything

Once I started teaching my clients some of the ways they could set up their emotional clearing techniques with intention, their results dramatically improved. After teaching these methods, I could visibly tell in their energy system at their next session whether they had been using them or not. Not only could I see the difference, but their sessions went more smoothly and they were able to release and heal more energy during the session.

## Chapter Challenge

Have you ever had a practice of setting intentions in your life?

When you set intentions, did it help you focus better, perform better, accomplish more?

Try setting daily intentions each morning for a week and see if it makes a difference.

This practice can increase your success with directing energy to set intentions in future chapters.

## Feel Better Five

- Before each technique, it is important to set an intention.
- Emotions can be released as a group or individually.
- If emotions are not addressed, they can manifest physical symptoms over time.
- Emotions can be related in our energy system in unexpected ways.
- Emotions are not standalone objects in our energy systems; they are part of a network.

# Transform in Five

Technique 4.1. Setting the Intention

Inside chapter 4, you will find more details about each step.

1. You can set the intention for an technique by simply saying, *"I choose to feel better"* or *"I choose to release the emotions I am feeling."*
2. If you have a further awareness of what emotion you are feeling, you can call out that emotion (or emotions) by name.
3. You can also name more than one emotion here, something like, "I choose to release all of the anger, sadness, and grief that I am feeling right now."
4. If you are not sure what the other emotions are, you can simply say, "I choose to release anger, sadness, and grief *and any other emotions that I need to release at this time in my best and highest good.*"
5. If you are interested in diving deeper and getting out more stuck emotions a little at a time, just add this statement onto the end of your intention statement: "…and whatever it is attached to." For example, "I choose to release this anger *and whatever it is attached to.*"

# Transform in Ten

These steps require a little more time but are worth it for quicker long-term results.

1. When you have time, sit with and release memory after memory that comes up for you around your root imprint by saying, "I choose to release (emotion or event) and whatever it is attached to." Refer to the section Going Deeper: Emotions Are Related in Unexpected Ways on page 51.
2. In the case of not being sure what emotion to call out, you can start with the general statement, *"I choose to feel better"* or *"I choose to release the emotions I am feeling."*
3. Then, try calling out to release just one emotion and see if you feel any different. This way, you can start to learn what each emotion feels like. Refer to your list of emotions from chapter 3 to help you.

Did you know that emotions and color are closely linked? In the next chapter, we talk about the relationship between emotions and color and how you can use this to your advantage to feel better fast.

# CHAPTER 5

---

# Color Is an Energy Vitamin

When I went to an energy healer for the first time, I had never given any thought to energy work. I didn't understand what it was or how it could help me. I just wanted to feel better and was trying to have an open mind.

I showed up to the office, and the lady had me lie on a massage table, close my eyes, and relax. She took my hand and started flicking my wrist around. She told me it was a form of muscle testing, which I was familiar with, so it really didn't seem that weird. I just did my best to let my body go and not think about anything.

To my surprise, things started to pop into my vision. I couldn't really explain it, but words, symbols, and colors, especially the color violet (purple), kept showing up. But my eyes were closed. Okay . . . this was weird. I told her what I was seeing, and she seemed interested but really didn't comment much on any of it.

When I asked her what it meant, she told me that it was just energy processing out of my energy system and that seeing things during an energy work session is fairly common. This put me at ease, but I was still very curious as to why I was seeing what I was seeing. It had to mean something. And later I would learn exactly what. I would start to understand why I was seeing the color violet. And why it was the foreshadowing of what was coming next.

Color is everywhere. The world wouldn't be what it is without it. As humans, we are drawn to color; some of us prefer bright and bold, while others of us prefer soft and muted. Some hate orange while others can't seem to get enough. But why?? While there are psychological reasons why we are drawn to certain colors, there are energetic reasons too. Depending on the individual, certain colors can either fill you up or drain you. So what determines this? When you understand how and why color affects you energetically, you can use it to further your healing journey.

# Your Energy System Is a Thumbprint of Color

When you look at a picture of the human energy system, the first thing you will notice is color. The chakras and aura are an array of color, and each color is representative of a different set of vibrational energies. If you search for images of aura or chakras on the internet, every picture looks basically the same, with the chakras being displayed from root to crown in the spectrum of color:

- Red: root chakra
- Orange: sacral chakra
- Yellow: emotional chakra
- Green: heart chakra
- ·Blue: throat chakra
- Purple or Indigo: third eye chakra
- White or Violet: crown chakra

But the truth is, no one's energy system looks exactly like that. Each person's energy system is like a fingerprint; no two are the same, and the colors change over a lifetime. Some people may have more red or yellow in their aura, while others have more blue and violet. Some people have brightly colored chakras in all the traditional colors, while some people have dull, sullen-colored chakras with dark spots in their aura. The reason for this is, no two people are the same. Each one has different traumatic and verbal inhibitory imprints playing out in their energy system, which is part of what determines the colors that are present and where they are located.

While we could really do a deep dive into the function of the energy system here, it's just a lot for anyone's brain and doesn't really help you with the reason you are reading this book. It's important to understand the correlation between your energy system, color, and emotions a little bit so you can comprehend how color plays a role in healing. That said, we are going to stay focused on how colors relate to emotions. It's the basis for some of the variations on the simple techniques found in the coming chapters on envisioning, breathing, and grounding, and using it can make a big difference in how you feel. It takes the simple concepts to a whole new level, and once you understand it a bit better, you can carry this knowledge into healing your emotional states.

Each color has a use, kind of like a vitamin that is providing a specific nutrient. There are times when it is great to use a certain color to balance something out or heal it, and there are times when using the same color can actually make something worse. While that is definitely a concern, the way I am going to teach you to use color is easy, simple, and safe. There are aspects of energy healing that use color in really complex ways, but that is not our focus here. While the techniques taught in the book are ones you can use to feel better quickly, the cumulative effect is deep and long-lasting. Color makes them work even better.

## The Safe Way to Use Color for Energy Work

Color can be powerful and effective when you are working with the human energy system. It has to be used the right way, though. The cool thing is, you can do this with very little effort on your part. That is because your energy system does all the thinking for you.

It's like this: when you eat a steak or a salad, what happens? You put it in your mouth, chew it up, and swallow it. Your body does the rest. You don't have to put any thought into which vitamins and minerals to extract out of the food you ate and send it to certain cells or organs in your body for nourishment. Your body knows what to do and takes care of it for you. The same is true for the energy system. Simply by taking it in, your energy system knows what to do with color in order to help you the most. It sends it to the areas in your energy system that are deficient in that color, and this in turn promotes healing in your energy system and supports emotional releasing of your traumatic and verbal inhibitory imprints.

## Too Much of a Good Thing

Now let's say you are one of those people like me who have to eat animal protein. Yeah, I kind of wish I didn't, but my body needs it. I get sick without it. But let's say I was on a salad kick for a few days and all I did was eat veggies and salad. I have done this, so I know what my body does. I get lethargic. I start to get spacey, feel depressed, and get bad headaches. At this point, I know my body is screaming for what it needs. It's getting too much of one set of nutrients and not enough of another.

Color is the same way. When you use color in working with your energy system, you can have the same reaction if it gets too much of one color over another. But just like you know what foods you can and can't eat for your optimum health, you kind of already know what colors are good for you. It's simple... what colors are you drawn to? Chances are, the colors that make you feel good are the colors you need to be taking into your energy system. You probably gravitate toward having certain colors around you. Whether it's the color you paint your walls or the main colors in your closet, you most likely have preferences. Later in the chapter, we are going to go over what colors are good for working with certain emotions. This way, you will have a better understanding of what colors to use when you are using techniques in later chapters.

## Brighter Is Not Always Better

While I am a big fan of a dark-red wall in a public space or an eye-popping yellow chair in a restaurant, those colors can wreak havoc if we take something that strong directly into our energy system. When we are surrounded by bold colors, we are soaking them up in small quantities, and this is fine. Each color carries a certain vibration, and being exposed to it in our environment lets a little bit of it seep into our energy system. However when we are working with color directly and intentionally pulling it into our energy system, bright, bold colors can be damaging. It's like putting a speaker on full blast directly up to your ear versus listening to the music with the volume turned up a quarter of the way. We have to dilute the color down to a muted form so that when we take it in, the color is healing versus damaging.

So in this chapter, there are examples to help you with the general idea of what colors to use when you are working with color in your energy system and emotional imprints. This way, you can feel confident you are working with it correctly for the best results.

## Feeling the Blues—How Color Impacts You

I used to go to a chiropractor who was brilliantly quirky and had more gadgets in his office than you could imagine. I'm a fan of these guys. I have been going to chiropractors since I was nine. My health would definitely be worse off without it.

This guy, though, seemed to have something new every time I went in. One day at my appointment, I was having a hard time with my depression. He did some extra work with my nervous system and then looked at me quizzically. He walked over to a drawer and pulled out a pair of red glasses. He asked me to stick my arm out and pushed down on it. It was strong. He was muscle-testing me to see if wearing the red glasses strengthened or weakened my body. A strong arm meant my body liked it. My energy system liked it.

He took those off my face and asked me to put on another pair. This time they were orange. My arm budged even less. Wow.

Okay, so maybe my body would like all the glasses colors and none of this meant anything. Yeah, I was thinking that. But then he pulled out the blue glasses. I put them on and held out my arm. Before he even touched it, it felt weak. He barely pushed on my arm, and it flopped to my side. I tried it again. No matter how hard I tried to hold it up, I couldn't. What's more, I started to feel even more depressed with them on. He put the orange glasses back on me for a second to perk me back up. And it worked.

I was intrigued by the whole thing, and the more I thought about it, the more I understood why I didn't like the color blue. I had never liked it. I didn't have a single blue piece of clothing other than jeans. I had no blue jewelry and I would never dream of painting my walls blue. I actually kind of hated the color, especially pure blue. Yuck. It just made me feel bad.

Red, on the other hand, was my favorite color at the time. So much so that in every house I had for years, I just had to paint one of my walls red. It energized me and made me feel powerful. Gold or orange was a close second. I didn't know it then, but my energy system was depleted in those colors due to traumatic and verbal inhibitory imprints that were impacting my ability to hold that color in my energy system. Preferring the color was my body's way of getting what it needed. Just like preferring to eat a salad or a steak.

The funny thing is that now, I wouldn't dream of painting a wall in my house red. It would feel like too much. It would agitate me if I had to look at it every day. Most of my house is a neutral palette of grays with touches of color. And shockingly, one of my paintings is primarily blue. Why the change? Because my energy system changed. I have been releasing the emotions from the traumatic and verbal inhibitory imprints that made my energy system depleted of red. I carry plenty of it with me now and don't need to add it very often. Actually, my closet is mostly black and white at this point, due to all of the releasing work I have done over the years. My energy system can hold an abundance of all the colors that it needs to be healthy. I still wear some color, don't get me wrong, but I don't need a lot of it. When I do, I know which colors to add, depending on how I am feeling or what emotions I need to release.

## White: The Multivitamin of Color

White is an interesting color. It goes with everything you put with it. Nothing looks bad with white. That's because white is a combination of all the colors. When I was a little kid, someone told me that, and I thought they were crazy (shouldn't that be black?), until my brother got me a prism for my birthday when I was eight. When white sunlight hit it, my room would flood with little bits of rainbows all over the walls. And the colors were always in the same order, no matter how the sunlight hit it: red, orange, yellow, green, blue, indigo, and violet. It's no coincidence it's the same order that the colors appear in a rainbow in the sky. Sunlight hits the droplets of water at precisely the right angle to break down the spectrum of white light into the individual colors in the white-light spectrum. The color that is displayed is determined by the wavelength of the light in it, with violet being the shortest wavelength with the highest frequency and energy, while red has the longest wavelength and lowest frequency and energy.

Does this order of color ring a bell? This is the same order of the chakra colors in the energy system, from the root chakra to the crown chakra. In the world of energy, everything has an interplay. Nothing stands alone as a separate piece. Color and the energy system are no exception.

So, back to our color here, white. Since white is the catchall color, it can be used no matter what you are doing. It's like a multivitamin. It has a little bit of everything you need without overdoing anything. Even if you don't particularly need blue, for instance, the amount you get out of white light really isn't a big deal. White-colored energy can be used in any of the emotional release techniques in the following chapters and is recommended for when you are getting used to using color.

## The Other Colors

After addressing the use of white, we are going to go through the colors in the order they are on the spectrum, starting with red and working our way to violet. Each color has a sort of personality, so to speak, and is useful in different situations, depending on what color you are deficient in. The surplus or deficiency of a particular color can be determined pretty easily, because each color is presented here with different character traits.

For instance, if you find yourself feeling insecure, red is a good color to add to your energy system. However, if you are working on releasing anger or you tend to be hyperactive, red would exacerbate these emotions and should not be used.

When color is used in conjunction with the emotional release techniques, it can increase the potency of the techniques when used correctly. If you use a color and find that you feel worse instead of better, look at the list and choose a different color. Some emotions are listed for more than one color. That is because some colors on the spectrum are a combination of colors. These are called secondary colors and hold attributes of more than one color.

Again, color is best utilized only after you have mastered the simple techniques in the chapter you are working on.

The idea is for you to understand how these different colors play into releasing emotions and healing your energy system. This way, you will have a good idea of what specific colors to use in the techniques in later chapters.

## Setting Intentions with Color

There really are no bounds in energy healing. That is why I love working with it. When it comes to color, it can be worked with in many different ways. Here, we are just going to talk about setting intention with it in regard to healing traumatic and verbal inhibitory imprints and clearing emotions, as this is the focus of this book. We're going to keep the concept simple so you can refer to the chart for the emotion you are feeling and bring in that color using techniques found in the later chapters.

## How to Use the Color Charts on the Following Pages

There are two categories for each color: when to use a color if you are feeling a certain emotion, and when not to use this color.

Let's take the example of red that we used above. If you are feeling insecure, this means that you have a deficiency of red in your energy system and need to add it in. This will help you to release the feeling of insecurity and replenish your deficiency of red. You can do this by using the techniques in the later chapters.

However, if you are working on releasing anger, red is not the color to use. Adding more red will only amplify your anger. In order to alleviate your anger, look to other colors in the chart until you see anger listed under the "when to use" category. In this case, the colors to use with anger are green and blue.

| Emotion | Use | Use | Use | Don't Use | Don't Use | Don't Use | Don't Use |
|---------|-----|-----|-----|-----------|-----------|-----------|-----------|
| Abandoned | Red | Orange | | Indigo | Violet | | |
| Aggressive | Blue | Green | | Red | | | |
| Anger | Green | Blue | | Red | Orange | Yellow | Violet |
| Anxious | Green | Blue | | Red | Orange | Yellow | Indigo |
| Betrayed | Green | | | Orange | | | |
| Confused | Blue | Yellow | Indigo | Green | | | |
| Controlling | Indigo | | | Orange | Yellow | | |
| Critical | Green | | | Indigo | Violet | | |
| Defensive | Green | | | Orange | | | |
| Depressed | Yellow | | | Blue | Violet | Indigo | |
| Detached | Red | Orange | Yellow | Blue | Violet | | |
| Discomfort -not phys | Green | Orange | | Indigo | | | |
| Disorganized | Blue | | | Violet | Indigo | | |
| Distrust | Blue | Green | | Red | Orange | Yellow | |
| Dramatic | Green | Blue | | Indigo | | | |
| Embarrassed | Indigo | | | Yellow | | | |
| Fearful | Red | Orange | Violet | Blue | | | |
| Flawed | Yellow | Orange | | Green | | | |
| Grief | White | | | Blue | Orange | Violet | |

| Emotion | Use | Use | Use | Don't Use | Don't Use | Don't Use | Don't Use |
|---|---|---|---|---|---|---|---|
| Guilty | Green | | | Red | Yellow | | |
| Hopeless | Green | Orange | | Indigo | | | |
| Hyperactive | Blue | Indigo | Violet | Red | Orange | Yellow | |
| Imbalanced | Green | Indigo | | Blue | | | |
| Imperceptive | Indigo | | | Green | | | |
| Impulsive | Green | Blue | Violet | Red | Indigo | | |
| Indecisive | Blue | Orange | Yellow | Indigo | Violet | | |
| Indulgence | Blue | | | Red | Orange | | |
| Ineffective | Violet | Orange | Indigo | Green | Blue | | |
| Insecure | Red | Green | | Blue | Indigo | Violet | |
| Jealous | White | | | Red | Orange | Yellow | Indigo |
| Lonely | Red | Indigo | | Orange | Green | Violet | |
| Manipulative | Blue | Indigo | | Red | Yellow | Orange | |
| Materialistic | Green | Indigo | | Violet | Orange | | |
| Negative (no anger) | Red | Orange | Yellow | Blue | Indigo | | |
| Overbearing | Blue | Green | Indigo | Red | Orange | | |
| Overly independent | Violet | | | Green | | | |
| Oversti-mulated | Blue | | | Red | Orange | Yellow | |
| Powerless | Red | Orange | Yellow | Blue | | | |
| Rage | Indigo | Blue | Green | Red | Orange | Yellow | Violet |
| Resentful | Green | | | Orange | | | |
| Sad | Yellow | | | Blue | | | |
| Selfish | Green | | | Yellow | Indigo | Violet | |
| Sleepless | Blue | | | Red | Orange | | |
| Stifled | Green | | | Violet | Indigo | | |

| Emotion | Use | Use | Use | Don't Use | Don't Use | Don't Use | Don't Use |
|---|---|---|---|---|---|---|---|
| Stressed | Green | Orange | | Violet | Indigo | Yellow | Red |
| Suicidal | White | | | Violet | Blue | Yellow | |
| Temperamental | Orange | Blue | Violet | Red | Indigo | | |
| Tired | Red | Yellow | Tired | Green | Violet | | |
| Unable to express self | Blue | Orange | Yellow | Violet | | | |
| Unable to speak truth | Blue | Yellow | | Indigo | | | |
| Unclear | Indigo | | | Violet | | | |
| Uncreative | Violet | Orange | | Blue | Green | | |
| Under whelmed | Red | Orange | Yellow | | | | |
| Unforgiving | Blue | | | Red | Orange | Yellow | |
| Ungrounded | Red | | | Violet | | | |
| Unintelligent | Violet | Orange | | Yellow | | | |
| Unloved | Green | | | Violet | | | |
| Unmotivated | Red | Green | Indigo | Blue | | | |
| Unsafe | Green | Yellow | | Red | | | |
| Unsuccessful | Indigo | Orange | | Yellow | Blue | Violet | |
| Untruthful | Blue | Green | Violet | Orange | | | |
| Unworthy | Violet | Orange | Green | Blue | | | |
| Vulnerable | Red | Indigo | | Yellow | Blue | | |
| Weak | Red | Blue | | Orange | Yellow | Violet | |
| Withdrawn | Violet | Orange | | Yellow | Green | Indigo | |

# Color Spectrum Chart

The color spectrum chart is so awesome that it was beyond fitting in the book, so I did the next best thing. Use the QR code below to access the color chart and other information that will help you to better understand and visualize when working with color in your energy system.

# Choosing a Color to Work With

When choosing a color to work with, you first need to have a good idea of what emotions you are trying to clear out of your imprints and energy system. Starting to work with just a random color is not ideal, unless it is the color white, which can be used for anything. Even then, using a soft white is best, because bright, strong colors are not the way to go with your energy system, as you learned earlier. There are examples of shades you can use on the following pages to keep within a safe range when working with color.

# Working with Primary versus Secondary Colors

It's recommended that you only work with one color at a time so that your intention is very clear and you get a good feel for it. This applies to primary versus secondary color, not just one color versus another. Meaning, if an emotion is listed under red, blue, or yellow, set your intention to work with that color first. Next, you can move on to the secondary colors of orange, green, indigo and violet if the emotion is listed under one of those colors. For example, if an emotion is listed with more than one color, such as abandonment, which is listed under both red and orange, start with red, as that is a primary color. Then move on to orange.

This technique is for setting the intention for working with color, and techniques for using it are in the following chapters on envisioning, breathing, and grounding.

### Technique 5.1. Setting the Color Intention

1. Choose an emotion that you want to release. Let's use anger as an example. Locate anger on the color chart. Some emotions may have more than one color, as does anger. Blue and green can both be used for releasing anger. Look at the chart and pick a color. Focus on using one of these colors. It is best to start with a primary color. In this case, that is blue.
2. After locating the emotion on the color chart, set the intention to work with this color for that particular emotion. This sets the intention for targeted work on that emotion, regardless of where it is in your energy system or physical body.
3. Say, *"I choose to bring (the color) into my energy system to clear (this emotion)."* For example: "I choose to bring the color blue into my energy system to release anger." While this statement is powerful on its own, when combined with the later techniques, it becomes even more potent.

# White

White is the multivitamin of color. While most emotions fall under a color or two, some emotions can become imbalanced by using this method because the emotion is too multifaceted or delicate, or it is stage-oriented. Therefore, white is the best choice.

# Red

Red is a color that is considered bold, outspoken, and strong. It demands attention. Red holds the energy of the life force and is strong in nature. Use this color if you are low in energy and have to get things done. If you are feeling extremely fatigued, use a very soft shade of red. Your energy system is most likely fragile and can only handle a little bit of this color at a time.

# Orange

Orange is also a bold color, and it holds the attributes and energy of both red and yellow. It is all about excitement and creativity. Orange stimulates the mind as well as hunger. Use it when you need to get your creative juices flowing or are lacking appetite. This is a great mind-reset color if you have a creative block or are low on energy.

# Yellow

Another high-energy color, yellow holds the energy of excitement, joy, and happiness. It's the pep-you-up color and is great to use if you experience depression and apathy. Yellow can be a little loud energetically, so if you are feeling overly sensitive and feel you need the color, use a very light shade of yellow.

# Green

Green is calmer in nature than the first three colors because it is a combination of yellow and blue. It is the color of nature and promotes relaxation and wholeness. Green denotes a feeling of balance and serenity. Use this color if you need to feel empowered but feel you have suppressed anger or excitability. It will keep these emotions in check while helping you to stand on your own two feet.

# Blue

Blue is the color of calm and clarity. Its depth demands contemplation but can take you deep into thought without causing you to become ungrounded. Use this color if you are having difficulty speaking up for yourself. Combine this with green if you are in need of the ability to speak up for yourself but do not want to hurt the feelings of another person.

# Indigo

Indigo stimulates thought and encourages extrasensory perception to kick in, expanding the intuition. Use indigo when you are working on things that require a high level of thought or are working on developing your extra senses.

# Violet

Violet is the color of transformation and denotes the energy of wisdom, intelligence, and spirituality. It is often used in meditations to enhance the meditative experience. This is a great color to use if you are working with the "tapping in" techniques in the chapter on journaling.

## Colors Can Be Part of an Energetic Imprint

Colors are a powerful element in energy work and when used correctly can amplify emotional healing and releasing. As you progress through the techniques in the envisioning, breathing, and grounding chapters, you will see how to effectively use them. While the emotions and related colors on previous pages are examples, they are by no means a be-all and end-all. Just like anything else, colors can be part of an emotional imprint and trigger a negative response. If you have a color aversion because of an emotional imprint, such as Sam had in chapter two in response to the green carpet, do not use that color right away. Chip away at releasing other emotions in the imprint before you use it so that the emotional charge is lessened.

For instance, if you feel that you are powerless and lack confidence, you might feel that you need to use the color red to shift this feeling. However, if you were in a car accident where a red car hit you, this color may cause an emotional trigger, since the color red is likely part of the traumatic imprint from the car accident. In this case, adding the color red to your energy system may cause a state of alarm rather than being a source of healing. The color has become a sort of energetic "allergy" and could cause physical symptoms to occur, such as a rapid heart rate and sweating, or emotional symptoms, such as anxiety or fear. It is then necessary to address the rest of the traumatic imprint before you try healing with that color. Use an intention statement to identify the emotions present in the imprint and combine it with techniques in the later chapters.

## Understanding Violet

After having studied color a bit, I now understand why I was seeing the color violet in my first energy work session. With this color flooding my energy system in such a large quantity, I was being prepared for my chakras to open and have my spiritual kundalini awakening in my second energy work session.

Since violet holds such a high vibration, it was preparing me to let go of anything of a lower vibration, namely, all of my lower-vibration emotions that had been trapped in my traumatic and verbal inhibitory imprints.

# Chapter Challenge

Observe your mood around certain colors: do they empower you, agitate you, or drain you?

Pay attention to what colors you are naturally drawn to, and surround yourself with them.

When you identify the colors that make you feel good, get a cup that color and drink water from it.

Eating foods that are of your color incorporate that color into your body.

Sunlight is a great way to get the full spectrum of color into your energy system and clear your energy.

## Bonus Chapter Challenge: Wearing Color for a Power Move

I was recently talking with a client of mine. I told her I was writing this book, and she volunteered to read it and give her opinion. Her feedback on this chapter was so good, I just had to add it. She told me that in her former business, she was a clothing consultant. She helped people dress in the styles and colors that best suited them. She pointed out that when she had her business, she used color in similar ways to what I have recommended in this chapter and recommended the following chapter challenge. I agreed.

Since color is such a powerful tool and holds the energetic vibrations of emotions, it makes sense that we should use it to our advantage whenever possible. Try the tips below tomorrow and every day when you are getting dressed.

It's important to note that sometimes you may need a color that does not look particularly great on you. If this is the case, wear it as the color of your underwear or a small accessory such as earrings, a purse, a belt, or shoes. This way you still get the benefit without feeling like you are washed out or overpowered by it.

### Technique 5.2. Dressing for your day

1. Think about what you have to do today. Is there an important meeting on your calendar, or are you having a chill day?

2. Take stock of how you are feeling. Are you confident, bold, depressed, anxious, or overwhelmed? Refer to the color and emotions charts to see what fits you best.
3. If you are having a big meeting and feel like you are lacking confidence, try out wearing something red or orange to bring on the power to boost you.
4. If you are relaxing after a long week, cuddle up in some soft off-white, pink, or gray loungewear for the morning.
5. If you're not sure which colors to wear, just open up your closet and see what clothes you are attracted to that day. Let your intuition guide you.

Confession: I sometimes buy clothes that I am guided to buy that I am not crazy about. Why? Because I wouldn't naturally buy it, but I sometimes need to wear it for the color. For instance, I used to have a bright orange shirt with sequins on it. Cute if your hair is blonde, but not for red hair like mine. It looks like I got dressed in the dark when I wear that thing. But if I am feeling down and I have a lot to get done that day, I will wear it around the house until I get all ready to go, and then I change into something else. It peps me up fast, and I don't have to wear it all day.

## Feel Better Five

- Colors correlate to different emotions.
- We are naturally drawn to colors that benefit us energetically.
- Color can be used in healing our energetic imprints.
- Color can be combined with other techniques in the book to increase efficacy.
- Dressing with color can help our mood.

## Transform in Five

Technique 5.1. Setting the Color Intention

1. Choose an emotion that you want to release. Let's use anger as an example. Locate anger on the color chart. Some emotions may have more than one color, as does anger. Blue and green can both be used for releasing anger. Focus on using one of these colors. It is best to start with a primary color. In this case, that is blue.

2. After locating the emotion on the color chart, set the intention to work with this color for that particular emotion. This sets the intention for targeted work on that emotion, regardless of where it is in your energy system or physical body.

3. Say, *"I choose to bring (the color) into my energy system to clear (this emotion)."* For example: "I choose to bring the color blue into my energy system to release anger." While this statement is powerful on its own, when combined with the later techniques in this book, it becomes even more potent.

# CHAPTER 6

---

# The Secret to Unlocking Your
# Buried Emotions

 I don't know how many times I came across the following scenario: I walk upstairs to get my youngest son up for school. Of course, he hasn't moved after I've called him ten times. I flip on the light and hear a groan.

"Get up! You're going to be late!"

"But I'm siiiiick!"

Sigh. My son is extremely sensitive to stress, and in his younger years, he had a lot of it. He is a child of divorce, like millions of other children, and unfortunately, going back and forth between two environments that included very different disciplinary styles, eating habits, and levels of conflict took its toll on him just about every other week. As a mom, you try to do what's best for your kids, and when you are faced with a child that is dealing with this level of stress, it's often a toss-up between dragging them out of bed and making them go to school and letting them sleep in because you know they had a rough weekend.

When we have stress pumping throughout our bodies, other emotions often accompany it. Fear, anxiety, anger, and despair are also common emotional companions. Stress alone causes a series of chemical reactions in our physical bodies that take their toll both immediately and over time. For children, an upset stomach and headaches are very common reactions to stress, and this is what my son had in spades.

While I did address his symptoms with the usual treatment—ginger tea, toast, and a hot pack on his forehead—I knew that wasn't enough. As parents and even adults, we are always tempted to just take care of the symptoms in front of us, because we have to get to school or to work and we "can't afford to miss." The problem is, if this is as far as we ever go in taking care of ourselves, we are never addressing the underlying cause. When low-vibration emotions are not dealt with in a way that we can process and remove them, the energy from them can settle into different parts of our bodies, causing ailment and disease. However, when we understand how emotions impact our physical bodies, we can begin to see the connection between health and our energetic and emotional states. This allows us to dig deeper and achieve healing on a whole new level.

## Emotions Are Drawn to Certain Parts of Our Bodies

Just as certain toxins have attractions to certain parts of our bodies, emotions are drawn to certain parts of our bodies too. Energetically speaking, each organ in our physical body holds a set of frequencies. These frequencies attract particular emotions to that area of the body, causing them to set up residence. As we stockpile these emotions, the pent-up emotional states eventually start to affect our physical bodies. The longer we stockpile emotions, the more congested and clogged the energy gets in the organ, and this can eventually lead to not only an ailment but a disease. That is why it is so important we release these emotions from our bodies so that we can live longer, healthier, happier lives.

## Back to the Sandwich Again

As we talked about in chapter 2, I like to use the body (physical body), mind (emotional states), spirit (energy system) sandwich analogy for translating the fact that all of these pieces of us are intimately connected. Although everything starts on the energetic level, we often don't have an awareness of what is going on in our energy system. We aren't taught to have an awareness of this system in general, much less are we able to tell when something is amiss. That is, until we start to FEEL that something is off or we have low-vibrational or negative emotional states that affect us. When this happens it's because whatever was in our energy system has now migrated to the middle of the sandwich, or the mind (emotional) layer. This is where we start to have an awareness. Oftentimes, though, we shove this aside. We get super busy, distracting ourselves with "doing" so we don't feel those emotions, or we cover the emotions up with food, exercise, pills, or alcohol. We are aware we don't feel good emotionally, but we don't know how to fix it, so we deal with it the best we can by using outside resources as a Band-Aid to cover it up. The problem is, those outside resources are exactly that, a Band-Aid. They aren't addressing the root of the problem, and those are the emotional and energetic imprints in the energy system that are causing the disruption in the first place.

(Now, to be clear, if you are on some sort of medication to assist you in functioning, I am not recommending you stop taking it. I can't do that. But I can offer ways to address the underlying cause so that you may have the opportunity for that conversation with your doctor one day.)

With all that said, let's take a minute to connect some dots from the energy system all the way to the physical body so you can see what I am talking about.

## Your Energy System: The Chakras' Role

We have touched on the chakras in this book, but they aren't the superstar here. I've just mentioned them to explain that they exist within the human energy system and are the base for everything we have going on in our lives. However, to successfully take you on the journey from your energy system all the way to things showing up in your physical body, the chakras are a necessary piece of the puzzle. They correspond to your organs on an energetic level, holding the vibrations of particular organs. When there is damage to the chakra or there is an emotional imprint present there, this starts the cascade of events that, if not dealt with, can lead to physical ailments.

In general, each chakra contains certain types of energy, much like certain organs in your body contain certain types of cells. These types of energy and emotional states correspond to the chakra, as well as the organs that are associated with that chakra.

Another cool thing here is that the colors of the chakras correspond with the colors that are associated with the emotional states from the color chapter. Are you starting to get the picture here? You are an intricate, divinely created being on all levels. And once you understand how all of this stuff fits together, you can heal in ways you never thought possible.

# Chakras, Colors, and Their Role in the Physical Body

It's a pretty straightforward association for the most part between the location of the chakras and the location of the organs they are associated with. According to Barbara Anne Brennan in *Hands of Light, A Guide to Healing through the Human Energy Field*, here they are below. I have also found these correlations to be true when working with clients.

Violet/White > Crown > top of the head, pineal gland > upper brain, right eye

Indigo > Head > pituitary gland > lower brain, left eye, ears, nose, nervous system

Blue > Throat > thyroid > bronchial and vocal apparatus, lungs, alimentary canal

Green or pink > Heart > thymus > heart, blood, vagus nerve, circulatory system

Yellow > Solar Plexus > pancreas > stomach, liver, gallbladder, nervous system

Orange > Sacral > Gonads > reproductive system

Red > Root > Adrenals > reproductive system, spinal column, kidneys

# Your Emotional States Relate to Particular Organs

Now that we have established how the chakras or human energy system relates to the organs, let's talk about how the emotional states relate to the organs.

Like we have said before, everything starts in the energy system, trickles down to the emotional states, and then eventually, if not addressed, becomes a physical ailment. So, if we are having some sort of physical ailment, how do we know which emotional states we need to work on to feel better? It so happens that this association has been around for thousands of years in Eastern medicine, and it gives us a pretty good idea of where to start the detective work if we have a physical disease. I have taken the general principles of which organs relate to each emotion based on Eastern medicine and expounded on them to include all of the emotions listed in the book. While there are no hard-and-fast rules to this, the chart on the following pages gives you an idea of why you may be having issues with certain body organs.

**Low-Vibration Emotion Locations in the Physical Body**

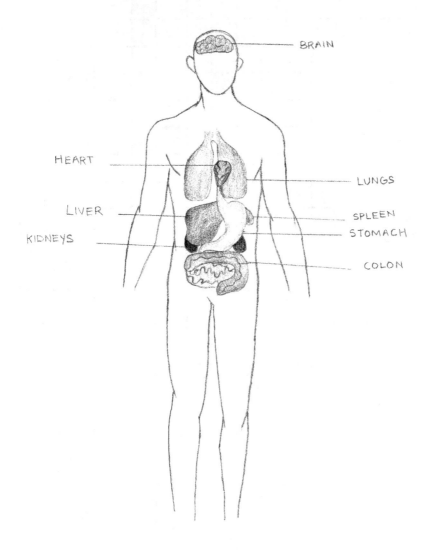

| Emotion | Brain/Head | Throat | Heart | Spleen | Lungs | Intestines | Stomach | Liver/gallbladder | Pancreas | Bladder/Kidney/Adrenals | Knees | Feet | Systemic |
|---|---|---|---|---|---|---|---|---|---|---|---|---|---|
| Abandoned | X | | | | | | | | X | X | | | X |
| Aggressive | | | X | | | | | X | X | | | | |
| Anger | | X | | | | | | X | X | | | | X |
| Anxious | | | | | | X | X | X | | X | | X | X |
| Betrayed | | | X | | | | | X | X | | | | |
| Confused | X | | | X | | | | X | | X | | | |
| Controlling | | X | | | | | | X | | | X | | X |
| Critical | X | | X | X | | | | X | X | X | | X | X |
| Defensive | X | | X | X | | | | X | X | X | | | X |
| Depressed | X | X | X | | X | | | X | | X | X | | X |
| Detached | | | | | X | X | | | X | X | | | |
| Discomfort - not phys | | | X | | X | | | | | X | | | |
| Disorganized | X | X | | | | | | | X | X | | | |
| Distrust | | | X | | | X | X | | X | X | | X | X |
| Dramatic | X | | | X | X | X | X | X | X | X | X | X | X |
| Embarrassed | | | | | | | X | | | X | | | |
| Fearful | X | | X | | | X | X | | | X | X | X | X |
| Flawed | X | X | X | | | X | | | X | X | | X | |
| Grief | | X | X | | X | | | X | X | | | | X |
| Guilty | | | X | | | | | X | X | | | | X |
| Hopeless | | X | | | X | | | | | X | X | | X |
| Hyperactive | X | X | | X | | X | | X | X | X | | | X |
| Imbalanced | | X | | | X | | | | X | X | X | | X |

| Emotion | Brain/Head | Throat | Heart | Spleen | Lungs | Intestines | Stomach | Liver/gallbladder | Pancreas | Bladder/Kidney/Adrenals | Knees | Feet | Systemic |
|---|---|---|---|---|---|---|---|---|---|---|---|---|---|
| Imperceptive | X | | | | | | | | | X | | | |
| Impulsive | X | | X | | | X | X | X | X | | X | | X |
| Indecisive | X | | X | | X | | X | | | X | | X | |
| Indulgence | | | X | | | | X | | | | | X | |
| Ineffective | | | X | X | X | | X | X | X | X | X | | |
| Insecure | | X | X | | X | X | | | | | | X | X |
| Jealous | | | | | | | | X | X | | | | X |
| Lonely | | | X | | | | | | | | | | X |
| Manipulative | X | X | X | X | X | | | X | | | | X | X |
| Materialistic | | | X | X | | X | | X | X | | X | | X |
| Negative (no anger) | | X | X | X | | X | X | X | X | X | | X | X |
| Overbearing | | X | | X | | | X | X | X | | X | X | |
| Overly independent | X | X | X | | X | X | | | | X | X | | X |
| Overstimulated | X | X | | X | | X | X | | | X | | X | X |
| Overwhelmed | | | | | X | | X | | | | | | X |
| Powerless | | | X | | X | X | | | X | | X | | X |
| Rage | X | X | X | | X | | | X | X | | X | | X |
| Resentful | | | X | X | | X | | X | X | | X | | X |
| Sad | X | | X | | X | X | | | X | | X | | X |
| Selfish | | X | X | | | X | | | X | X | X | | X |
| Sleepless | X | | | X | X | X | X | | | X | | | |
| Stifled | X | X | | | X | X | | X | X | X | | X | X |

| Emotion | Brain/Head | Throat | Heart | Spleen | Lungs | Intestines | Stomach | Liver/gallbladder | Pancreas | Bladder/Kidney/Adrenals | Knees | Feet | Systemic |
|---|---|---|---|---|---|---|---|---|---|---|---|---|---|
| Stressed | X | | X | X | X | X | X | X | X | X | | | X |
| Suicidal | | X | X | | X | | X | X | X | X | | | X |
| Temperamental | X | | X | | X | X | X | X | X | | X | | X |
| Tired | X | | | | X | | X | | | X | | X | |
| Unable to express self | X | X | | X | X | | | | | X | | | X |
| Unable to speak truth | | X | X | | | | X | | | | | | X |
| Unclear | | | | | | | X | | X | X | | | X |
| Uncreative | | X | | | | | | | | X | | X | |
| Underwhelmed | | | | X | | | | | X | X | | | |
| Unforgiving | | X | | | X | | | X | X | | X | | X |
| Ungrounded | | | | | | | X | | | X | X | X | X |
| Unintelligent | X | X | | X | | X | | X | X | X | | | |
| Unloved | X | | X | | X | | | X | X | | X | | X |
| Unmotivated | X | X | X | X | | | | X | | | | X | X |
| Unsafe | X | X | X | | X | X | X | X | X | | | X | X |
| Unsuccessful | X | | X | | | | X | | X | X | | | X |
| Untruthful | | X | X | | | | X | X | X | | X | | X |
| Unworthy | X | X | X | | X | X | X | | X | | | | X |
| Vulnerable | | X | X | X | X | X | | | X | | X | X | X |
| Weak | X | | X | | X | | | | X | X | X | | X |
| Withdrawn | | X | X | | | X | X | X | X | X | | X | X |

# Setting the Intention for Releasing Emotions from Organs

There are a couple of different ways you can go about setting the intention to release emotions from your organs. You can focus on a particular organ, or you can focus on a particular emotion to release. As you can see from the previous pages, most emotions have a propensity for more than one organ.

If you are experiencing a certain emotion strongly and you want to address it specifically, such as anger, use the chart to locate all of the organs anger is found in and set the intention by addressing the emotion to release from those particular organs.

If you are having issues with a particular organ, such as having a chest cold, you might want to focus on releasing all of the emotions found in the lungs, instead of just targeting one emotion. If you are also having a sore throat and stuffy head, you would want to add those organs in too.

Lastly, you can be very specific and just target one emotion from one organ. For example, if you are having anxiety before a test, you can set the intention to just release anxiety from your stomach.

The plus side is, the intention is very narrow, so all of the energy of intention to release the emotion is going to a particular area. The minus side is that, since everything is related, being that specific may not give you the results you desire. So if focusing on one organ and one emotion doesn't alleviate it, look at the chart on previous pages and also call out any other organs that have "anxious" within them. In this case, the bladder/kidney/adrenals, intestines, liver/gallbladder, and feet also tend to hold anxiety. Sometimes an upset stomach (nausea) can be caused by a drop in blood sugar that is brought on by stressed adrenals. Nausea from anxiety can also be caused by poor digestion involving the liver, gallbladder, and intestines, so it can help to target all body areas in your intention. As far as the feet go, with anxiety, rubbing them can help, since sore spots on the feet correspond to particular organs.

**Technique 6.1. Releasing an Emotion(s) from Several Organs**

1. Start by choosing an emotion to work on. Let's use the example of anger.
2. Locate all of the organs anger is found within on the chart on previous pages. It is found in the throat, liver/gallbladder, and pancreas.

3. You can set the intention to release this emotion by saying, "I choose to release anger from my throat, liver, gallbladder, and pancreas."
4. If you want to dig deeper, add the ending of "and whatever it's attached to." For example, "I choose to release anger from my throat, liver, gallbladder and pancreas *and whatever it's attached to.*"

### Technique 6.2. Releasing Emotions from a Particular Organ

1. Start by choosing an organ to work on. Let's use the example of the lungs.
2. You can set the intention to release the emotions located in the lungs by saying, "I choose to release all of the low-vibration emotions from my lungs."
3. If you want to dig deeper, add the ending of "and whatever it's attached to." For example, "I choose to release all of the low-vibration emotions from my lungs and *whatever they are attached to.*"

### Technique 6.3. Releasing One or More Emotions from a Particular Organ

1. Start by choosing an organ on the chart and an emotion or emotions that are found in that organ.
2. You can set the intention for an organ by simply saying, "*I choose to release (the emotion) from (the organ).*" Example: "I choose to release anxiety from my stomach."
3. If you feel that you need to release more than one emotion related to the organ, you can simply add it onto the statement, such as: "I choose to release anxiety and fear of new things from my stomach."
4. If you want to dig deeper, add the ending of "and whatever it's attached to." For example, "I choose to release anxiety and fear of new things from my stomach *and whatever they are attached to.*"

As we have said before, adding this little ending of *whatever it is/ they are attached to* is pretty powerful. It digs a little deeper to start unwinding the roots of the low-vibration emotions that trigger you. In the long run, you will start seeing fewer physical symptoms if you do this. It may take some time, as the physical body takes a while to stop reacting to your emotional states. This is due to your body being used to reacting this way. It has to unlearn the behavior, but by unraveling and releasing the underlying energetic structures that caused it to begin with, you can start to heal.

## Acute Illnesses

Afflictions such as colds, stomach bugs, or bacterial infections all have an energetic root to them, and releasing emotions around them can help. While you may not see a difference right away if you are in the thick of being sick, releasing the low-vibration emotions in your organs that are affected can help your physical body heal faster and strengthen your immune system.

So next time you feel a tickle in your throat, look at the list of emotional states and see if you have anything going on in your life right now that may be triggering a specific emotion to let illness set in. Have you been holding back speaking your truth, or have you been swallowing anger? Check in with yourself and start working on releasing those emotions before you get sick. You may be able to lessen the illness or prevent it all together.

## Chronic Ailments and Disease

This is a big topic and really warrants a book of its own. Chronic ailments and disease take years to form, and the roots of them are often formed in childhood. Emotional traumas can set up long-term physical complications by impacting the energy system first and then trickling down to the physical body. Physical traumas contribute to these illnesses as well.

By releasing the energy behind the traumas, you can improve your physical symptoms over time. They may not go away completely, but many clients state that even though they may not be all the way physically better, releasing the root causes have helped them be in a much better place mentally, therefore improving their lives.

Doing the techniques in this book daily as part of a routine is a good way to start chipping away at the years of traumatic and verbal inhibitory imprints that are arresting your energy system and causing your physical ailments.

If you are taking medications or seeing doctors for your ailments, these techniques/energy work are not a substitute for seeing your doctor but can safely be used in conjunction with your health routine. You may start to physically heal as a result of working on yourself.

Talk to your doctor about adjustments in your prescribed health care routine before making any on your own.

## Putting It All Together

I had a client, Mary, come to me several years ago complaining of being tired and stressed all the time. She had gained weight and was in a state of depression. Her voice was faint. Mary had gone through a tough divorce and was doing her best to coparent with a narcissist. She felt disregarded, and her children were being manipulated in the situation and pitted against her. She was at her wits' end as to how to survive the next several years in this situation.

When I started diving into her physical ailments, she mentioned offhand that she had Hashimoto's disease, which is an autoimmune condition of the thyroid. She also had digestive issues (Crohn's disease and bouts of nausea). These conditions made it even harder to deal with her life situation. When I asked her how long she had been dealing with these ailments, she remarked that they were present for most of her marriage. Before that she had been fairly healthy.

At this point, she felt as if she had no voice in her life. And after taking one look at her energy system, I could see why. Her throat chakra was very dark blue and almost invisible. It was shriveled and wilted. Her solar plexus or emotional chakra looked as if it had been unraveled, and the bright yellow color that should have been present there was a dingy gray-yellow. Her sacral chakra was enlarged, flaccid, and no longer rotating as it should.

So let's break down what that means a little bit and connect the dots. As we have said before, everything present in the energy system trickles down to the physical body, and her physical body was screaming at her.

The state of her throat chakra was related to her constant recoil from not being heard or seen in her life and being disregarded. She was unable to speak her truth and swallowed her anger, so her energy system made that chakra smaller and smaller, since she wasn't using it. The less she used her voice, the less it was able to function, until eventually this effect trickled down to her physical body, leading to her thyroid disorder and weak vocal cords.

Her emotional chakra was not bright yellow as it should have been. It was frayed and sullen. Energy was not flowing in that part of her body, as it was damaged by stress, nervousness, and dread. This trickled down and lent itself to her bouts of nausea and Crohn's disease.

The sacral chakra was enlarged from trying to please others by overgiving and not receiving anything in return. Her boundaries were pretty much nonexistent. She was constantly exhausted and felt like a failure in her life. This was reflected in her physical body with the depletion of her endocrine system, throwing her hormones out of balance and lending itself to her thyroid disorder. This chakra's depletion also played a part in her Crohn's disease, since this is the area of the intestines.

Mary was in a complicated place. Since her physical body was manifesting symptoms of this magnitude, this was not a quick fix. She had had these conditions for years.

We started by talking about how she could better manage her mindset in the situation so that she felt she had more control. I helped her understand the link between her physical ailments, her emotions, and her energy system. She then learned some basic releasing techniques and was instructed to use them any time she was triggered. I also instructed her to teach these techniques to her children to help them manage their situation with their father and stepmother so as to help them not exhibit the same physical ailments she was facing.

After she went through a few rounds of the releasing techniques, her voice shifted. It was more solid and confident. She reported feeling a bit better.

I then performed some energy work on Mary to address her damaged energy system directly. After the session was finished, she was standing up straighter and was smiling . . . something she hadn't done since she'd walked through the door.

I saw Mary a few more times, and she reported feeling better overall. She now had ways to manage her daily stress and found herself able to hold her own more in life situations. Even though her physical ailments did not vanish completely, she reported that her bouts of nausea had lessened and her doses of thyroid medication had stabilized, something she did not initially mention having an issue with.

Through using energy techniques, she learned to empower herself and manage her emotions. She was finally taking her life back.

# Chapter Challenge

Think about any ailments you have. Maybe you just have recurring bouts of bronchitis or you have allergies on a regular basis. Some of you may have more serious ailments, such as autoimmune disorders or cancer. While food and environment can play a role in physical illness, looking at the emotional and energetic links to physical ailments is worth doing on a personal level to better understand why your body is functioning like it is.

Do you currently have any ailments?

What organ or organs do they correspond to?

Locate the organs on the chart and see which emotions correspond to that organ.

Which emotions are you experiencing?

Do you have any ailments now that you did not have previously?

If so, what changed in your life?

What emotions are present now that weren't present before the change?

Did you used to have ailments that you no longer have?

If so, what changed in your life?

What emotions are present now that weren't present before the change?

# Feel Better Five

- Every ailment begins energetically and eventually trickles down to the physical body.
- Emotions are drawn to certain organs of our bodies.
- Chakras, color, emotions, and organs are all linked.
- Releasing emotions from organs helps them to function better.
- Even chronic illness can be improved by releasing emotions.

# Transform in Five

Technique 6.1. Releasing an Emotion(s) from Several Organs

1. Start by choosing an emotion to work on. Let's use the example of anger.
2. Locate all of the organs anger is found within on the organ chart on pages 78-80. It is found in the throat, liver/gallbladder, and pancreas.
3. You can set the intention to release this emotion by saying, "I choose to release anger from my throat, liver, gallbladder, and pancreas."
4. If you want to dig deeper, add the ending of "and whatever it's attached to." For example, "I choose to release anger from my throat, liver, gallbladder, and pancreas *and whatever it's attached to.*"

Technique 6.2. Releasing Emotions from a Particular Organ

1. Start by choosing an organ to work on. Let's use the example of lungs.
2. You can set the intention to release the emotions located in the lungs by saying, "I choose to release all of the low-vibration emotions from my lungs."
3. If you want to dig deeper, add the ending of "and whatever it's attached to." For example, "I choose to release all of the low vibration *emotions from my lungs and whatever they are attached to.*"

Technique 6.3. Releasing One or More Emotions from a Particular Organ

1. Start by choosing an organ on the chart on pages 78-80 and an emotion or emotions that are found in that organ.
2. You can set the intention for an organ by simply saying, "*I choose to release (the emotion) from (the organ).*" Example: "I choose to release anxiety from my stomach."
3. If you feel that you need to release more than one emotion related to the organ, you can simply add it onto the statement, such as: "I choose to release anxiety and fear of new things from my stomach."

4.  If you want to dig deeper, add the ending of "and whatever it's attached to." For example, "I choose to release anxiety and fear of new things from my stomach *and whatever they are attached to.*"

In the next chapter, we will start flexing your imagination muscle, and you will learn how to use this powerful tool to heal.

# CHAPTER 7

# Your Imagination Is the Key to Manifestation

When I first had my awakening, it was all a jumbled mess of emotions, visions, and sounds. I didn't know how I was going to come out the other side okay, let alone how to get there, or where I even was to begin with. What was going on, and how was I going to move through it?

A couple of months after my awakening happened, the mentor and teacher of the woman who facilitated my awakening came to town. I was so excited. I knew I had to get in to see her while she was here. She had been doing energy work for a long time, and I felt if anyone could help me, she could.

When I arrived at the office and met her, I was in awe. She was so grounded and seemed to emanate light. I felt intimidated and a little embarrassed. I was such a hot mess with so many questions.

She greeted me and immediately started channeling information about me, although at the time, I had no idea what was going on. She started talking to me about how when I am cooking dinner and I hear a voice say a word or a phrase, I should write it down. *How did she know I was hearing voices while I was making dinner?!* Next she told me that when I get overwhelmed by emotions in the middle of vacuuming my living room, I need to stop and go perform a certain energy technique. This would calm my emotions. *What?! I had just gotten overwhelmed like that while I was vacuuming the day before.* This lady was really starting to freak me out. I felt really vulnerable and embarrassed.

After a few more of these statements, I finally stopped her. "How do you know that's what I've been going through?"

"I can see it," she said simply.

"See it?" I asked.

I was seeing things, but nothing was clear. I didn't understand it right then, but she was about to teach me how to turn those jumbled random flashes of visions into the most powerful tool for getting me to the other side.

When most people are experiencing overwhelming emotions, they don't know what to focus on to feel better. They don't have a plan for finding a way out of the place they are in. In life, we aren't taught emotional management tools. We are told to calm down, take it easy, or relax. But when we are severely triggered and overwhelmed, that is not so easy to do. When people are told to shift their emotional states, they do not have a framework or focus for releasing emotions. They may try to let things go, but without a structure of how to do it, they feel lost.

One of the ways to make releasing emotions easier is to use the power of visualization. *When we visualize something in the mind, the physical and energetic bodies respond accordingly.* When we simply visualize something, our mind and body follow suit with whatever we are focusing on. This allows us to have a great deal of control over what our energetic bodies are doing and how. But how do we know what to focus on or even where to start? For some of us, we have to go waaaay back.

## The Secret to Start Visualizing

Think back to when you were a child. What did you use to daydream about? Was it visions of what you wanted to be when you grew up, far off lands, or imaginary friends? When you closed your eyes, how big did you dream? For most kids, I would say it's big. And often. When our imaginations run wild, anything is possible. We could be a knight storming a castle or an astronaut going to the moon. But as we get older, "reality" sets in. Our worlds tend to get smaller, and we daydream more about things like what it would be like to have a new car or how to ask our boss for a raise. The childlike dreams seem like they were a waste of time now, and we spend our energy on thinking about our day-to-day. For the most part, that's okay, but what if I told you that the childlike daydreaming you did when you were younger is the key to feeling better fast? Would you consider revisiting it? Would you even know how to get back there?

The good news is, it's like riding a bike. You *can* get back there again. In this chapter, we are going to talk about getting back there and give you some images to help you jar your imagination muscle so that you can start using it to release stuck emotions in your energetic imprints.

## Step One, Stretch the Muscle . . . but with Some Rules

But what about meditating? Aren't I supposed to meditate??

Meditation is a powerful tool, but in this book, we are starting at step one. When someone is told to meditate, I find that it often brings up anxiety and self-judgment for people. They have ideas around what meditating looks like and what they are supposed to do. Some say they can't clear their mind or get it to be still long enough to meditate. So I say, don't. Start somewhere else. By reopening your imagination, you are engaging your third eye in a way that allows your mind to "bridge" the activity of imagining into a place where you can have deeper access to a state that is more meditative. Using the imagination is like engaging a "back door." Your mind is looking for something to do, so let it. When you reengage your imagination, you will start to see the same types of things that would show up if you were purposefully trying to meditate. You will start to "see" things that you were not consciously thinking about, such as colors, shapes, beings, memories, symbols, and so on.

In addition, there are certain types of people that do not benefit from deep meditation. If you are the type of person that "checks out" or freezes when you are triggered, you are already in a dissociated state. For you, meditating by relaxing into meditation can make things worse. The technique of imagining, however, engages your brain in a way that allows you to access your emotional states while remaining connected to your physical body, which is super important. Otherwise, you have no ability to access the emotions trapped in your physical body, and you can get stuck in the pattern of just reliving events and not releasing them.

Deep meditation takes practice and is worth exploring if you are not dissociative and are so inclined, but imagining is a way to get there NOW without the stress of wondering if you are doing it "right."

We're going to practice a bit to remind you of what daydreaming feels like. If you feel like you have this down, you can go through the techniques quickly, but it's worth running through them and will make the envisioning to let go of emotions happen more easily.

The goal of these techniques is to stretch your imagination past the everyday and into a very different space. The first step is to brainstorm. Brainstorming is the closest thing adults have in their lives to structured daydreaming. It feels productive, and it is, but here we are using it as a stepping stone to bigger things.

The rule is this: **Do not judge where your mind goes.** It doesn't matter where it goes or what it does. Let it go.

### Technique 7.1. You with No Limits

1.  Imagine yourself completely free of the emotional blocks you have right now.
2.  If you had nothing holding you back, would you be living in the same place? With the same people? Would you live in a different country, have a different job? Would you have lots of money or peace of mind?
3.  Allow yourself to dream as far as you can possibly go.

**The only rule is, if you find yourself saying, I can't do that or say that or leave that behind, push past it and dream it anyway.** You are not going to hurt someone's feelings by dreaming about something. This is your dream, not theirs. Try to do this for about five minutes or until it naturally ends. You can write things down if you want to, but it is not required.

You can repeat this technique a few times if it helps you. If you have not done this much, it can be really liberating to dream this way.

Questions:
Did your imagination go places that you didn't expect?
Did you think of things that perhaps you had forgotten about or had never dreamed of before?

If you did, congratulations! That is a good sign. If it went to places of worry or limitation, don't be too concerned. It just means that you have some limiting energetic imprints that need to be cleared of stuck emotional states. We will address this in the book. Simply redirect and try again.

Using the brain to daydream brings the subconscious mind to the forefront. Using your imagination engages what is called the "third eye." It is located in between your eyes on your forehead and is where the third eye chakra is located. When one is intuitive or psychic, this is the part of the energy system that is activated. By daydreaming and imagining, you are flexing this energy system "muscle." The imagination turns it on. The more you use it, the easier it gets and the better you are at it.

The next step is to be a little more free with your daydreaming. I'm going to give you a basic structure, but let your mind go as free and far as it possibly can. The more outrageous, the better. This time, try to let your mind go more, as in, just watch the "movie" that your imagination is playing in front of your eyes. Relax and let your mind wander free. Don't worry about being able to put words to what you are seeing, and don't try to make it make sense. This takes daydreaming a step further. It lets your subconscious and third eye engage at a higher level.

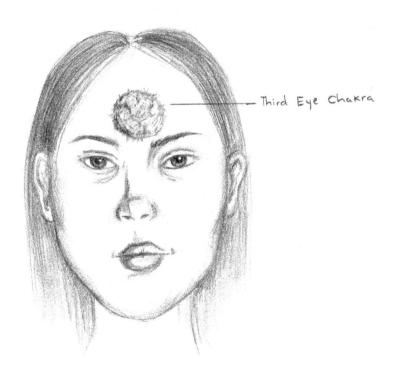

Third Eye Chakra

**Technique 7.2. Dream It**

Try one or all of these:

1. Imagine a far-off land.
2. Imagine living on another planet.
3. Imagine living in a time period that fascinates you.

Questions:

1. Where did you go, and did it have a name?
2. Who did you meet?
3. What time period were you in?
4. What happened when you went to these places in your imagination?
5. If it had a taste, what would that be?
6. If it had a smell, what would that be?

You may have found this technique a little tougher, but hopefully you were able to let your mind go. Repeat these techniques a few times. If you feel led, write down things that stand out to you about your daydreams in this Section.

As you start to activate your third eye with these techniques, your energy system starts to open up as well. The disconnection that has formed over your lifetime between your awareness of your conscious mind, subconscious mind, and energy system starts to heal. When this happens, you gain access to your energy system in your conscious mind and third eye. This is what allows you to start being able to "see" what is going on in your energy system and, therefore, to heal it. It allows you to envision letting go of the emotions that are stuck in your emotional energetic imprints. When you can "see" what is going on, it becomes infinitely easier. Just think of how many things you do with your eyes open. Probably just about everything. Have you ever tried to fix your hair with your eyes closed? Why would you? The same goes for releasing emotional states. If you can envision it, even in your imagination, that is the start to being able to fully use your inner vision to see your energy system and interact with it.

# A Word about Using Your Imagination and Third Eye

When you use your imagination, should your eyes be open or closed? The answer: it doesn't matter. If you are just starting out, it will probably be easier to get a "blank slate" to use your imagination on if your eyes are closed. People often see colors with their physical eyes when their eyes are closed if they are relaxing and doing releasing techniques or energy work. Others may feel more comfortable with their eyes open and staring off into space or looking down at a forty-five-degree angle. Whatever works for you is fine. The key is to allow your mind to wander freely so that you can tap into your third eye vision.

## Visualizing Your Emotions

Now that you have done the techniques 7.1 and 7.2 and have a comfort level with using your imagination again, let's start on the first releasing technique.

The idea is that you are going to be visualizing the emotions you are letting go. This is also a really great way to grow your intuition and gain an in-depth understanding of energy, but to start, just visualizing your body releasing the emotion is the simple technique.

What is it *supposed* to look like?

That's a great question, and there isn't a straightforward answer to this. To start with, you will be envisioning something specific, and as you grow in your understanding and intuition, your envisioning will probably shift. This is normal and just shows that your third eye/imagination muscle is getting stronger.

What if I don't see anything?

That's perfectly fine. I myself tend to see things vividly. It's how I can do detailed energy work. Other people may feel, sense, or just know things instead. These are all different types of intuition. So, if you can't "see" things, don't worry about it. Just imagine it, and eventually your seeing sense strength will grow.

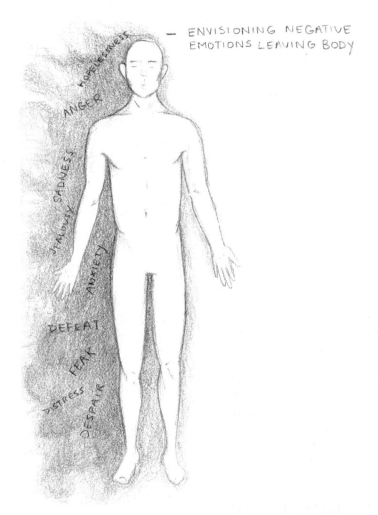

— ENVISIONING NEGATIVE EMOTIONS LEAVING BODY

HOPELESSNESS
ANGER
SADNESS
JEALOUSY
ANXIETY
DEFEAT
FEAR
DISTRESS
DESPAIR

### Technique 7.3. Envisioning for Emotional Release

1. Make a note of how much an emotion is affecting you on a scale of 1–10. This will help you assess your progress with the technique.
2. Get in a quiet place if you can, but in a pinch, just get quiet in your mind as much as you can.
3. Identify the emotion(s) you want to release. Say it out loud, if possible, as the intention statement you have learned: "I choose to release (emotion) and whatever it is attached to." If you have

to say it in your mind, do so. I agree it would look a little weird to say it out loud in the middle of class or in a meeting.

4. Next, envision the emotion(s) leaving your body.
5. You can take a couple of deep breaths to help.
6. When you envision the emotions coming out of your body and floating away, simply envision a gray-to-black or dull-colored cloud of energy or smoke that rises out of you and floats off.
7. The more relaxed you are, the easier this is to do.
8. Keep up the envisioning technique until you feel like the emotion has dissipated or you don't "see it" anymore.
9. Take a couple of more deep breaths.

You can repeat this technique with additional emotions by stating other emotions that come to mind that you need to release. If you are still feeling "off" but nothing specific comes to mind, you can make a more general statement, such as, "I choose to release any other emotions that I need to let go of right now that are in my best and highest good." Now repeat the envisioning technique: a gray-to-black or dull-colored cloud of energy or smoke that rises out of you and floats off.

Important note: We aren't going to get into all of the reasons why here (we will talk about it later), but when you are envisioning the emotions floating off, direct the cloud of emotions out a window or door if at all possible. You don't want those low-vibration emotions sticking around in your space.

## You May Not See or Feel a Cloud of Emotions

It's also good to note that for some people, the emotions take different forms when they are leaving the body. This is determined by which of your chakras are more highly developed, so it is unique to each person. Here are some other things you might experience when you are releasing emotions:

- You may see other colors than black or gray. This is perfectly fine. If the emotions are leaving, they need to go. Don't worry about letting go of something you shouldn't. It doesn't work that way.
- The emotional energy may have a different texture or feel to it. It can be stringy or sticky, like yarn, dust, or a blob. It may look or feel like something else too. All are fine. Each person lets go of energy in a different way.
- Each time you release emotions, it may look different. Sometimes it may be a cloud, and other times it may be stringy. This is fine too.

- You may experience physical sensations such as pressure, pain, crying, shaking, shivering, twitching, or muscle contraction. It's usually nothing too crazy. These are actually really good signs that things are leaving. If you are having these reactions, keep going. You can tap on the area to help your body release the emotions if any of these are going on, and it will help the process along. Personally, if I am releasing a really big mess of emotions, I have strong muscle contractions. I breathe through it and keep going. I feel sooo much better after it is over.

## Addressing the Imprint Directly

After you have been working on releasing purely named emotions for a while, you may start to make connections as to where the roots of the emotions lie. Memories and thoughts of traumatic events or inhibitory statements may start to pop up that are connected to the emotions you have been releasing. As we talked about in chapter 2, traumatic and verbal inhibitory imprints are what contain these low-vibration, restrictive emotions that limit us in our lives. Releasing the emotions individually or as a group is great and can work really well, especially in the moment, but the goal is to get to the root of things.

In chapter 4, we talked about the emotional string of beads that forms as a result of these imprints and, as a result, how they can form a series of imprints containing emotions and memories that are seemingly unrelated. However, we learned they are related because our energy system and subconscious mind have put them into the "root imprint" or original traumatic or verbal inhibitory imprint. Even if we have no understanding of how our emotions or memories are related to an event, that emotion or event is vibrationally similar to something that we are experiencing now. Somehow, they were part of the creation of the original imprint.

It's important to understand that you do not ever have to figure out why or how these things are related. What's important is that by working on releasing the energy or emotions contained in the root imprint, you can actually save yourself a lot of time in releasing other emotions and memories.

That's right. Working with the "root imprint" allows you to go straight to the source of the original imprint on that string of beads. Oftentimes when those emotions in the root imprint are addressed, the rest of the string of beads simply disappears, or at the very least, those other emotional imprints or beads that are linked to the root lose their intensity. That is because when you address the root of the issue, all of the other emotional imprints that are attached to it lose their power. There is no signal being sent to the attached imprints that they are supposed to be reacting to the emotions and memories in the root imprint. Simply put, if you unplug an appliance from a wall, does it still work (assuming it doesn't have batteries)? The appliance is no longer receiving the charge that it needs to operate. Traumatic and verbal inhibitory imprints are the same. When you address the root imprint (the electrical charge), the other imprints (appliances) that are inhibiting you no longer do.

Once you identify the root imprint, you can address it by first setting the intention with your intention statement. This will look a little different from intention statements we have used before, since we are addressing the imprint directly.

Let's use an example here that is near and dear to me. It's an experience that left me with a fear of water and pretty much anything to do with it. When I was nineteen, I was being pulled in a tube on a jet ski. The tube flipped over, pinning me underneath it. My head became stuck between the mesh at the bottom of the tube and the side, pulling me along by the head. My body was dragged behind the tube. I couldn't move the tube off my head due to the force created by the water, and I could not breathe. It was absolutely terrifying. While this experience lasted probably a matter of seconds before the jet ski stopped, right then I would have sworn I was under for a minute or more. The event left me with neck problems and headaches that I still struggle with today. Anytime I get stressed or eat the wrong foods, I can get a headache from it. It's annoying, to say the least. Before I understood the value of releasing the emotions attached to this event, I would get severe headaches that would last for several days. What's more, I would get so nervous around water and boats that I could barely function, and it felt like I was being tortured. "But shouldn't I be having fun?" I thought. I wasn't still under that tube in the lake. I was on a boat with different people in a different place. But that traumatic root imprint was causing alarm bells to go off in my energy system that said I was in danger, even though I was perfectly safe.

My now husband was recently talking about getting a boat, and I found myself in a panic. I had worked on this event so much that I thought I had addressed it all, but here it was again, only this time I addressed the traumatic imprint differently, and I can honestly say now the thought of being on a boat or even living on one, for that matter, doesn't alarm me at all.

So, to address this root imprint, I simply said, "I choose to release the fear of being pinned underneath that tube and everything it is attached to." I watched the event before my eyes like a movie, and as I felt the emotions come up, I envisioned them leaving my body in a cloud of energy. I took a few deep breaths to help clear them out.

It's important to note that you may have some degree of emotional reaction, depending on the intensity of the imprint. I did get emotional when I said that sentence. I had never cried in relation to that event, so I did have a physical reaction as the emotions left my body. This is not abnormal, and feeling the emotions as they leave can be part of releasing them. It doesn't mean they are sticking around. It's just them waving goodbye on the way out the door.

After I said that intention and envisioned it leaving, another memory popped up that I had forgotten about. I almost drowned in swim class when I was eight. I had worked on this imprint multiple times after being dragged under the tube when I was nineteen but still had a fear of all things water as an adult afterward. I always assumed that the event when I was eight was stronger because it was first. In the beginning, this was true, because the other one had not occurred yet, but after the other event happened at nineteen, it sort of "took over" as the root imprint later in my life.

That may seem really confusing. The subconscious often is. Remember, there is no linear path here. In chapter 4 we talked about the emotional string of beads and how sometimes, some of the beads from different parts of the string get stuck together with "glue." That is what happened here. Since the second imprint was stronger, it became the dominant traumatic imprint. I had already addressed the traumatic imprint from almost drowning when I was eight many, many times, so it had lost most of its charge. But the imprint that occurred when I was nineteen stuck to it and reignited it to a point, since it was vibrationally similar. This is what caused it to pop up after I worked on the nineteen-year-old root imprint. The good thing is, when emotions are released from an imprint, they don't come back. So the eight-year-old imprint only had a small amount of the original emotion in it when the nineteen-year-old imprint stuck to it.

When the memory of almost drowning when I was eight popped up, I simply said, "I choose to release all of the emotions from the event of almost drowning in swim class when I was eight and anything that it is attached to." I didn't feel fear, but I felt a little anxiety come up. It left me easily.

I had one additional memory pop up during this technique. It was one of being chased in a pond by water moccasins when I was twelve. This memory kind of made me laugh, but I did feel some fear surface as I envisioned the event. I simply said, "I choose to release all of the emotions around being chased by water moccasins and everything it is attached to." I had no emotional reaction, and no other memories or emotions came up after that. It was the end of that string of beads. And the belief that water was dangerous had left me. In case you were wondering, this whole process took me about ten minutes. When you are just starting out, it could take fifteen to twenty, just because you are new to the techniques. If I had stopped after the root imprint (this process took about two minutes), I would have gotten the majority of the emotions that needed to come out, and the emotions from the two other imprints might have left on their own. After you learn the process, though, digging deeper doesn't take that much more time.

When you are addressing traumatic and verbal inhibitory imprints, it's important not to judge what comes up or in what order. Only our subconscious has a rhyme or reason to it. But if you follow that string of beads, you are honoring your energy system, emotions, and physical body by releasing it in the order that will work the fastest with the best results.

**Technique 7.4. Releasing from the Root Imprint**

1. Make a note of how much the emotion is affecting you on a scale of 1–10. This will help you assess your progress with the technique.
2. Get in a quiet place if you can, but in a pinch, just get quiet in your mind as much as you can.
3. Identify the imprint you want to release emotions from. Say it out loud (describe it or name it): "I choose to release (the emotions of the root event) and whatever it is attached to." If you have to say it in your mind, do so.
4. Next, envision the emotions leaving your body and floating away.
5. You can take a couple of deep breaths to help.

6. When you envision the emotions coming out of your body and floating away, simply envision a gray-to-black or dull-colored cloud of energy or smoke that rises out of you and floats off.
7. The more relaxed you are, the easier this is to do.
8. Keep up the envisioning technique until you feel like the emotions have dissipated or you don't "see them" anymore.
9. Take a couple more deep breaths.

# Variations of the Technique

These technique variations can be used independently or together, and the more you use them, the better results you will get. As your emotions clear from your imprints, you will have more clarity overall, and your intuition will increase. Which in turn makes you better overall.

Where do you "see it" and "feel it"?

We talked about just releasing these emotions in general; now let's focus on where you are seeing and feeling them.

As you gain greater awareness, you will start to feel emotions in certain parts of your body. For example, just about everyone has experienced "butterflies" in their stomach or felt heartache when we end a relationship or lose a loved one. While these are physical sensations, they are driven by emotional states. As we talked about in chapter 6 on the organs, certain emotions relate to specific organs, and in many cases, one emotion can be found in more than one place in the body. It's important to note, however, that you may tend to have a particular emotion housed mainly in one or two places in your body. Everyone is different. You may feel sensations such as tightness, pain, or a congested feeling where the emotion is kept or have an ailment in that area. By combining where you are feeling these sensations with the following technique below, you can start to really connect the dots about where your body stores particular emotions.

### Technique 7.5. Feeling and Releasing a Stuck Emotion

1. Make a note of how much an emotion is affecting you on a scale of 1–10. This will help you assess your progress with the technique.

2. Get in a quiet place if you can, but in a pinch, just get quiet in your mind as much as you can.
3. Identify the emotion you want to release.
4. See if you can feel where the emotion you named is stuck.
5. Set your intention: "I choose to release (emotion) in my (body organ/area) and whatever it is attached to."
6. Next, envision the emotion rising up and floating off from its location in your body.
7. You can take a couple of deep breaths to help. The more relaxed you are, the easier this is to do.
8. Let this technique continue until it no longer feels like the emotion is stuck in that place and/or you don't "see it" anymore.
9. Take a couple more deep breaths.
10. Now, using envisioning, scan your body from top to bottom to see if you can "see" or feel that emotion stuck anywhere else.
11. Repeat the technique for each area you feel it stuck. Doing it this way helps you bring a new level of awareness to where you are storing these emotions in your body and developing your intuition in sight and feeling for releasing them.

## A Shortcut

If you like this technique but want to use a shortcut after you have developed the skill doing one area at a time, you can use the intention setting statement to help facilitate a quicker release of all the areas where these particular emotions are stuck.

**Technique 7.6. Feeling and Releasing a Stuck Emotion (Entire Body)**

1. Make a note of how much an emotion is affecting you on a scale of 1–10. This will help you assess your progress with the technique.
2. Get in a quiet place if you can, but in a pinch, just get quiet in your mind as much as you can.
3. Identify the emotion you want to release.
4. See if you can feel where the emotion you named is stuck.
5. Set your intention: "I choose to release (emotion) and whatever it is attached to."
6. Next, envision the emotion rising up and floating off from its locations in your body.
7. You can take a couple of deep breaths to help. The more relaxed you are, the easier this is to do.

8. Let this technique continue until it no longer feels that the emotion is stuck in those places and/or you don't "see it" anymore.
9. Take a couple more deep breaths.
10. Now, using envisioning, scan your body from top to bottom to see if you can "see" or feel that emotion stuck anywhere else.
11. Repeat the technique until you feel it is gone from all its locations.

So why would I care where they are releasing from if I can do it all at once?

It's definitely optional to care, and frankly, you may not always have the time to think about it, hence the name of the book. However, if you are looking to have deeper long-term results, knowing where you have tendencies to store stuck emotions can give you clues as to why you may be having physical ailments in certain areas of your body or where you are likely to develop them. By having an awareness, you can start to understand how your energy system functions at a deeper level and use your increased intuition to assist you in other areas of your life.

## Addressing Specific Parts of the Body

If you are having uncomfortable physical sensations or ailments, refer to the chart in chapter 6 to get an understanding of what emotions might be lending to your discomfort. For example, if you are having foot pain, you have a couple of options on how to address it. This is assuming your foot has not suffered a physical trauma, although the emotion probably contributed to the injury, but that is another subject altogether.

**Technique 7.7. Envisioning Release for Specific Body Parts**

1. First, make a note of how much an emotion is affecting you on a scale of 1–10. In this case, you can use the scale to denote your level of pain. This will help you assess your progress with the technique.
2. Get in a quiet place if you can, but in a pinch, just get quiet in your mind as much as you can.
3. Identify the area of the body and the emotion you want to release from it.
4. Set your intention: "I choose to release (emotion) and pain from my (body part) and whatever it is attached to."

5.  Next, envision the emotion and pain rising up and floating off from its location(s) in your body.
6.  You can take a couple of deep breaths to help. The more relaxed you are, the easier this is to do.
7.  Let this technique continue until it no longer feels that the emotion is stuck in those places and or you don't "see it" anymore.
8.  Take a couple more deep breaths.
9.  See if you can envision or feel the emotions leaving your body from any place other than the body part you released from.
10. If you do, check the chart and address the emotional states in the other areas that apply, as they are most likely to be connected on the same string of emotional beads.

## Calming the Nervous System

This technique is a little different from the others, but it is very helpful in a pinch if you get super nervous, scared, or excited and are having trouble calming down. While it can be used on its own, it is meant to be used in conjunction with other emotional releasing techniques if you have severe overwhelm or are experiencing shutdown. Relying on it solely does not address the underlying issue, but it can be helpful in the beginning stages of working on releasing your emotions.

This technique is basically an instant "chill pill." It addresses the amygdala, the area of the brain that is responsible for processing emotional memories. Disruptions in this part of the brain have been linked to PTSD and are what lead to the fight-or-flight response. When this area of the brain is overstimulated, the front part of our brain, the prefrontal cortex, which is responsible for making rational decisions and moderating behavior, is turned down or off, depending on the severity of the stimulus. We become reactive or freeze. We may do things as a reflex or just not be able to calm down. This is tied to our emotional imprints and can also be part of our negative coping mechanisms. We may feel we are "hardwired" to react a certain way in the moment. That is because we are, but you can train yourself out of these knee-jerk reactions by combining this technique with other techniques in the book. With repeated emotional releasing, this technique will be needed less.

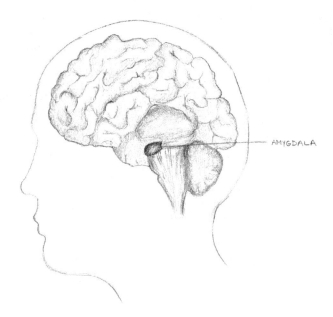

AMYGDALA

**Technique 7.8. Calming Your Fight-or-Flight Response**

Although you can use this technique every time you do emotional release, do use this technique if you have a highly traumatic imprint or emotion (one that registers between 6 and 10) before you begin to work with the imprint and related emotions. If releasing becomes too intense, repeat the amygdala technique below so that emotional releasing is easier.

1. Envision your amygdala (shown in the illustration above). When it is overstimulated, the cells in it go into a rapid-fire mode, sending a flood of signal between the cells. Think of it like turning on a strobe light in that part of your brain. By using an envisioning technique, you can slow this back down, calming it and taking yourself out of panic. The other benefit of doing this is that as the amygdala calms down, it actually allows the prefrontal cortex, which is responsible for rational decisions, to fire up, which is what we want.
2. Simply take a few deep breaths and focus on envisioning the rapid-fire signals calming to a slow pulse.
3. As you envision this decline in activity, your physical body will respond by mimicking your vision. This may take a little practice, but in time, you can master this technique.

4. To practice, wait until you are in a calm state and access a memory that brings up some anxiety or fear. Don't choose anything too overwhelming at first.
5. You can look at your assessment in chapter 3 and choose memories that you rated 4 or 5.
6. Next, envision the amygdala and focus on the strobe signals flooding between the cells.
7. Intentionally envision the cell signals calming to a slow pulse.
8. After you have calmed down your amygdala signals, you should be able to feel the shift in your body.
9. Next, use one of the techniques in the book to release the emotions out of that energetic imprint so it no longer causes a reaction for you.
10. By combining the amygdala calming technique with the emotional release technique, you are rewiring your energy system and physical body to react differently in response to a stimulus.

## Envisioning with Color

As we talked about in chapter 5, emotions have color. As you gain practice in envisioning, you may start to see some color when you see the low-vibration emotion clouds float out of your body. This is perfectly normal. Personally, sometimes I see color, and sometimes I don't. It just depends on what type of emotions are being released. If you look back at the color chart in chapter 5, you will see that there are colors to avoid using with each emotion and colors to use with each emotion. The colors to avoid with each emotion are colors that the emotion holds. Using those colors will aggravate and intensify the emotion rather than release or heal it. For example, colors to avoid when working with anger are red, orange, yellow, and violet. These colors can intensify anger, which is not what you want if you are trying to release it. Colors that calm anger are green and blue.

Later in the book, we will revisit color and talk about bringing it into your body to heal by using the colors in the "colors to use" category for each emotion.

For the purpose of this stage, use the following technique to help you further develop your envisioning skills.

### Technique 7.9. Envisioning and Releasing Emotional Color

1. Choose one emotion to release. By choosing one emotion, you have a better chance of seeing a specific color, rather than a muddle of colors.
2. Say the intention statement, "I choose to release (emotion) and anything that it is attached to."
3. Now, envision the cloud of low-vibration emotions rising up out of your body and floating off. Out a window, preferably, if you are indoors.
4. What colors do you see or sense?
5. Now, look on the chart for that emotion and see if the colors match up.

If you asked to release anger, for example, you may see a mix of red, yellow, orange, or violet. It may be mixed with gray and black as well. If you don't see color, it doesn't mean you did it incorrectly; these things just take practice.

# Sage Advice

As I sat there in my session with that larger-than-life healer, I was intimidated. I told her that I didn't understand what I was seeing.

"It takes time to understand. Don't judge yourself for not grasping it at first. And don't judge yourself for what you are seeing or feeling."

She then taught me that the only thing I needed to pay attention to were things that upset me. These were the things that were keeping me in a state of emotional upheaval. By seeing flashes of upsetting images and feeling emotions with them, my energy system was trying to clear out the emotions that were ready to be released. She taught me to envision these emotions leaving my body and floating away.

I started using this technique many times a day. This is when I started to see a difference in my emotional stability. By remaining as calm as possible when I would see or feel things and simply setting an intention for it to leave and watching it float off, I started to find my true self for the very first time.

# Chapter Challenge

When doing the daydreaming techniques to flex your third eye "muscle" for envisioning, take notes on where your mind goes. If it goes to negative things or emotions, ask yourself some questions:

Does my daydream remind me of an event in my past that was traumatic or limiting?

Do the emotions in my daydream remind me of past events?

How did I react to what was happening in the daydream?

These are clues into where your subconscious is driving the bus, so to speak, and what traumatic and verbal inhibitory imprints need to be addressed. Use the techniques below to address them.

# Feel Better Five

- Reengaging your imagination is the key to envisioning.
- Meditation is not required for envisioning.
- You can address individual emotions or imprints directly with envisioning.
- Envisioning can tell you where emotions are stuck in your body in order for you to release them.
- Envisioning with color can help bring more insight to releasing emotions.

# Transform in Five

Technique 7.1. You with No Limits

1. Imagine yourself completely free of the emotional blocks you have right now.
2. If you had nothing holding you back, would you be living in the same place? With the same people? Would you live in a different country, have a different job? Would you have lots of money or peace of mind?
3. Allow yourself to dream as far as you can possibly go.

Technique 7.2. Dream It

Try one or all of these:

1. Imagine a far-off land.
2. Imagine living on another planet.
3. Imagine living in a time period that fascinates you.

Questions:

1. Where did you go, and did it have a name?
2. Who did you meet?
3. What time period were you in?
4. What happened when you went to these places in your imagination?
5. If it had a taste, what would that be?
6. If it had a smell, what would that be?

Technique 7.3. Envisioning Emotional Release

1. Make a note of how much an emotion is affecting you on a scale of 1–10. This will help you assess your progress with the technique.
2. Get in a quiet place if you can, but in a pinch, just get quiet in your mind as much as you can.
3. Identify the emotions you want to release. Say them out loud, if possible, as the intention statement you have learned: "I choose to release (emotion) and whatever it is attached to." If you have to say it in your mind, do so. I agree it would look a little weird to say it out loud in the middle of class or in a meeting.
4. Next, envision the emotions leaving your body.
5. You can take a couple of deep breaths to help.
6. When you envision the emotions coming out of your body and floating away, simply envision a gray-to-black or dull-colored cloud of energy or smoke that rises out of you and floats off.
7. The more relaxed you are, the easier this is to do.
8. Keep up the envisioning technique until you feel like the emotion has dissipated or you don't "see it" anymore.
9. Take a couple more deep breaths.

Technique 7.4. Releasing from the Root Imprint

1. Make a note of how much an emotion is affecting you on a scale of 1–10. This will help you assess your progress with the technique.

2. Get in a quiet place if you can, but in a pinch, just get quiet in your mind as much as you can.
3. Identify the imprint you want to release emotions from. Say it out loud (describe it or name it): "I choose to release (the emotions of root event) and whatever it is attached to." If you have to say it in your mind, do so.
4. Next, envision the emotions leaving your body and floating away.
5. You can take a couple of deep breaths to help. The more relaxed you are, the easier this is to do.
6. When you envision the emotions coming out of your body and floating away, simply envision a gray-to-black or dull-colored cloud of energy or smoke that rises out of you and floats off.
7. Keep up the envisioning technique until you feel like the emotions have dissipated or you don't "see them" anymore.
8. Take a couple more deep breaths.

After addressing your root imprint, see if any other memories or imprints come to mind. If so, these are on the same string of beads as the root imprint. To go deeper in healing, repeat the imprint technique above until no other memories come to mind.

## Transform in Ten

Technique 7.5. Feeling and Releasing a Stuck Emotion

1. Make a note of how much an emotion is affecting you on a scale of 1–10. This will help you assess your progress with the technique.
2. Get in a quiet place if you can, but in a pinch, just get quiet in your mind as much as you can.
3. Identify the emotion you want to release.
4. See if you can feel where the emotion you named is stuck.
5. Set your intention: "I choose to release (emotion) in my (body organ/area) and whatever it is attached to."
6. Next, envision the emotion rising up and floating off from its location in your body.
7. You can take a couple of deep breaths to help. The more relaxed you are, the easier this is to do.
8. Let this technique continue until it no longer feels that the emotion is stuck in that place and or you don't "see it" anymore.
9. Take a couple more deep breaths.

10. Now, using envisioning, scan your body from top to bottom to see if you can "see" or feel that emotion stuck anywhere else.
11. Repeat the technique for each area you feel it stuck. Doing it this way helps you bring a new level of awareness to where you are storing these emotions in your body and developing your intuition in sight and feeling for releasing them.

Technique 7.6. Feeling and Releasing a Stuck Emotion (Entire Body)

1. Make a note of how much the emotion is affecting you on a scale of 1–10. This will help you assess your progress with the technique.
2. Get in a quiet place if you can, but in a pinch, just get quiet in your mind as much as you can.
3. Identify the emotion you want to release.
4. See if you can feel where the emotion you named is stuck.
5. Set your intention: "I choose to release (emotion) and whatever it is attached to."
6. Next, envision the emotion rising up and floating off from its locations in your body.
7. You can take a couple of deep breaths to help. The more relaxed you are, the easier this is to do.
8. Let this technique continue until it no longer feels that the emotion is stuck in those places and/or you don't "see it" anymore.
9. Take a couple more deep breaths.
10. Now, using envisioning, scan your body from top to bottom to see if you can "see" or feel that emotion stuck anywhere else.
11. Repeat the technique until you feel it is gone from all its locations.

Technique 7.7. Envisioning Release for Specific Body Parts

1. First, make a note of how much an emotion is affecting you on a scale of 1–10. In this case, you can use the scale to denote your level of pain. This will help you assess your progress with the technique.
2. Get in a quiet place if you can, but in a pinch, just get quiet in your mind as much as you can.
3. Identify the area of the body and the emotion you want to release from it.
4. Set your intention: "I choose to release (emotion) and pain from my (body part) and whatever it is attached to."
5. Next, envision the emotion and pain rising up and floating off from its location(s) in your body.

6. You can take a couple of deep breaths to help. The more relaxed you are, the easier this is to do.
7. Let this technique continue until it no longer feels that the emotion is stuck in those places and/or you don't "see it" anymore.
8. Take a couple more deep breaths.
9. See if you can envision or feel the emotions leaving your body from any place other than the body part you released from.
10. If you do, check the chart and address the emotional states in the other areas that apply, as they are most likely to be connected on the same string of emotional beads.

Technique 7.8. Calming Your Fight-or-Flight Response

1. Envision your amygdala (see page 106) . When it is overstimulated, the cells in it go into a rapid-fire mode, sending a flood of signals between the cells. Think of it like turning on a strobe light in that part of your brain. By using an envisioning technique, you can slow this back down, calming it and taking yourself out of panic. The other benefit of doing this is that as the amygdala calms down, it actually allows the prefrontal cortex, which is responsible for rational decisions, to fire up, which is what we want.
2. Simply take a few deep breaths and focus on envisioning the rapid-fire signals calming to a slow pulse.
3. As you envision this decline in activity, your physical body will respond by mimicking your vision. This may take a little practice, but in time, you can master this technique.
4. To practice, wait until you are in a calm state and access a memory that brings up some anxiety or fear. Don't choose anything too overwhelming at first.
5. You can look at your assessment in chapter 3 and choose memories that you rated 4 or 5.
6. Next, envision the amygdala and focus on the strobe signals flooding between the cells.
7. Intentionally envision the cell signals calming to a slow pulse.
8. After you have calmed down your amygdala signals, you should be able to feel the shift in your body.
9. Next, use one of the techniques in the book to release the emotions out of that energetic imprint so it no longer causes a reaction for you.
10. By combining the amygdala calming technique with the emotional release technique, you are rewiring your energy

system and physical body to react differently in response to a stimulus.

Technique 7.9. Envisioning and Releasing Emotional Color

1. Choose one emotion to release. By choosing one emotion, you have a better chance of seeing a specific color, rather than a muddle of colors.
2. Say the intention statement, "I choose to release (emotion) and anything that it is attached to."
3. Now, envision the cloud of low-vibration emotions rising up out of your body and floating off. Out a window, preferably, if you are indoors.
4. What colors do you see or sense?
5. Now, look on the chart for that emotion and see if the colors match up.

In the next chapter, you will learn the importance of breathing in releasing emotions and how effective it can be for calming the mind and body.

# CHAPTER 8

---

# Focus Your Breathing for Power Vibes

 When I had been doing this work for about six years, I came upon a very stressful time in my life. I was planning to get a divorce, so in order to get myself in the best place possible before that happened, I decided to start attending counseling. It was something my angels and spirit guides actually recommended for me to do, which I found interesting. After I started attending sessions, I began to see why. Even with all of the abilities I had to tap into the spirit realm and plug into and get guidance from Source, it was comforting to have someone who was actually another human to talk to, and they knew I needed that.

I would go into my sessions a stress ball and just start talking nonstop. The more I talked, the thinner my voice got, and sometimes I would start to get light-headed. My counselor would just smile at me and say, "Breathe." I remember in one session, when I'd had a particularly stressful week, she managed to say it to me four times in one session.

I was getting annoyed. "Why do you keep saying that? I'm breathing!"

"No, not really," she said. "Don't just take a breath. *Breathe.*"

Up until this point, the main focus of my work had been learning all I could from my guides and angels in regard to techniques, practicing on myself, and then bringing these tools into sessions. The techniques were advanced, which I thoroughly enjoyed, but by focusing on these techniques, I had skipped some really important steps without even realizing it. Because of the way I had opened up to the spirit world and became psychic in an instant, I didn't go about it like everyone else. I didn't have to go through the process of learning to connect. It was just like, boom! I was plugged in. The techniques that most people use to open their energy up and connect to Source were foreign to me. I thought I didn't need that.

Like me at the time, most people don't even think twice about breathing. We just do it, and if we are told to breathe, we might take a couple of quick deep breaths and go right back to whatever we were doing. But I was missing a really important point. Breathing is for more than just surviving. *Breathing is a simple yet powerful tool for transforming energetic, physical, and emotional states.* It is not only something that is fundamental; it is a tool we can use to shift us into an optimum state for opening up our energy and releasing emotions.

That brings us to the fundamental technique in this chapter: breathing. Just like I said before, most people don't think about it, but in this chapter, we are going to create an intentional practice of doing it. We are going to be learning what it means to truly breathe versus just taking breaths. Using breath as an intentional technique opens up the energy system. It creates a welcoming, relaxed space for energy to flow within. When people are stressed, anxious, or afraid, this creates a constricted state. In this state, we tend to hold our breath; our bodies are tight. Energy, emotions, oxygen, and blood don't flow well. Breathing intentionally takes our mind off of what is stressing us. It brings us to our present space, and we can't help but relax. In this place, it is easier to focus on releasing emotions.

## The Simple Technique

To start working with this technique, it helps to lie down on your back so you can get a good feel for it. It's easier to tell where you are breathing from and easier to relax. We all have a natural way of breathing. This technique may challenge you a bit, depending on your habits.

## Shoulder Breathing versus Belly Breathing

Take a deep breath without thinking about it. Does your belly go out, or do your shoulders go up? If you are constantly moving and tend to have nervous energy, chances are your shoulders go up instead of your belly going out. This makes it more imperative to practice belly breathing. Why? Because belly breathing will help you to ground yourself too (more on this in chapter 9). People who pull up their shoulders to breathe are ungrounding themselves when told to take a breath. This is still contractive versus expansive. Belly breathing activates your lower chakras, which is imperative in calming and grounding yourself. You can relax much easier.

Some people may find it physically difficult to belly breathe. This can be due to a hiatal hernia (where a portion of the stomach sticks up through the esophageal opening in the diaphragm) and can cause a physical limitation to belly breathing (I know, I have one), but it is still possible in most cases; it just takes some patience and training.

**Technique 8.1. Belly Breathing**

1. Start by breathing in through your nose, filling your chest with air while keeping your shoulders down. Then move on to belly breathing from there.
2. If you are lying down (sitting works too), place your hands over your belly.
3. Now breathe in a deep breath through your nose.
4. As you breathe in, focus on breathing in so that you breathe into your belly, moving your belly under your hands.
5. Now breathe out completely, through your mouth.
6. Do this a couple of times to get the feel for it.
7. Once you get the hang of belly breathing, you don't have to put your hands on your stomach. This makes it easier to use this technique when you are driving a car, or something else where you need to use your hands.
8. Next, take a deep breath in through your nose and hold your breath for four seconds.
9. Now breathe out completely through your mouth. Do this ten times.
10. This will get you to a relaxed state, but not so relaxed that you can't get up and go do something afterward.

# Quick Technique Version

No matter where you are or what you are doing, taking some really deep, slow breaths can calm your body, mind, and energy system, bringing you back to center. Next time you are stressed, try taking some deep breaths in through your nose, holding for about three to four seconds, and out through your mouth to reach a calmer state.

**Technique 8.2. Relaxing Fast**

1. Belly breathe in through your nose as described above.
2. As you breathe in, tense every muscle in your body.
3. Hold for ten seconds and exhale through your mouth as you relax every muscle in your body at the same time.
4. Repeat this ten times.
5. This will release pent-up tension in your body and get you into a deeply meditative state.

6.  Doing this technique two to three times can help you to just get relaxed quickly. Perform no more than three times if you have a "freeze" coping mechanism.

This technique variation is often used in meditation classes to obtain an altered state, so use it carefully. You don't want to do this ten times and then go right out and try to drive a car or chop vegetables in the kitchen. However, reaching a deeply meditative state can make it easier to go much deeper into your energy system and release more embedded emotions. Just keep in mind, if you already tend to disassociate (or freeze), you don't want to overdo this one (no more than three deep breaths). In that case, deep meditation isn't your friend.

# Additional Techniques

Now that you have an understanding of how to do the simple technique, it's time to play with some variations, diving deeper into breathing and mixing in some energy work.

### Technique 8.3. Breathing In White Light

The breathing techniques on the following pages combine the envisioning and feeling techniques you learned in the previous chapter with the new breathing techniques you are learning now. Combining these increases the potency for releasing emotions.

WHITE LIGHT

NEGATIVE EMOTIONS

1.  Start by saying your intention: "I choose to release (emotion[s]) and anything that it is attached to."
2.  Next take a deep breath in through your nose, only this time, envision breathing in white light.
3.  Hold your breath for about five seconds, and then breathe it out through your mouth.
4.  As you breathe out through your mouth, set the intention that you are breathing out congested energy, or breathing out the emotions you are releasing.
5.  With each breath, deeply breathe white light in through your nose, hold for five seconds, and breathe out the emotions through your mouth.

As we discussed in the color chapter, white light contains all of the colors you could possibly take in, since white is the entire spectrum of color all in one. It is a sort of catchall color and is effective for general clearing of energy and emotions. Where light is present, darkness, or low-vibration, heavy emotions, can't reside. Breathing in white light pushes these emotions out and is therefore a great addition to just the simple breathing technique.

## Breathing In Other Colors

As we discussed in chapter 5, each emotion has colors that it holds and colors that help to remedy that emotion. When breathing in other colors, it's important to work with the specific colors for the emotion or emotions you want to address. For example, anger can contain the colors red, orange, yellow, and violet. These are colors you want to avoid setting an intention to breathe in if you are trying to release anger, since adding more of the color the emotion is made of can exacerbate your emotional state. Instead, breathe in colors that remedy the emotion, which are blue and green. It is a good idea to start with the primary color of blue, because you are only dealing with one color, versus green, which is a mix of blue and yellow. Yellow is one of the colors that can be representative of anger, and a little bit of yellow may be enough to make you feel worse, depending on how much yellow is present in that emotion for you.

The following technique is a little more advanced, but it is very effective at nipping emotions in the bud. Try it next time you are heavily emotionally charged in the moment for quick relief.

### Technique 8.4. Breathing In Color

1.  Set your intention. Say, *"I choose to release this emotion and whatever it is attached to."* Example: "I choose to release this anger and whatever it is attached to."
2.  Set another intention for the color to come into your body and energy system: "I choose to breathe in the shade of (color) in my best and highest good." Choose a remedy color for the emotion you are releasing.
3.  Breathe in the color, and breathe out the energy of the emotion (see if you can feel and or sense it leaving you).
4.  Envision the cloud of energy leaving your body through your breath and floating off.
5.  Remember to direct the energy out of your space, such as through a window.

## Further Increase Your Awareness

Part of the purpose of this book is to increase your awareness of not just your emotional states but your energy system as a whole. All of us have the ability to be our own healers, and you are doing it right now! Increasing your awareness of what is happening and "tuning in" to your energy system can also increase your awareness of others, as well as your own intuition in all areas of your life. I can't even stress how helpful this can be, and we will talk more about it in another book. But for now, let's talk about what that looks like in relation to breathing light.

### Technique 8.5. Tactile Breathing

1.  Set an intention: "I choose to release (emotion) and whatever it is attached to."
2.  Breathe in white light.
3.  Breathe out the emotion you set your intention for.
4.  To increase your intuitive skills while you are breathing out your emotions, bring your awareness to your exhale.
5.  Notice: Does your breath feel thick? Does it have a strange taste or texture? Do you see color (it's usually a smoky color or colors) in your mind's eye?

Working on increasing this part of your intuition will help you know when you are done with a technique, or when you have released all of the emotion you are working on. Sometimes you just feel complete, or you might feel empty in some way. Sometimes you might just feel calmer. It may be hard to tell at first, but this is where practice comes in. Doing this "breathing in light" technique ten times will clear a good amount of emotions out of your energy system. So if you are having a hard time telling if you are "done" with the technique, this is a good stopping point.

**Technique 8.6. Breathing In White Light through the Crown**

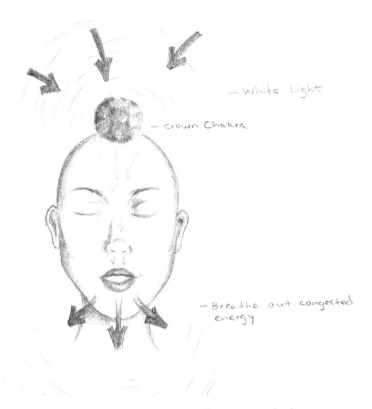

This technique is a general clearing technique, with the main focus being on how you are bringing light into your physical body and energy system. The top of your head contains the crown chakra, and the bottoms of your feet contain your foot chakras. While energy can be intentionally pulled in through all of the chakras, in general, the crown of the head is the top of the energy system, and the foot chakras are the bottom. When energy is pulled in through these spots, it is easier to direct the energy in a linear fashion, which is easier to keep up with in our minds.

1. Start by saying your intention: "I choose to release (emotion[s]) and anything that it is attached to."
2. Breathe in white light.
3. When you breathe in white light, don't breathe it in through your mouth in your mind, but breathe in through the top of your head.
4. Do this by envisioning white light entering through the top of your head when you inhale.
5. Try to breathe in very deeply, and envision filling your body up with light.
6. Hold your breath for about five to ten seconds, and breathe it out through your mouth.
7. While you are holding your breath, envision it "breaking loose" the stuck emotions.
8. Now when you breathe out, envision these being released through your mouth.
9. Do this technique until you feel like it is complete, that the emotion you set the intention to release is gone.

Sometimes, when you release emotions in this way, it can leave you a bit light-headed. To balance this feeling, you can also breathe the same Source light in through your feet. If you have a tendency to be ungrounded or dissociative, you can just do this technique and skip breathing in through the crown. Your top chakras are dominant if you are inherently ungrounded, so it is better to pull the light in through your feet to balance you out.

**Technique 8.7. Breathing In White Light through Your Feet**

1. Start by saying your intention: "I choose to release (emotion[s]) and anything that it is attached to."
2. Breathe in white light.
3. When you breathe in white light, don't breathe it in through your mouth in your mind, but breathe in through the bottoms of your feet.
4. Do this by envisioning white light entering through the bottoms of your feet when you inhale.
5. Try to breathe in very deeply, and envision filling your body up with light.

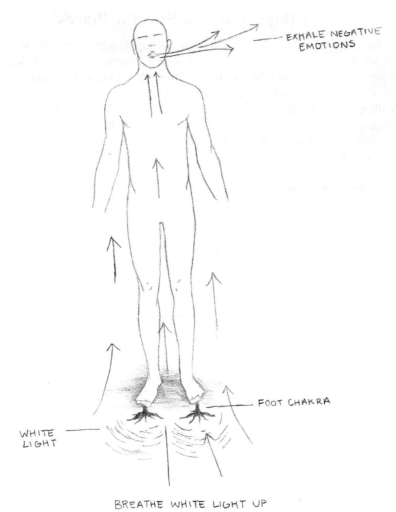

EXHALE NEGATIVE EMOTIONS

FOOT CHAKRA

WHITE LIGHT

BREATHE WHITE LIGHT UP THROUGH FEET

6. Hold your breath for about five to ten seconds and breathe it out through your mouth.

7. While you are holding your breath, envision it "breaking loose" the stuck emotions.

8. Now when you breathe out, envision these being released through your mouth.

9. Do this technique until you feel like it is complete, that the emotion you set the intention to release is gone.

# Breathing Light into Specific Places

We have talked about breathing in light through your crown and feet, but what if you want to direct it to a specific place, such as a chakra or organ? What if you know you have anger to let go of, for instance? You can direct the light to go to this specific place with your hands. While this can be done with your mind as well, involving your hands brings a tactile element to the technique that can be helpful in engaging the chakras in your hands. These are the chakras that healers use in hands-on healing.

### Technique 8.8. Breathing to Direct White Light

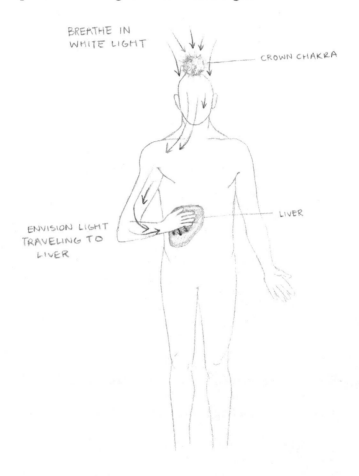

1. Place your hands over where you want to direct the white light.
2. In the Diagram on the previous page, we chose to work with anger, and we know one of the major areas anger is stored in is the liver/gallbladder.
3. After you place your hands over your liver, say your intention: "I choose to release this anger and anything that it is attached to."
4. You can also use a variation of this to make the statement more specific: "I choose to release this anger in my liver and anything the anger is attached to."
5. With your hand over your liver, breathe white light in through your crown. Envision it traveling through your heart and down your arm to your hand, entering your liver.
6. As you hold your breath for five to ten seconds, envision the light filling up your liver and breaking free all of the anger stored there.
7. Exhale it out fully through your mouth.
8. After working on the liver, check in with yourself and see how you feel.
9. If you want to work on it further, you can refer to the chart to see where else anger is stored in your body and repeat the technique.

# Breathing for Relieving Physical Discomfort

Try this technique for when you are not feeling well, for example if you have a headache or a stomachache. In these cases, think about what you have had going on lately. Have you been stressed about something in particular? Think about the emotions present in your situation, and address the emotions with your intention. If nothing comes to mind or you just feel too bad to think about it, put your hand over the area that hurts and set the intention on releasing the pain and whatever it is attached to. This can help alleviate discomfort. **This is not meant to replace medical attention. If you feel you need to go to the doctor, do so**, but this is helpful if you just don't feel well and are waiting for the pain to pass. It can speed up your recovery time and is also an opportunity to reach emotions that are at the surface that may not normally be easy to reach to be released.

### Technique 8.9. Breathing In White Light for Pain Relief

1. Place your hands over where you want to direct the light.
2. After you place your hands over your area of discomfort, say your intention: "I choose to release this emotion and anything that it is attached to."

3. You can also use a variation of this to make the statement more general: "I choose to release this (discomfort, pain, nausea, etc.) and anything it is attached to."
4. With your hand over the area, breathe light in through your crown. Envision it traveling through your heart and down your arm to your hand, entering the area of discomfort.
5. As you hold your breath for five to ten seconds, envision the light filling up the area and breaking free all of the energy stored there that is causing the discomfort.
6. Exhale it out fully through your mouth.
7. Since you are dealing with the physical body, it may take some time to alleviate the discomfort. If you feel up to it, look up that body organ or area and see what emotions might be present that could be affecting you.
8. You can call out these emotions specifically with an intention and work through the technique if you feel that the general technique is not enough.

## Breathing Makes All the Difference

Sitting there in my counselor's office, it never occurred to me that there was a difference between taking breaths and breathing. She explained to me that truly breathing involved opening yourself up and trusting your environment around you in order to take a breath. She walked me through expanding myself out rather than contracting my energy and body inward and then had me take some breaths. It made all the difference in how I felt. After that day, I returned to it again and again when I needed to remind myself to feel expansive, be present, and relax.

## Chapter Challenge

When you breathe, do you belly breathe or chest breathe?

When you breathe in, does your body feel tight or relaxed?

Bringing an awareness to how you breathe can help you shift the way that you breathe to a more relaxed state. This will shift your energy and improve your physical health.

## Feel Better Five

- Breathing is a simple yet powerful tool for transforming energetic, physical, and emotional states.

- Belly breathing grounds and relaxes the physical body, mind, and energy system.
- Breathing in light can help clear emotions out of traumatic and verbal inhibitory imprints.
- Envisioning, feeling, and breathing can be combined for clearing emotions.
- Breathing in light can be used for grounding.

# Transform in Five

Technique 8.1. Belly Breathing

1. Start by breathing in through your nose, filling your chest with air while keeping your shoulders down. Then move on to belly breathing from there.
2. If you are lying down (sitting works too), place your hands over your belly.
3. Now breathe in a deep breath through your nose.
4. As you breathe in, focus on breathing in so that you breathe into your belly, moving your belly under your hands.
5. Now breathe out completely, through your mouth.
6. Do this a couple of times to get the feel for it.
7. Once you get the hang of belly breathing, you don't have to put your hands on your stomach. This makes it easier to use this technique when you are driving a car, or something else where you need to use your hands.
8. Next, take a deep breath in through your nose and hold your breath for four seconds.
9. Now breathe out completely through your mouth. Do this ten times.
10. This will get you to a relaxed state, but not so relaxed that you can't get up and go do something afterward.

Technique 8.2. Relaxing Fast

1. Belly breathe in through your nose.
2. As you breathe in, tense every muscle in your body.
3. Hold for ten seconds and exhale through your mouth as you relax every muscle in your body at the same time.
4. Repeat this ten times.
5. This will release pent-up tension in your body and get you into a deeply meditative state.

6. Doing this technique two to three times can help you to just get relaxed quickly. Perform no more than three times if you have a "freeze" coping mechanism.

Technique 8.3. Breathing In White Light

1. Start by saying your intention: "I choose to release (emotion[s]) and anything that it is attached to."
2. Next take a deep breath in through your nose, only this time, envision breathing in white light.
3. Hold your breath for about five seconds, and then breathe it out through your mouth.
4. As you breathe out through your mouth, set the intention that you are breathing out congested energy, or breathing out the emotions you are releasing.
5. With each breath, deeply breathe white light in through your nose, hold for five seconds, and breathe out the emotions through your mouth.

Technique 8.4. Breathing In Color

1. Set your intention. Say, "I choose to release this emotion and whatever it is attached to." Example: "I choose to release this anger and whatever it is attached to."
2. Set another intention for the color to come into your body and energy system: "I choose to breathe in the shade of (color) in my best and highest good." Choose a remedy color for the emotion you are releasing.
3. Breathe in the color, and breathe out the energy of anger (see if you can feel and/or sense the emotion leaving you).
4. Envision the cloud of energy leaving your body through your breath and floating off.
5. Remember to direct the energy out of your space, such as through a window.

Technique 8.5. Tactile Breathing

1. Set an intention: "I choose to release (emotion) and whatever it is attached to."
2. Breathe in white light.
3. Breathe out the emotion you set your intention for.
4. To increase your intuitive skills while you are breathing out your emotions, bring your awareness to your exhale.

5. Notice: Does your breath feel thick? Does it have a strange taste or texture? Do you see color (it's usually a smoky color or colors) in your mind's eye?

Technique 8.6. Breathing In White Light through the Crown

1. Start by saying your intention: "I choose to release (emotion[s]) and anything that it is attached to."
2. Breathe in white light.
3. When you breathe in white light, don't breathe it in through your mouth in your mind, but breathe in through the top of your head.
4. Do this by envisioning white light entering through the top of your head when you inhale.
5. Try to breathe in very deeply, and envision filling your body up with light.
6. Hold your breath for about five to ten seconds and breathe it out through your mouth.
7. While you are holding your breath, envision it "breaking loose" the stuck emotions.
8. Now when you breathe out, envision these being released through your mouth.
9. Do this technique until you feel like it is complete, that the emotion you set the intention to release is gone.

Technique 8.7. Breathing In White Light through Your Feet

1. Start by saying your intention: "I choose to release (emotion[s]) and anything that it is attached to."
2. Breathe in white light.
3. When you breathe in white light, don't breathe it in through your mouth in your mind, but breathe in through the bottoms of your feet.
4. Do this by envisioning white light entering through the bottoms of your feet when you inhale.
5. Try to breathe in very deeply, and envision filling your body up with light.
6. Hold your breath for about five to ten seconds and breathe it out through your mouth.
7. While you are holding your breath, envision it "breaking loose" the stuck emotions.
8. Now when you breathe out, envision these being released through your mouth.

9.  Do this technique until you feel like it is complete, that the emotion you set the intention to release is gone.

Technique 8.8. Breathing to Direct White Light

1.  Place your hands over where you want to direct the white light.
2.  As indicated in the diagram on page 124, we chose to work with anger, and we know one of the major areas anger is stored in is the liver/gallbladder.
3.  After you place your hands over your liver, say your intention: "I choose to release this anger and anything that it is attached to."
4.  You can also use a variation of this to make the statement more specific: "I choose to release this anger in my liver and anything the anger is attached to."
5.  With your hand over your liver, breathe white light in through your crown. Envision it traveling through your heart and down your arm to your hand, entering your liver.
6.  As you hold your breath for five to ten seconds, envision the light filling up your liver and breaking free all of the anger stored there.
7.  Exhale it out fully through your mouth.
8.  After working on the liver, check in with yourself and see how you feel.
9.  If you want to work on it further, you can refer to the chart to see where else anger is stored in your body and repeat the technique.

Technique 8.9. Breathing In White Light for Pain Relief

1.  Place your hands over where you want to direct the light.
2.  After you place your hands over your area of discomfort, say your intention: "I choose to release this emotion and anything that it is attached to."
3.  You can also use a variation of this to make the statement more general: "I choose to release this (discomfort, pain, nausea, etc.) and anything it is attached to."
4.  With your hand over the area, breathe light in through your crown. Envision it traveling through your heart and down your arm to your hand, entering the area of discomfort.
5.  As you hold your breath for five to ten seconds, envision the light filling up the area and breaking free all of the energy stored there that is causing the discomfort.

6. Exhale it out fully through your mouth.
7. Since you are dealing with the physical body, it may take some time to alleviate the discomfort. If you feel up to it, look up that body organ or area and see what emotions might be present that could be affecting you.
8. You can call out these emotions specifically with an intention and work through the technique if you feel that the general technique is not enough.

In chapter 9, we will talk about one of the most important concepts when it comes to your energy system: grounding. You will learn why this is so important, how to tell if you are grounded or ungrounded, and how to change if you aren't grounded.

# How to Effortlessly Command Your Life

**A**s Susan walked into the apartment, she was visibly shaking. Her gaze darted around, as if she thought she was being followed or secretly recorded. Her skin was sallow. After our greeting, she sat down and held her purse tight in her lap.

With a big sigh, she said, "I am thinking about leaving my husband. I really want to. I have to. I'm so unhappy."

She proceeded to tell me about her history with her husband and how difficult it had been. We talked about what she needed to do if she chose that route. I wasn't a lawyer, I told her, but I had been through it. The longer we talked, the more relaxed she got. She wrote down a list of suggestions I gave her and put them in her purse.

As we started the energy work session, I noticed something strange right away. While most people have roots from their feet going into the ground, the roots on the bottom of her feet had this strange bubble around them. They were small, bright white, and very healthy, but for some reason not in the ground at all. I asked her guides about it. They told me they had put it there to protect her, to keep her where she was until she was ready to move on. She was ready now, and they wanted me to remove the bubble. I knew this was all that was stopping her.

Grounding is a term most people don't really understand. It's a popular phrase to throw around when you are talking about energy or about someone's presence. As far as "getting grounded" goes, it can be hard to achieve without direction or framework if you are not inherently wired that way. Most people feel lost or do the opposite when trying to ground by over activating the top of their energy system versus the bottom. When they over activate the top chakras, they will feel different, but the reality is they are more ungrounded.

*When we properly ground, we are more effective in our lives overall.* Being grounded keeps up from "toppling over" emotionally if something in life goes awry and allows us to keep a clear head when everything else around us is frantic.

## What Does Being Grounded Mean?

Let's start by talking about electricity. Have you ever seen a lightning rod on the top of a building? These rods of metal are meant to direct the electricity from a lightning strike into the ground. The **rod** is connected to the ground through a cable that is attached to a **stake** that is driven into the **earth**. Hence the term "grounded." It directs the electricity away from the structure where it could harm the building or the people in it.

When we use the term *grounded* in terms of our energy system, we are talking about our energy system being connected to the earth, just like a lightning rod. When the proverbial lightning strikes in life, such as being late for work or someone yelling at you, if you are not grounded, that energy is going to go haywire in your system, causing you to feel out of control. If this happens when you are grounded, it is going to be much easier to keep your wits about you and respond in a calm manner.

## Grounding Assessment

Are you grounded or not? You may not have any idea, or what that even means. It's easier if you just think about the following questions and choose A or B.

1. You find out that your deadline for your assignment at work got moved up, and you have too many other things to do to get it done on time.
   A. Your heart starts racing and your mind spins, fearing the worst possible outcome, like losing your job or looking like a failure to your colleagues. You start to frantically pull out everything you need to complete the project, and you freeze; your mind is blank.
   B. Your blood pressure goes up a bit. You know how much this project means to your boss and your department. You remember that your coworker finished a similar project last month and said, "If you need help getting yours done next month, let me know." You shoot a

quick email over to them explaining your situation, and they respond saying they are happy to help.

2.   Your alarm doesn't go off and you are late. Again.
   A.   Frantic, you jump up out of bed and get in the shower. In your frenzied state, you accidentally put shower gel in your hair instead of shampoo. You wonder what you were thinking even getting in the shower, because now you are even later.
   B.   You get up, realize you are late, and think up a quick strategy. You comb through your hair and pull it back. Messy is the new neat. Throw on an easy dress and a little blush, and you are out the door in fifteen minutes or less.

3.   You have to give a big presentation at work.
   A.   You go over it in your mind a million times and dwell on all the things that could possibly go wrong, even though you are overprepared. Once you are in the meeting, you keep dropping everything, and you talk so fast your boss actually has to tell you to slow down.
   B.   You prepare for the meeting and list any questions that you think might come up. During the presentation, you are calm and speak articulately. Some questions come up that you don't anticipate, but you calmly explain that you don't know the answer and tell them you will find out and get back to them.

4.   You just mopped the floor after being up until 3:00 a.m. the night before. You feel so accomplished. Until your two-year-old starts dumping a gallon of apple juice on the floor five minutes later.
   A.   You start screaming at the two-year-old and they drop the juice, smashing the bottle. All this wakes the baby up from its nap. Then you start crying and just sit down in the apple juice.
   B.   You manage to keep your wits and calmly walk over to the two-year-old, taking the glass jug and saving half of the juice. You lift them out of the puddle of juice. You throw some towels on the floor and take a break to watch a video with your toddler, letting the towels do most of the work. Later you toss the towels in the wash and mop. Again. Mom life!

If you saw yourself mainly in the A group, you tend to be ungrounded. If you answered mainly B, you are most likely in a grounded state by nature. Our energy system has habits in how it works, just like our body and mind do. We come in with a particular energy makeup, just as we come in with certain genetics. As we go through life, the experiences we have cause certain energy system habits to form. Some of these habits are due to imprints, namely traumatic imprints. If we are initially wired to be ungrounded in our energy system and then we have traumatic imprints on top of this, it is much more difficult to be in a grounded state on a regular basis. When our imprints get triggered, we tend to "pull up our roots" and flee, either emotionally, physically, or both. We simply don't feel safe. Our energy system has to be trained to be grounded.

If you found yourself in group B, congratulations. Chances are you stay pretty calm most of the time and things don't rattle you that much. It's not that you don't experience stress, but you tend to handle it well, keeping your wits about you. Even if you are grounded by nature, though, certain things that are in your traumatic imprints may cause you to "pull your roots up" and have difficulty functioning.

The good news is, whether you tend to be mostly grounded or ungrounded, there are simple techniques that can get you back on track.

## Energy System Anatomy: Your Roots

We have talked about the chakras a little in this book, but here in this Section, we are going to go into a little more detail about two chakras in particular that aren't included in the main set of chakras: the foot chakras.

The foot chakras are located on the bottoms of your feet right below the ball of the foot. The purpose of these chakras is to draw up energy from the earth to ground you. In addition, these chakras have roots coming out of them that actually go into the earth. Think of them like your own personal lightning rods.

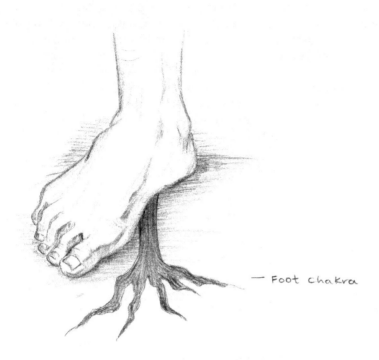

— Foot chakra

When your energy system is functioning correctly, these "roots" penetrate the earth from about two to ten feet down. They pull up the earth's energy, helping you to feel confident, clear, and strong. People who have a healthy root system have a commanding presence about them that is magnetic. You notice when they enter the room, and everyone listens when they speak. They are calm, rational, and wise. Good examples of people who are grounded are Charlize Theron, Deepak Chopra, and Oprah Winfrey.

When your energy system is not functioning correctly, there are a number of things that can be going on with your roots. Since we are talking about being grounded in this section, we will stick to that. In an energy system that is not grounded, the roots are basically not in the ground or are very shallow. I have even seen people's roots pulled all the way up inside their legs to their knees. As we discussed before, people who are not grounded struggle to get things done in life. They typically overthink things and take very little or erratic action. They try to do things quickly and, in the process, make lots of mistakes. They are nervous and often complain of anxiety and sleeplessness.

When we are in a hurry, the best thing we can do is to take a moment to make sure we are grounded before we go about doing anything. This may seem counterintuitive. It might seem like it would make sense to "pull up your roots" so that you can move about more quickly to get things done, but the opposite is true. By doing this, you pretty much ensure whatever you are trying to do will wind up being a disaster. If you have a habit of getting frantic, you are not alone. The good thing is, it's easy to train your energy system to ground itself. You just have to know some simple techniques.

**Technique 9.1. Grounding Your Roots**

1.  Ask yourself, do I feel grounded right now? Am I calm or nervous? Am I overthinking things or is my mind clear? Observe how you feel overall and have a number in your mind (1–10), with 1 being ungrounded and 10 being very grounded.
2.  Envision roots coming out of the bottom of your feet, like we talked about on the previous page.
3.  How far in the ground are they?
4.  What color are they? Are they bright and look 'healthy'?
5.  If they are fairly shallow, push them farther into the ground. Focus on them going deeper instead of just spreading out.
6.  After pushing them farther into the ground, how do you feel?

# Using the Grounding Technique for Working with Traumatic Imprints

Traumatic imprints are by nature ungrounding. When we are working on clearing emotions from these imprints, it can get pretty intense. By grounding really well before we dig deep to work with high-trauma memories, we can remain calmer through the process and actually access more of the emotions that need to come out. Use the Set an Intention variation 9.3 of the simple technique on the following pages when working with traumatic imprints for better results.

# Variations of the Technique

In these variations, we combine a couple of techniques you have learned in this book.

## Technique 9.2. Grounded Root Breathing

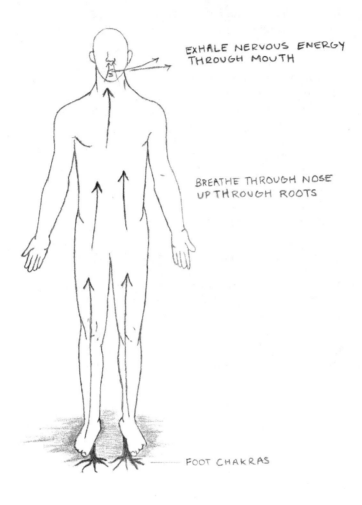

EXHALE NERVOUS ENERGY THROUGH MOUTH

BREATHE THROUGH NOSE UP THROUGH ROOTS

FOOT CHAKRAS

1. First, perform the technique 9.1 and get your roots into the ground.
2. Next, take a deep belly breath through your nose and breathe up through your roots.
3. Hold it for about eight seconds.
4. Feel the energy coming into your body and calming you down.
5. Now breathe the nervous energy out through your mouth.
6. Repeat this a few times until you feel calm and your thinking is more clear and rational.

### Technique 9.3. Setting Grounded Intention

1.  You can also add an intention statement beforehand, such as, "I choose to release this nervous energy (i.e., anxiety, fear) and whatever it's attached to."
2.  Now envision your roots.
3.  If your roots are not in the ground very far, sink them deeper into the ground.
4.  Now envision your roots deeply in the ground and breathe up through them.
5.  Hold your breath for eight seconds.
6.  This process grounds the nervous energy and dispels it. You should be able to feel this happening.
7.  Now breathe out through your mouth and feel your system calm down.
8.  Repeat this a few times until you are calmer and more focused.

# Pulling Colors Up through Your Roots

Just like we can breathe in colors through our crown, we can breathe in colors through our roots too. When we do this, it infuses the grounding energy into the colors, shifting the frequency of the color to a more grounded state. If you are extremely ungrounded, this may be a better option for you than breathing in colors through your crown until your energy system is more balanced.

# Choosing a Grounding Color

To choose a color to work with, you need to first know what emotions you are working with. Refer to the color chart in chapter 5 to choose a color that works to diffuse and release the emotion. For example, anxiety is a common emotion that is identified with being ungrounded. You can envision the colors blue and green and pull them up through the feet chakras to assist in grounding. Remember that starting with the primary color is always best, in this case, blue.

### Technique 9.4. Breathing Color through Your Roots

1.  Set the intention: "I choose to release (emotion) and whatever it is attached to."
2.  To pull colors up through your roots, envision your roots going deep into the ground, as in the simple technique (9.1).
3.  Next, envision the color you want to pull up into your body through your roots and breathe it in; breathe in through your nose, pulling the colored energy up through your roots.

4. Hold your breath for about five seconds.
5. This process pulls in the grounded color to where it is needed in your energy system, grounds the nervous energy there, and dispels it. You should be able to feel this happening.
6. Now breathe out through your mouth fully, breathing out the anxious energy.
7. Repeat this several times.
8. After you feel like the first color is complete and if you need more grounding, you can move on to the next color.

## You Can Ground Anywhere

Grounding can be done while literally standing on the ground, but it does not have to be the case. Grounding can be done while you are over water, in a high-rise building, or even in an airplane. It really is a matter of just envisioning the simple technique or one of the variations and performing the technique. Your state of mind about grounding plays an important role in your ability to ground. Energetically, your physical location is irrelevant to the process. It may take some practice to wrap your mind around that concept, but the more you practice, the easier it will get.

## What to Do If It's Hard to Ground

For some people, grounding is a very difficult thing to do. They can get really frustrated trying to put their roots in the ground, and if they do manage to get that far, pulling energy up through their roots and into their body feels impossible.

First, this is not your fault. Several different things can cause this to happen. One of those things is an imprint being in the way of the energy moving in that part of your energy system and your body. So how do you know if that is what's going on? One indicator is that you appear "clumsy" in your legs and feet. You might trip over things easily or are constantly hitting your legs, knees, and feet on things. This is from your physical body trying to get energy to move in those areas, as well as you not having a sense of where that part of your body is because not much energy is flowing through it. Getting the energy unblocked from your legs can be a process, but the following technique (9.5) is a way to get things moving again.

You have a main energy channel running in the top portion of your body, from the top of your head all the way down to your root chakra. You also have two branches coming off of this and going into your legs, down to the bottom of your feet. If the energy is blocked in these channels, grounding energy (or any energy) has trouble moving throughout the body.

**Technique 9.5. Cleaning the Pipes**

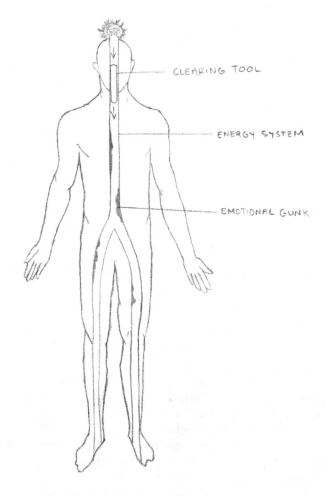

CLEARING TOOL

ENERGY SYSTEM

EMOTIONAL GUNK

"CLEANING THE PIPES"

This technique is advanced and may take some practice to get down. This is one of the most advanced techniques in the book, but it is powerful if you are having difficulty grounding.

1. Envision the channels (on the previous page) in your body.
2. Starting in the channel at the top of your head, imagine you have a rod that fills that channel all the way to the sides, about four inches long.
3. Now in your mind, envision putting the rod in the channel that starts on the top of your head.
4. Then push that rod slowly through the main channel until you reach the point where it splits to go down your legs.
5. Finish this motion by pushing the rod through the bottom of your pelvis. This will push out the "energy gunk" that is clogging this channel, as well as the rod.
6. When you do this technique, you may feel strange, like there is pressure in your body. That is normal. What you are doing is cleaning this channel out. Think of it as cleaning the gunk out of the inside of a pipe.
7. Next run the rod under some "water." Envision doing this to clean the rod off.
8. Next take the rod and, starting at the bottom of your pelvis where the channels branch down your legs, repeat the process for each leg, pushing the rod down the leg slowly until you reach the bottom of the foot and then pushing it through the foot.
9. After the first leg, clean the rod with "water" again before you repeat the process with the other leg. Doing this will clean out all of your main channels so that you can pull energy up through your body.

At this point, try the simple technique 9.2 and see if it works better. How do you feel before and after? If you feel better after you perform the simple technique now, you will know your "clean out" worked.

## If the Rod Gets Stuck

When you are performing the "clean out" technique, you may come to spots in your main channels where you feel like the "rod" you are pushing through is stuck. There are a couple of main reasons for this. There could be a sizable "clog" in your main channel that you need to push through, or the channel could have a narrow spot in it. Most of the time, you can simply push it through the clog with some persistence. If it's not budging, try the following technique.

**Technique 9.6. Unsticking the Rod**

1. Put your hands over where the clog is and set the intention: "I choose to release this clog of energy and whatever it is attached to."
2. When you breathe in through your nose, envision breathing into the clog, decongesting the energy to clear the block. (If you like to work with breathing in light, you can use light with this step.)
3. Breathe the congested energy out through your mouth.
4. Do this three times and then see if you can push the rod farther.

**Technique 9.7. Expanding a Narrow Channel**

Sometimes, the main energy channels are narrowed in spots. This can be an inherent energy structure, or it can be from some sort of energetic damage due to traumatic or verbal inhibitory imprints. If you are not sure whether the channel is just narrow or there is a clog, try the technique to release the clog first. If this doesn't work, try the technique below.

1. Set the intention: "I choose to release the restriction in my energy channel and whatever it is attached to."
2. Place your hands over where you feel the restriction, or where the rod is stuck.
3. Take in a deep belly breath and make a deep "OM" sound as you exhale, setting the intention for the vibration to relax and expand your channel.
4. Do this three times and then try pushing the rod farther through your channel.
5. Continue to move the rod down to clean your channels. If you feel it stick again, repeat the techniques.

# What If You Are Unhappy Where You Are? How Do You Ground There?

There are factors that can influence our ability to ground. One of those things is not being happy with where we are. This could be where we are physically located, where we are in our lives at the moment, or both. When we are in this space, we tend to daydream, projecting our energy wherever we want to be.

I once had a client that was in this very predicament. She had moved to go to college in a different state. After arriving, she realized that this wasn't what she wanted after all. Everything felt off about it—the people, her classes, the intensity. Her heart was not in it, and she was beating herself up for feeling this way. She tried to find ways to connect and integrate herself into the college life, but it just felt wrong and it was draining her. She longed to be at a different school in a different state that she had visited a few weeks prior. It felt like a much better fit, and she was energized being there. She had applied to go there next semester, and it was all she could think about. The problem was, it was making her feel more disconnected than before from where she was going to school now. Everything felt like an increasing struggle, and her health was suffering as a result. As we talked, her energy was stirring, but nothing was really sticking as far as creating a positive shift. We talked about grounding where you are and calling back your energy from where she was projecting it to be present. This is what I normally do to help clients ground when they are having this sort of issue, but that seemed to make her feel worse. Then I was shown something in her field that made me shift what I was telling her. I saw pieces of where she was projecting her energy coming into her field. She was wanting to go to school in Colorado, and I saw a pine cone and pine branches in her energy system. They were under her feet, and it seemed to be recharging her energy.

Instead of having her ground where she was physically, we brought where she wanted to ground to her. Think of it as carrying a memento with you to remind you of someone or something that makes you feel good.

We simply set the intention of calling in energy from where she wanted to be and put it under her feet. I told her to sink in her roots, and before she even did that, she felt better. The pine cone and branches were pulling her energy system out of the alarm state it was in from not being where the vibrations were more supportive. In allowing her energy system to have contact with something that felt good, it relaxed, and she started to perk back up. It was apparent in her voice. She felt that the time she had left at her present school was more manageable now and had a renewed focus.

## Grounding Where You Want to Be, Not Where You Are

This is a great tool to use if you have already made a decision to change something in your life and the timeline is just longer than you would like. It is great for getting boosts of energy to make the most of where you are right now instead of projecting your energy out into the future and causing energetic, emotional, and physical issues.

Note: This technique is not to be used in place of making tough decisions, but it can assist you in bringing in the energy to make a decision if you are on the fence about making it. When we introduce the energy of a new time or place into our energy system and it relaxes, this is a sign that it is what our soul wants. Always listen to that.

**Technique 9.8. Surrogate Grounding**
1. Set the intention: "I choose to ground my energy in (time or place)."
2. Envision something small, if possible, that represents that time or place to you.
3. Bring the envisioned object into your energy field underneath your feet.
4. Envision sinking your roots deep into the ground around the object.
5. If the energy the object represents is in line with you and the decision you have made, you should feel calm, focused, and grounded.
6. If the energy the object represents is not in line with you and the decision you have made, you will most likely feel more ill at ease. If this happens, reevaluate your decision and the energy you have brought in. It may not be a good fit.
7. If you find it is not a good fit for you, envision returning the object to where it came from.
8. Take a few deep breaths and breathe out the energy from the object to clear it.

# Susan Gets Her Roots

Grounding is such a key piece of the puzzle when it comes to emotional stability and getting things done. As was the case with Susan, who had the bubble around her otherwise healthy roots.

As she was lying on the massage table, I told her what I was seeing. I asked her to envision taking a pin and popping the bubble around her feet. As she did, I witnessed something straight out of *Jack and the Beanstalk*. Her roots instantly grew. Fast. They got bigger around and longer, spreading out and driving themselves into the ground. As the roots did this, she took a deep breath and told me her body felt really warm. I told her that was normal, as I was dodging her mutant roots from running me over. Thankfully, her eyes were closed.

I performed a little energy work on her as well, but her roots going into the ground took care of most of what she needed for healing.

After the session was done, she sat up and commented she felt stronger and more solid. I told her that made sense, given the state of her roots. Her guides wanted her to come back in two weeks, so she made another appointment.

When I saw her two weeks later, she looked like a different person. She had taken all of the steps I recommended: gotten an attorney, filed for divorce, and rented an apartment. She was standing up straight, and color had started to return to her face.

Her second session was just teaching her how to clear her emotions and the stagnant energy she had let go of. We continued to work together over the next year.

When she was ready to date again, we talked about what that might look like. Her biggest concern was to not repeat her last relationship. I told her that the most important thing to do to prevent that from happening was to heal herself. She was on a good track, but I recommended she get a therapist to help with the finer details to compliment what we were doing. She did. A year later, she was engaged to a wonderful man. I have never seen Susan shine brighter.

# Chapter Challenge

Are you primarily grounded or ungrounded?

Think about the traumatic and verbal inhibitory imprints you listed in your chapter 3 assessment. Do you see how they might be linked to being ungrounded?

Walk across a room. Feel your body and how you move. Now, do a grounding technique from the chapter and walk across the room again. Do you feel different? If so, how?

Look in the mirror at yourself for a moment and observe your facial features, especially around your eyes. Now step away for a moment and perform a grounding technique. Look in the mirror again. Do you look more confident and calmer?

# The Feel Better Five

- Being energetically grounded is the same as the principle of grounding lightning.
- Our energy system has roots that come out of our feet and into the ground.
- Our roots can help us to be calm, focused, and productive.
- Being ungrounded causes us to be nervous, unclear, and frantic.
- By combining breathing and envisioning with grounding, we can get calm fast.

# Transform in Five

Technique 9.1. Grounding Your Roots

1. Ask yourself, do I feel grounded right now? Am I calm or nervous? Am I overthinking things, or is my mind clear? Observe how you feel overall and have a number in your mind (1–10), with 1 being ungrounded and 10 being very grounded.
2. Envision roots coming out of the bottom of your feet.
3. How far in the ground are they?
4. What color are they? Are they bright and look "healthy"?
5. If they are fairly shallow, push them farther into the ground. Focus on them going deeper instead of just spreading out.
6. After pushing them farther into the ground, how do you feel?

Technique 9.2. Grounded Root Breathing

1. First, perform the technique 9.1 and get your roots into the ground.
2. Next, take a deep belly breath through your nose and breathe up through your roots.
3. Hold it for about eight seconds.
4. Feel the energy coming into your body and calming you down.
5. Now breathe the nervous energy out through your mouth.
6. Repeat this a few times until you feel calm and your thinking is more clear and rational.

Technique 9.3. Setting Grounded Intention

1. You can add an intention statement beforehand, such as, "I choose to release this nervous energy (i.e., anxiety, fear) and whatever it's attached to."

2. Now envision your roots.
3. If your roots are not in the ground very far, sink them deeper into the ground.
4. Now envision your roots deeply in the ground and breathe up through them.
5. Hold your breath for eight seconds.
6. This process grounds the nervous energy and dispels it. You should be able to feel this happening.
7. Now breathe out through your mouth and feel your system calm down.
8. Repeat this a few times until you are calmer and more focused.

Technique 9.4. Breathing Color through Your Roots

1. Set the intention: "I choose to release (emotion) and whatever it is attached to."
2. To pull colors up through your roots, envision your roots going deep into the ground, as in the simple technique (9.1).
3. Next, envision the color you want to pull up into your body through your roots and breathe it in; breathe in through your nose, pulling the colored energy up through your roots.
4. Hold your breath for about five seconds.
5. This process pulls in the grounded color to where it is needed in your energy system, grounds the nervous energy there, and dispels it. You should be able to feel this happening.
6. Now breathe out through your mouth fully, breathing out the anxious energy.
7. Repeat this several times.
8. After you feel like the first color is complete and if you need more grounding, you can move on to the next color.

Technique 9.8. Surrogate Grounding

1. Set the intention: "I choose to ground my energy in (time or place)."
2. Envision something small, if possible, that represents that time or place to you.
3. Bring the envisioned object into your energy field underneath your feet.
4. Envision sinking your roots deep into the ground around the object.
5. If the energy the object represents is in line with you and the decision you have made, you should feel calm, focused, and grounded.

6. If the energy the object represents is not in line with you and the decision you have made, you will most likely feel more ill at ease. If this happens, reevaluate your decision and the energy you have brought in. It may not be a good fit.
7. If you find it is not a good fit for you, envision returning the object to where it came from.
8. Take a few deep breaths and breathe out the energy from the object to clear it.

# Transform in Ten

Technique 9.5. Cleaning the Pipes

This technique is advanced and may take some practice to get down. This is one of the most advanced techniques in the book, but it is powerful if you are having difficulty grounding.

1. Envision the channels (on page 142) in your body.
2. Starting in the channel at the top of your head, imagine you have a rod that fills that channel all the way to the sides, about four inches long.
3. Now in your mind, envision putting the rod in the channel that starts on the top of your head.
4. Then push that rod slowly through the main channel until you reach the point where it splits to go down your legs.
5. Finish this motion by pushing the rod through the bottom of your pelvis. This will push out the "energy gunk" that is clogging this channel, as well as the rod.
6. When you do this technique, you may feel strange, like there is pressure in your body. That is normal. What you are doing is cleaning this channel out. Think of it as cleaning the gunk out of the inside of a pipe.
7. Next run the rod under some "water." Envision doing this to clean the rod off.
8. Next take the rod and, starting at the bottom of your pelvis where the channels branch down your legs, repeat the process for each leg, pushing the rod down the leg slowly until you reach the bottom of the foot, then pushing it through the foot.
9. After the first leg, clean the rod with "water" again before you repeat the process with the other leg. Doing this will clean out all of your main channels so that you can pull energy up through your body.

Technique 9.6. Unsticking the Rod

1. Put your hands over where the clog is and set the intention, "I choose to release this clog of energy and whatever it is attached to."
2. When you breathe in through your nose, envision breathing into the clog, decongesting energy to clear the block. (If you like to work with breathing in light, you can use light with this step.)
3. Breathe the congested energy out through your mouth.
4. Do this three times and then see if you can push the rod farther.

Technique 9.7. Expanding a Narrow Channel

Sometimes, the main energy channels are narrowed in spots. This can be an inherent energy structure, or it can be from some sort of energetic damage due to traumatic or verbal inhibitory imprints. If you are not sure whether the channel is just narrow or there is a clog, try the technique to release the clog first. If this doesn't work, try the technique below.

1. Set the intention: "I choose to release the restriction in my energy channel and whatever it is attached to."
2. Place your hands over where you feel the restriction, or where the rod is stuck.
3. Take in a deep belly breath and make a deep "OM" sound as you exhale, setting the intention for the vibration to relax and expand your channel.
4. Do this three times and try pushing the rod through your channel farther.
5. Continue to move the rod down to clean your channels. If you feel it stick again, repeat the techniques.

Writing about things can really help you to shift your perspective and process emotions. In the next chapter, you will learn how to constructively journal. Even if you don't like to write, this chapter has nuggets you can use and apply to other techniques in the book, such as how to tap into your intuition more.

# CHAPTER 10

## Scripting a Plan for Change

I got a stressed call from one of my long-term clients. She had been dating a guy during the summer, and while they still cared about each other a great deal, they decided to part ways. They had just graduated high school, and my client left for a summer academic program that had her traveling with a group of students her age. She felt that being in a relationship was not going to work for her during this time, wanting the freedom to just focus on her studies rather than having her energy and mind pulled somewhere else.

But as it often does, the Universe had something else in mind. A guy in her program kept asking her out. While she liked him, she really didn't want to commit herself to anyone at that point. Further, she still had feelings and a great deal of respect for her past boyfriend and wasn't sure if that was truly over yet. Something, though, kept pulling her to say yes and go out with this new guy.

"I just don't know what to do," she said. "My heart is torn. I like this new guy, but I still have feelings for my old boyfriend. My head keeps telling me to just move on, but I just can't decide. What should I do?"

When I get questions like this from my clients, I am oftentimes getting a clear read on what is best, but it's not my journey—it's theirs. It's just my job to present perspective for them to make their own choice and trust their intuition. She was usually pretty clear with herself, so this struggle was out of character for her.

What came through in her session was that she needed to journal. I told her, "When your head and heart don't agree, stop asking them what to do. Ask your soul. It may have a different answer than you expect."

Journaling can be a powerful way of getting things down on paper or can just make a record of what is going on in your life at the time. Most people don't have any sort of journaling structure, though, which can leave them feeling even more confused than when they put the pen to paper. When you have a constructive plan for journaling, it becomes a powerful problem-solving tool. While other methods of processing emotions and information are good, journaling allows your body to get involved in the process in a different way, and sometimes that can make all the difference when you are dealing with something difficult.

## It's Not for Everyone, but Hang on a Sec

When I told my husband that I was putting a journaling chapter in this book, he got concerned.

He said, "I don't know if that's a good idea. People may think they have to do that to let things go. You know me, journaling would drive me crazy. I would think, 'I can't do that,' and I might just toss the book aside and give up." Mind you, this is a guy that I have learned a thing or two from about releasing emotions. He makes it a practice to do emotional releasing anytime he has something come up he needs to let go of, but journaling is not his thing. He prefers to do it in some of the other ways presented in this book.

So if this sounds familiar, this part of the chapter is for you. If you find that writing is super frustrating and you don't process well this way, **don't do it**. For some people, it just isn't going to work, and that's fine. Writing can be super helpful, but if you have read this far into the book, you know by now there are lots of other ways to release emotions.

Before you flip to the next chapter, though, hold on a second. . . . Even if writing isn't your jam, I encourage you to read this chapter. The reason is, the base of the techniques you learn can be used in conjunction with other techniques in the book. These techniques have you "tap in" to different things, such as your traumatic and verbal inhibitory imprints, as well as any part of your physical body, before you do the writing technique. This act of "tapping in" can be applied when you are doing other releasing techniques and increases their potency.

If you aren't planning on journaling, for now, put writing in the scrap bucket and just focus on learning the base "tapping in" technique that is found after the simple technique in this chapter.

## Writing versus Typing . . . Does It Matter?

While you may have a preference to type, let's talk a little about what writing something out the old-fashioned way can do versus just clicking away on a keyboard. Confession time: I do have a journal that I type. It's faster for me and works most of the time. But if I am super stuck on something and am having a hard time processing, I will write it down. It doesn't matter how much like chicken scratch it looks (my handwriting is not the best). What matters is that I am able to better process difficult things more easily if I write it down. It opens my energy and mind up in a different way than typing, and here's why.

Writing by hand uses a different part of your brain than typing. For notetaking, it increases memory recall, and this can be really effective for journaling as well. It turns on the part of the brain that remembers things. So whether you are recalling what you did recently or several years ago, it can help jog your memory centers, which can really help if you are releasing emotions that you have been holding on to for a long time.

Writing things out creates spatial relations between the bits of information you are writing and can help you remember a series of events—first, second, third. This can be helpful in moving traumas from your subconscious mind to the conscious, so that they can be processed and released. It also activates the part of the brain that is involved in thinking and working memory, which can be helpful in emotional processing. This allows for the mind and emotions to work through a process of releasing that we lay out later in the chapter.

When you are writing things down, your brain engages in making connections between things, which can be extremely helpful when you are trying to make sense of your emotions and let them go. Writing allows you to problem solve more easily by activating critical thinking, which we will also be using in the journaling technique.

Energetically speaking, writing is a great way to move energy through your body. Since your brain is engaged in a different way, writing can often access thoughts and emotions that are difficult to get to any other way. I find that when I am super stuck on releasing something and I write it down, it flows out of me better and differently than if I was doing some other sort of releasing technique. Writing also can be powerful when you are declaring something to yourself or the Universe (writing a "Dear Universe" letter is how I manifested my husband). Your handwriting has the energy of you in it. Written words carry vibration just as spoken words and thoughts do. Everything is energy, and vibration and written words are a concrete form of that. So when you write it down, it's like saying, "I really mean business here!!"

With all that said, if you still aren't feeling it and you want to type your journal, I totally get that too. It has its own benefits of getting down more information more quickly than handwriting. Sometimes that is helpful, and like I said, I do it both ways, depending on my goal for the writing technique. So let's get into the techniques and start journaling.

Journaling can be done a number of ways, but for the sake of this technique, we are going to focus on constructive journaling for releasing emotions. This type of journaling has you coming to some resolve at the end versus just venting and stopping. This way, at the end you have something constructive and actionable. You've moved energy through and have done some problem-solving. Another benefit is that once you learn how to journal this way and make a habit of it, it trains your mind to start thinking this way, which is helpful if you have trouble processing through situations and releasing emotions.

Disclosure: This is one of the few techniques in the book that will most likely take more than five minutes.

I have had a few clients tell me that they make themselves sit there with their journal for at least thirty minutes, because sometimes it takes a while for a stream to start coming out onto paper, so just play with it a bit and see what works for you.

## Express Yo' Self

I mean, sometimes you just have to vent it out, right?? When you are in a highly charged emotional state, you have to express it. If you don't, that stuff will soak into your energy system, causing more problems later and making it tougher to get out. It's kind of like spilling red wine on the couch. You better get it up right away, or it is most likely *never* coming out!! And while it's always possible to release emotions, it's much easier when they are on the surface. Around my house, we call emotions being brought to the surface "a gift." I must admit, sometimes I say this tongue-in-cheek, and that is usually when I need to sit down and do some good old-fashioned journaling. The last thing you want to do is blow up at someone in the moment and regret it later. Journaling lets you say whatever you want on paper, moving the energy through so you can blow your stack without blowing up the house.

**Technique 10.1. Vent. Reflect. Think Positive. Resolve.**

1. Write out everything that has you upset.

You may not have a clear idea of what that even is when you start writing, but once you start, you will be amazed at what you put down on paper. It doesn't have to make a ton of sense, be spelled correctly, or have the right grammar; you are venting here. Do this part of the technique until you feel like you are done. This may take a while, especially if it has been a while since you let things out.

As you write any of these steps, you may find yourself returning to the venting step. That's okay. Emotions aren't linear. Other thoughts or feelings may come up that you need to get out. You can keep going back to it until it stops coming up. This will make the other steps easier.

2. Put the shoe on the other foot.

After you get your frustrations down on paper, it's time to shift your perspective. If you are upset with a person, think about their point of view. Whether you know the person or you don't know the person, you can ask yourself a few questions to help you look at the situation a different way. If a trauma or tragedy "happened to you" or someone you love, it may be hard to understand why. Sometimes, there is no seemingly good answer, but if you can manage to shift your perspective, even a little, it can help you to reframe it in your mind so you can let go and heal.

Ask yourself the following questions that apply:

1. Did you say something or do something that could have been offensive to the person?
2. Did you possibly have a lack of understanding for the person or situation?
3. If you know the person, did you trigger an emotional reaction in them because they had some kind of past trauma? (You may or may not know, but this gives you an idea of the possibility.)
4. If something happened that you weren't expecting, as in, you didn't get the job you were hoping for, what would be their reasons for not hiring you? (If they didn't hire you, know you are awesome and it's their loss ;).)

Just as we discuss in other parts of the book, traumatic imprints can trigger emotions to come up when we least expect them. That applies to everyone. Sometimes you don't know what someone else has been through or what they are going through. They react like you don't expect. Shifting your perspective to move to a place of compassion can help you let go and move from a place of judging and anger to forgiveness or helping them to resolve.

You can journal here about what you think might have caused it. If you don't know the person (like someone that cuts you off in traffic) or aren't sure, you can create a scenario that supports the behavior in your mind. Maybe they were running late for work, or maybe they are in the middle of a divorce and are stressed. Maybe they just have to go to the bathroom. It could be anything; it doesn't matter. The point of the technique is for you to shift your mindset into understanding that everyone and everything around you focuses and functions on its own agenda and mindset. All emotions are valid, even if you don't understand them, but you have the power to choose how they affect you.

Note: If you have someone in your life who is repeatedly abusive or hurtful to you in some way, this is a whole other type of situation. While you need to release your emotions around the situation or person for your own sake, you will ultimately need to create healthy boundaries for yourself here. Addressing that is beyond the scope of this book. Abuse is never okay, and there is no excuse for it. Seek help if this is what's happening to you.

3. The silver lining.

Now it's time to take a step further and ask yourself:

- What did I learn from this situation?
- If it happened again, what would I change about my reaction to it?
- Did the situation highlight or trigger any of my traumatic or verbal inhibitory imprints that I can work on healing?
- Would I take any additional or different actions?

This not only helps your mind to reframe the situation, but it helps you to explore other outcomes mentally. Remember, our problem-solving brain is activated when we write things down. This is where you put that to good use. Brainstorming what you would do differently next time, knowing what you know now, is a great way to cement other options in your mind and possibly head off future drama.

4. The resolution.

If what you are journaling about requires some type of action on your part to make amends or solve a problem, this is where you write that down. Think out your resolution and write out the whole thing in your journal. This way, you can go back and read it, memorizing the dialogue if necessary to help you come to the best resolve.

If it is something that requires amends, wait until the person is calm to approach them. Nothing goes farther than an apology. If you have an awareness of why you reacted the way you did and it was out of line, help them understand where your reaction was coming from, such as, "I get angry when people are trying to be funny and jump out to scare me, because I was assaulted. I'm working on healing this, but it takes time." Letting them know you are aware your behavior was "off" and that you are working to resolve it moves people from a place of disdain to compassion for you.

If it was someone else that had a behavior you felt was out of line and you feel comfortable talking to them, wait until they are calm to approach them, and have a conversation if you feel it would be helpful. Sometimes, people aren't aware of how they come across to others, and it can be of benefit for you to tell them. Again, do this only if you feel it is constructive. Some people are extremely wounded and will not react well to this type of input. Use your best judgment.

If you were upset by a situation, say you didn't get hired for a job, then what is your next step? Make a resolve to start fresh tomorrow sending out resumes, or make a list of all the contacts you can think of that could help.

This simple technique obviously takes some time, and you may not do it all in one sitting. That's okay. You might want to just vent and come back to it, but doing all of the steps here to some extent will help you to process emotions and situations better in the long run if you make a practice of journaling them from time to time.

# Variations of the Technique: Tapping In

In this Section, we are going to introduce a new concept that I call "tapping in." It is basically the premise that you can open up a dialogue with just about anything and get information. This idea may seem a little far-fetched, but I swear to you, it works. This technique combines some of the other techniques in the book and kind of requires that you have your imagination/envisioning muscle, your third eye, opened up and strengthened some. You may have heard this concept called other things, and it can sound really woo-woo . . . Okay, maybe it is, but if dipping your toe into woo-woo a bit made all the difference in how you felt, would you do it?

The way I look at it is that you are just having a conversation you wouldn't normally think of having with something you wouldn't normally think of having it with. Let's start small . . .

Have you ever talked to your pet? If you have a pet, chances are you have had a conversation or two. It can be easy to forget that they can't actually answer you with words, because they communicate so well in other ways. Maybe your dog gets excited when you ask it, "Do you want to go for a walk?" They know what you are saying and vice versa. Studies show that 70 to 93 percent of all communication is nonverbal. So, words are only a small portion of the equation.

What about a plant? Studies have been done on the effects of words on plants and even on pond water. There was even a whole study done (and a book published) on the effect words had on water as it formed into ice crystals. I won't get too scientific on you here, but the results went something like this: when harsh words were said to the subjects in the experiments, the subjects did not thrive. The plant withered, the pond water got super gross, and the ice crystals formed erratic configurations. However, when the identical plant, pond water, and pre-frozen water were communicated with in a positive way, they all thrived. The plant grew vibrantly, the pond water did not turn dark and start to stink, and the frozen water formed beautiful configurations. The plants, pond water, and ice crystals all gave a nonverbal response to the words that were spoken to them. But what if I told you it could be a two-way conversation instead? What if you could get feedback from whatever it was by asking it a question? Weird, right? Maybe not. Everything carries a certain vibration, including words. They are powerful. By learning and practicing the "tapping in" technique, you can have an insightful two-way conversation with anything.

That is what I am going to teach you in this Section. Once you learn how to do this, you will be amazed at the feedback you get from whatever you are talking to. Let's take the example of my client at the beginning of the chapter. This client of mine had been working with me for many years when she came to me with her guy predicament. She had learned to flex her imagination/envisioning muscle and had become pretty intuitive. So when I told her she needed to ask her soul what it thought she should do in this situation, she knew what to do and how to do it.

The technique is really pretty simple, although it may take some practice to get a steady flow of dialogue to journal. You may only get bits and pieces of things at first, and that is okay. We are learning to crawl before we walk, so to speak.

Like we have mentioned before in the book, emotions are stored in either traumatic or verbal inhibitory imprints. These imprints are in your energy system, affect your emotional states, and if they are inhibiting energy flow long enough in your energetic body, they can start to affect your physical body. Also, as we have discussed in the book, different parts of the physical body tend to store certain emotions more than others.

Once this energy trickles down to the physical level and starts to show up as illness and disease, it's a whole new ball game. Your physical body has to be addressed to help it heal. (You should seek a doctor in this case, and the following technique is not meant as a substitution for any medical treatment.) But the problem is, if you don't address the underlying cause of emotional baggage and energetic disruption, it's going to heal a lot slower, and the illness will likely become chronic or keep returning. This is where tapping in can help to get to the bottom of the illness and heal it from the inside out.

## My Tapping In Journey

Before we talk about the technique, I want to give you an idea of what the process of learning to tap in looked like for me. The reason I am sharing this is that I don't want you to get discouraged, thinking you aren't doing it well or right. It's a process and is an advanced technique that I was guided to share in this book. The cool thing is, with practice, I do believe that anyone can learn this technique, whether you had an experience like mine or not. I have taught it to many of my clients, and they use it with great results.

When I first had my spiritual kundalini awakening, I had a jumble of messages, sounds, and visions coming into my mind. One of the things that an experienced healer suggested I do was start carrying a notebook with me and writing things down. At first, what I wrote down were words that seemed to mean nothing. I would hear or see names of people, places, or things and write them down. I remember one time, I just kept hearing the word *fruit*. I mean, I literally heard it all day. I kept writing it down, thinking maybe I would get more information than that. Fruit . . . I must have written it down fifteen times. By that evening, I wasn't feeling well. I felt like I was coming down with a cold, and I started craving oranges. So I ate two of them. The next morning, I woke up and I felt infinitely better. Both of my kids, on the other hand, woke up coughing with a stuffy nose.

Since I had eaten the oranges, I felt fine and was able to take care of them. Midmorning, after filling up humidifiers, rubbing Vicks on the kids' chests, and making them tea, I happened to glance down at my notebook in the kitchen . . . FRUIT. Something was telling me what my body needed; I just had no idea what it meant until after the fact. I was receiving communication. My body was saying, Hey, you need to pay attention here, but all it could manage to get across was one word. And that was enough.

As time went on, over the course of several months, I started getting phrases, then whole paragraphs, then pages. It got easier and easier. It truly is like tuning into another language.

At first I didn't think this concept could really be taught, but over the years, my guides taught me a process that would work for people to learn it. So, I am excited to share it with you. Give it a whirl. It will change your life to be able to talk to your body and soul this way.

**Technique 10.2. Tapping In**

1.  To start, we are going to simply envision what you are wanting to open up a dialogue with. Let's say you are having gallbladder issues, such as gallbladder attacks or gallstones. The gallbladder and liver are intimately linked, and the liver typically houses anger, frustration, and rage. Maybe you have already worked on this using techniques earlier in the book. That's great! This is a different way of addressing it that can shed more light on the emotions and energy that are trapped there by giving the energy a chance to directly have a voice.

Imagine for a second that something was wrong and you needed to get someone's attention. Has this ever happened to you? You are trying desperately to get someone to listen to you, but whatever you try doesn't work. Now imagine all of a sudden you got to let it all out and speak your mind after years of being silenced. In this case, that's what you are doing for your liver and gallbladder. You are giving them a voice. You are allowing them to tell you what's wrong.

2. So let's envision your liver with your gall bladder right underneath it.

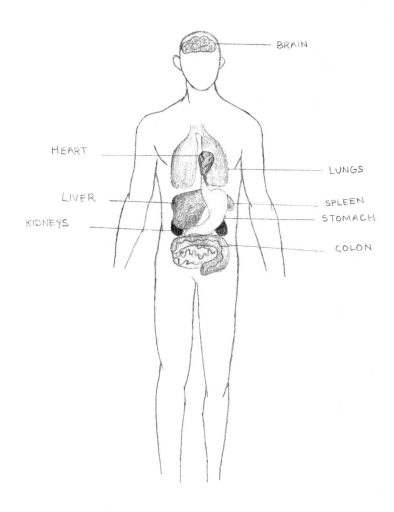

For other areas of discomfort or ailments, see the organ diagram on the previous page to help you envision it:

3. Now hold the image of that in your mind.
4. Next envision a cord that is connected to your liver and gallbladder. This cord allows for the transmission of information: visions and pictures, emotions, and words all travel between the liver/gallbladder and the mind. This cord allows you to understand what the liver and gallbladder are saying so that you can give them voice.

For the sake of this technique, you will be journaling what you see, feel, hear, and know. The information could come to you in a variety of ways.

5. At first, just write down whatever comes into your mind from that translation cord. It may just be images or memories, emotions, or sensations. There is no right or wrong way to receive the information.
6. Once you get a little practice of tapping into the liver and gallbladder in this way, you will start to have more of a conversational flow with it.
7. You can ask questions directly to it, like the following:

    • What do you want to say?
    • What is making you ill?
    • What emotional imprints are you storing?
    • What emotions do you need to release?
    • What can I do to help you?

8. Just write down the question in your journal and envision the information coming through the translation cord. Then write down the information you get.
9. You can repeat this process with any organ in your body, any body system, and even cells! Whatever you are having an issue with, you can give a voice to. Giving your body a chance to speak up can also shift your mindset about your body in general. Your illness is your body trying to communicate with you. It is not against you and is not your enemy. It's trying to tell you, Hey, you need to pay attention to me. It's like a puppy chewing up your shoes. It just wants attention. Once you give it that, things can truly shift for the better.
10. You can use the tapping in technique in conjunction with the simple journaling process in this chapter if you would like, but

it can also be used with any of the other emotional releasing and healing techniques in the book. We will talk about that in the "putting it all together" chapter.

## Tapping in Further

I couldn't really end the chapter without talking about a bit more abstract concept here. In the story at the beginning of the chapter, I talk about telling my client to tap in to her soul. You can call it your higher self if you want. It really doesn't matter what you call it. The premise is the same. The easiest way to envision tapping in to your soul is to imagine something like the picture below. For your mind, it is easier to envision something next to you rather than tapping into yourself, even though that is exactly what you are doing. It brings a little concreteness to the mind and the whole idea.

While this technique can be helpful with releasing emotions or giving you direction on what emotions or imprints to work on, it is also helpful if you are struggling with a tough decision. This is especially true if you are getting input from a lot of different people and don't want to hurt anyone's feelings. A lot of the time, you have a gut feeling of what the right thing to do is, but you are torn, just like my client. By tapping into the soul, you are staying in alignment and honoring what is best for you.

When tough decisions are put in front of you, it can trigger a whole host of emotional states, especially if you are prone to anxiety and stress. Do use the other techniques in the book (or the simple journaling technique) to clear these emotions, as you will make a clearer decision with them. However, if you take it a step further and tap in to your soul and ask what it wants you to do, you will be getting the information from the source, so to speak.

**Technique 10.3. Tapping In to Your Soul**

1.  For this technique, envision the image on page 165 with your soul standing in front of your physical body, to help the mind grip the concept of connection. Envision a translation cord from your physical body to your soul. This cord acts just like any other translation cord, such as those connected to the physical organs. While the soul actually is the essence of you and is inside your physical body, holding it as something outside of yourself for this technique gives the mind something to grasp, rather than the soul being an abstract idea.
2.  At first, see what visions, emotions, or words come to you through the cord. Write them down. After you get some practice at this, you can ask questions.
3.  You can ask your soul anything, just as you can ask your organs anything, but here are some questions to try:

    - What do you want me to know?
    - Are you happy?
    - What imprints are holding you back?
    - What emotions do you need to release right now to feel better?
    - What should I do about (a decision)?
    - What job should I take?
    - Is (a relationship) good for me?

You can even ask it what college you should go to and journal the answer. That is precisely what my client that had the guy dilemma did. But what about her guy situation?? A couple of days after we talked about her journaling what her soul thought she should do, I saw pictures on her Instagram of her with the new guy. Later she told me that the journaling had helped immensely. She got "advice" from her soul on how to talk to her ex-boyfriend about it and honor that connection, as well as how to move on. She followed it. And two years later, she and the new guy are still in a relationship and are attending the same college. I have even heard whispers about wedding bells . . . "Not yet, though," she assures me.

## Chapter Challenge

Start a journal, no matter what it looks like or how often you do it.

Does journaling help you process in a different way? Why or why not?

How did you feel before and after journaling? Did things come up that you didn't expect?

## Feel Better Five

- Journaling isn't for everyone.
- Journaling can help you process things in a different way.
- Writing engages your brain differently than typing.
- Having a structure for journaling can help you problem-solve more effectively.
- The tapping in technique can be used to dialogue with anything in your body or soul to give it a voice.

# Transform in Five (*journaling may take longer)

Technique 10.1. Vent. Reflect. Think Positive. Resolve.

1. Write out everything that has you upset. You may not have a clear idea of what that even is when you start writing, but once you start, you will be amazed at what you put down on paper.
2. Put the shoe on the other foot. After you get your frustrations down on paper, it's time to shift your perspective.

3. The silver lining. It's time to take a step further and ask yourself:

- What did I learn from this situation?
- If it happened again, what would I change about my reaction to it?
- Did the situation highlight or trigger any of my traumatic or verbal inhibitory imprints that I can work on healing?
- Would I take any additional or different actions?

4. The resolution. If what you are journaling about requires some type of action on your part to make amends or solve a problem, this is where you write that down.

Technique 10.2. Tapping In

1. To start, we are going to simply envision what you are wanting to open up a dialogue with.
2. Now hold the image of that in your mind.
3. Next envision a cord that is connected to what you are dialoguing with. This cord allows for the transmission of information: visions and pictures, emotions, and words all travel between the subject and the mind.
4. At first, just write down whatever comes into your mind from that translation cord. It may just be images or memories, emotions, or sensations. There is no right or wrong way to receive the information.
5. Once you get a little practice of tapping into something in this way, you will start to have more of a conversational flow with it.
6. You can ask questions directly to it, like the following:

- What do you want to say?
- What is making you ill?
- What emotional imprints are you storing?
- What emotions do you need to release?
- What can I do to help you?

7. Just write down the question in your journal and envision the information coming through the translation cord. Then write down the information you get.
8. You can repeat this process with any organ in your body, any body system, and even cells!

Technique 10.3. Tapping In to Your Soul

1. For this technique, envision the image on page 165 with your soul standing in front of your physical body, to help the mind grip the concept of connection.
2. Envision a translation cord from your physical body to your soul.
3. At first, see what visions, emotions, or words come to you through the cord. Write them down.
4. You can ask your soul anything, just as you can ask your organs anything, but here are some questions to try:

   - What do you want me to know?
   - Are you happy?
   - What imprints are holding you back?
   - What emotions do you need to release right now to feel better?
   - What should I do about this decision?
   - What job should I take?
   - Is this relationship good for me?

Practicing self-care is important, and while emotional releasing is part of that equation, it's not the whole picture. In the next chapter, we talk about physical products and how they can support you on the journey of emotional healing.

CHAPTER 11

# The Feel Better Product Checklist

About a year after I had my kundalini awakening, I was still discovering my new talents and gifts. By that point, I had become fluently audiovoyant and clairvoyant and was beginning to regularly channel recipes and formulas—everything from food to herbal remedies. It was fun, and I was beginning to help people with them.

One day I was at my chiropractor, and I noticed she wasn't feeling well. "I never get sick," she said, "but I have been under stress, and my immune system got low. I think I am getting a cold." She had a pile of chewable vitamin C on her desk, along with a slew of other vitamins she was taking to stay afloat.

My guides told me I was going to make her something, so I told her what I was hearing. She looked intrigued. "What are you going to make?"

I just stared back at her and blinked. "I have no idea. They didn't tell me yet."

"Well, if it can make me feel better, I'll try anything." She turned her head to cough at the wall.

I nodded and left my appointment. I was a little nervous. I had never made anything for her before, and she was someone I really looked up to. What if I was guided to make something that didn't help her, or worse yet harmed her in some way? I decided to trust my guides and just do as I was told. I seriously wish I still had that recipe. I didn't fully understand at the time how my guides operated or why they would tell me to add in certain things to a formula. I was just blindly listening to what they told me to add to this pot on the stove. I added at least four kinds of cooking oils, some essential oils, vitamins, salt, cereal, oatmeal, and the weirdest ingredient—fish food. There were at least fifty ingredients in that mix . . . and it was the nastiest, slimiest thing you have ever seen. All I had to put it in was a Ziplock bag. I carried it to her office and handed it to her in the waiting room that was full of patients.

"Here," I said, "for something that looks as bad as you feel. Dump all of this in a bath and soak for twenty minutes and take a nap."

She laughed and nodded. "As soon as I get home."

I just hoped she still spoke to me after that.

The marketplace is full of well-meaning products that vow to make us feel better; whether it's to lose weight, get more sleep, or have more energy, there are a wide variety to choose from, and they work, with varying results. Most of us, me included, have no less than a cabinet full of them. The problem is, unless we address the underlying issue, these products often don't do much. However, when we use these products in conjunction with emotional clearing techniques, they can be extremely helpful in assisting our bodies in processing out emotions and other low-vibration energy.

As we have mentioned throughout the book, physical ailments are a manifestation of energy being congested somewhere in the body. Energetic imprints and low-vibration emotions limit the flow of energy through the energy system. Taking out these emotions through setting an intention, envisioning, breathing, grounding, or journaling can be tremendously helpful in clearing these emotions so that the energy system, mind, and physical body function better. Sometimes, though, having some physical products to assist in the process helps us focus on self-care more, as well as amplify our emotional clearing results.

## A Few Ways to Use This Chapter

The products in this chapter can be used at any point in the emotional clearing techniques process to assist you in releasing lower-vibration emotions. While the products can work on their own, they are better when used with other techniques in the book. Most of the physical products listed include a description to let you know how and when it would be most helpful in regard to releasing specific emotional states. These products can be combined in endless ways to amplify your results. Some combinations are laid out in chapter 12.

Bringing other elements into the mix is sometimes helpful to create an environment that is supportive of releasing emotional energy. It also gives our mind something more tangible to do and to relate this practice to, which can be helpful, especially if this is all new to you. Pretty much anything that is emotionally supportive to you can be used to help you create a space that feels comforting and relaxing. The more relaxed you are, the easier it is to get into a state to process or release emotions.

## Clearing the Space

It is important to use some type of energy clearing to clear the emotions you release from a space. Some of the following suggestions below will do this. I'm not going to go too deeply into this here, but emotions are energy, and just as you had the emotions in you, they can travel to other people and affect their energy system as well. It's important to give the emotions you release somewhere to go so that they don't affect others. This is why, if you have ever been to some sort of group meditation or energy clearing event, you sometimes feel bad afterward. A lot of emotions get released in those spaces, and it's pretty much guaranteed you picked something up from someone else. This is why personally I am not a big fan of them. Especially if you tend to pick up the emotions of others easily.

When releasing emotions, at the very least, do it outside if you can, or open a window and let in sunlight if possible. Just as you are responsible for your actions affecting other people, you are responsible for making sure the energetic emotions you release are dealt with so they do not migrate to those around you.

When you are choosing how to create your space, experiment with what works for you. These elements are by no means mandatory for releasing or processing, but they can be helpful.

## Candles

Candles have been used for hundreds of years in spiritual practice. They are often used on altars and are symbols for the state of enlightenment. Some feel they are representative of the impermanence of form, bridging the physical reality and spiritual realms. Lighting candles can be helpful to set a calm and relaxing mood, as well as assist us in providing focus to create an intention. The light of the candle is said to help call in angels and spirit guides for rituals and ceremonies. Energetically, the flame of a candle can help "burn up" emotions that are released when practicing emotional releasing techniques like the ones found in this book. The elimination of diffusing, dispelling, or burning up low-vibration emotions after you release them is very important. Otherwise, they will hang around, where you or someone else can pick them back up.

## Types of Candles

There are many types of waxes that are used for candles. Less expensive candles are made of waxes derived from petroleum, such as paraffin. These candles emit small amounts of volatile organic compounds when burned, which are toxic and can cause eye, nose, and throat irritation.

Other waxes, such as beeswax and soy, are natural alternatives. As an added plus, they last longer than paraffin too.

## Scented Candles

Candles come in a variety of scents and can be used in emotional clearing, although I personally prefer unscented candles for this purpose. Certain scents can make it more difficult to clear emotional states, and this varies from person to person. If you are going to use scented candles, use ones with natural fragrances and/or essential oils instead of synthetic fragrance. Reputable candle companies do use fragrances that are cleared for use in candles, whether they are natural or synthetic, but energetically speaking, natural fragrances or essential oils are best. When in doubt, stick to unscented candles that are made of soy or beeswax.

## Colors of Candles

This section assumes you are lighting candles with no scent accompanying them. These are just unscented candles with color. Color can play a big role in the releasing and healing of emotional states, and candles can assist in this process.

## White

As we talked about in the color chapter, white is the multivitamin of color, so white candles can be used for just about anything. In candle therapy, it represents the crown chakra and is used for destruction of negative energy, peace, truth, and purity. Given this, it is a perfect candle to light when you are releasing negative or low-vibration emotions. Grief and suicide are complicated emotions that use this color as a remedy, and if you have ever noticed, candlelight vigils often use white candles to show respect to loved ones that have passed on.

## Violet or Purple

Violet or purple is the color that also represents the crown chakra, but the energetic aspects of this color are closer to those of the third eye chakra. Spiritual awareness, wisdom, and tranquility are attributes of violet or purple in candle therapy. When you are working on releasing emotions such as fearful, hyperactive, impulsive, overly independent, temperamental, uncreative, unintelligent, untruthful, unworthy, or withdrawn, purple or violet is a useful color.

## Indigo

This color is between purple and blue and represents the third eye chakra. In candle therapy, the color represents meditation, healing, and inspiration. The third eye is the source of clairvoyance and your envisioning ability. This color is good to use if you are working to release the emotions of confused, controlling, embarrassed, hyperactive, imbalanced, imperceptive, ineffective, lonely, materialistic, overbearing, rage, unclear, unmotivated, unsuccessful, and vulnerable.

## Blue

The throat chakra is represented by the color blue and in color therapy represents forgiveness, fidelity, and open lines of communication. This is a good candle to light to obtain clarity in your voice and is also good for a meditative state. If you are working to release the emotions of aggressive, anger, anxious, confused, disorganized, distrust, dramatic, hyperactive, impulsive, indecisive, indulgence, overbearing, overstimulated, rage, sleepless, temperamental, tired, unable to express self, unable to speak your truth, unforgiving, untruthful, or weak, a blue candle can assist you.

## Green and Pink

The colors green and pink represent the heart chakra. In candle therapy, green represents money, fertility, luck, abundance, success, and health (do not use it if diagnosed with cancer). The color pink in candle therapy represents more of the heart-centered qualities, such as positive self-love, friendship, harmony, and joy. If you are feeling aggressive, angry, anxious, betrayed, critical, defensive, discomfort (not physical), distrust, dramatic, guilt, hopeless, imbalanced, impulsive, insecure, materialistic, overbearing, overwhelmed, rage, resentful, stifled, stressed, unloved, unmotivated, unsafe, untruthful, or unworthy, both green and light pink are good colors of candles to use when releasing these emotions.

## Yellow

Yellow is the color of the emotional chakra, and in candle therapy it represents realizing and manifesting thoughts, confidence, bringing plans into action, creativity, intelligence, and mental clarity. A yellow candle is good for bringing more energy into a space and pepping it up if things in the room have gotten lethargic. If you are feeling confused, depressed, detached, flawed, indecisive, negative (with no anger), powerless, sad, tired, unable to express self, unable to speak your truth, or underwhelmed, lighting a yellow candle can help you to dispel and burn up these emotions as you release them.

## Orange

Orange is a powerful color that represents the sacral chakra. When used in color therapy, it represents joy, energy, education, strength, attraction, and stimulation. Orange is a great color for bringing energy into a space that is all about taking action. Creativity and focus thrive in the light of an orange candle. If you are working on releasing emotions of abandoned, detached, discomfort (not physical), fearful, flawed, hopeless, indecisive, ineffective, lacking abundance, negative (with no anger), powerless, stressed, temperamental, unable to express self, uncreative, underwhelmed, unintelligent, unsuccessful, unworthy, or withdrawn, lighting an orange candle in your space while releasing these emotions can be helpful in coming back to a powerful, actionable state.

# Red

The grounding color of red is representative of the root chakra and in candle therapy is used for passion, love, lust, relationships, sex, energy, vitality, and courage. Like orange, red is a power color. It is all about being in the physical world and functioning well in it. If you are processing and releasing emotions such as abandoned, detached, fearful, insecure, lonely, low ambition, low on life, negative (with no anger), powerless, tired, underwhelmed, ungrounded, unloved, unmotivated, vulnerable, or weak, the candle color of red can help release and extinguish those emotional states.

**Technique 11.1. Candles for Emotional Clearing**

1. Choose the emotion or emotions you would like to work with.
2. You can choose one emotion or just choose to work with the color associated with its group of emotions.
3. Look at the list of emotions on the color chart in chapter 5 for each color and see if a large number of the emotions under that color (or the one you are wanting to work with) resonate with the emotions you are working on releasing.
4. Light a chosen-color candle.
5. Set your intention: "I choose to release (emotion[s]) and whatever they are attached to."
6. Envision releasing the emotion or emotions into the space around you and watching the emotions burn up in the flame of the candle.

# Incense

The practice of burning different herbs, spices, resins, and woods has been around for thousands of years to promote relaxation, meditation, focus, and emotional release. Incense is also good for clearing released emotional energies from a space, which is important, when you are dealing with low vibrational energy.

Today, for convenience, most incense is found in the form of sticks to burn rather than in a loose form. While there are many types of incense sticks on the market, all are definitely not created equal. You've heard the saying "you get what you pay for," and with incense, it's no exception. Less expensive types of incense sticks are unscented. They are covered with a mix of sawdust and charcoal powder mixed with a binding agent formed onto a bamboo stick and then dipped in diluting chemicals and fragrance oils to simulate herbs and spice scents. The result is that you are burning chemical oil with a small amount of fragrance. If incense has ever given off black smoke when you light it, made your eyes burn, or given you headaches, this is most likely why. These chemicals are toxic and were never meant to be burned.

The traditional method of making a good-quality incense stick starts with raw ingredients of spices, herbs, resins, fragrant woods, and flower petals that are ground into a fine powder. They are then mixed with honey and aromatic oils to make a dough and rolled onto a bamboo stick and coated with aromatic wood powder so that the wet sticks do not stick to each other.

## Don't Smoke Yourself Out

Always use incense in a well-ventilated area, and if you are asthmatic or prone to breathing difficulties, use with caution. If you start experiencing issues with your incense, make sure that it is made from natural ingredients. If it is and you are still having problems such as coughing or watery eyes, you may just be sensitive to the ingredients. Switch to another kind or use an essential oil diffuser instead.

**Technique 11.2. Incense for Emotional Clearing**

1. Light incense and let it smoke for a few minutes before you begin your emotional clearing techniques. This allows the scent to spread in your space and be present to dispel the low-vibration emotional energy once you start releasing it.
2. It is best to use in a ventilated space so it does not overwhelm you.
3. Be sure to use an incense holder and be mindful of the ash from the burned incense.

## Common Incense Ingredients

While incense can be made from a variety of natural ingredients, here are some common components of incense that have been used over the centuries.

## Sandalwood

This is personally my favorite scent, and it's such a workhorse of the aromatherapy world. It is both grounding and energizing to the physical body and the mind. Sandalwood allows you to go deep inside yourself and be honest with what is there. This awareness allows you to get to more emotions than you might have been able to access before and brings more clarity to what you need to release. If you have ever been to a yoga studio, chances are you have gotten a whiff of sandalwood, as it is commonly used in yogic practice. While it can be used in a blend, it is often a standalone incense.

# Cinnamon

Essential for emotional release, cinnamon digs deep to help us unearth emotions and memories that we have buried. It allows us to release and find clarity with people and situations that may have felt impossible in the past. This scent is good by itself or in a blend.

# Frankincense

This is a key ingredient when you are releasing any kind of fear or have anxiety or stress about change. It has been used since ancient times in meditation practices and is known for carrying oxygen and nutrients to the brain. Clarity, focus, and centeredness are easier to achieve with frankincense by your side.

# Myrrh

While this is not the best-smelling ingredient, it is often blended with frankincense for a more pleasing aroma. Myrrh is a great compliment to frankincense because it opens our minds to seeing ways to achieve our dreams and promotes inspiration. After frankincense clears your fear, myrrh swoops in and opens your mind so that you can see what's possible.

# Patchouli

If you are working on releasing fear, anxiety, or indecision, patchouli is your friend. It's very calming and centering, bringing about a cooperative effort between your heart and your head. Clearing out what ifs and self-imposed barriers and beliefs are easier with patchouli, as the scent specializes in digging to the core of your true self to let it shine.

# Sage or Cedar "Sticks" or "Smudges"

Smudging or burning herbs have been used by Indigenous peoples around the world for generations in ceremonies and to clear energy from spaces and energy fields. While burning herbs in a bowl is still in practice today, you can also purchase cedar and sage smudge bundles, often called "sticks." They burn longer than loose herbs in a bowl and are easier to deal with for moving them around a room or waving them around a person.

### Technique 11.3. Using a Smudge Stick in a Room

While you can let a smudge stick simply burn in a fireproof container in a space, it is more often used as a tool to clear energy from a room or a person's energy field. The following process can be used before an emotional release session but is very beneficial after emotional releasing to help burn up and neutralize the low-vibration emotional energy that is released. It is best used in a well-ventilated space.

1. To use in a room, simply light it and blow it out.
2. When it starts smoking, carry it around the room and let the smoke permeate the space.
3. Go around the edges of the room first and then through the center of the room.
4. If emotional releasing is being done in a certain area of the room, focus on that area with the smoking smudge stick.

### Technique 11.4. Smudging a Human Energy Field

1. To use in someone's energy field, simply move the smoking smudge stick slowly around the person, roughly two to ten inches away from their body, starting close to them and moving outward in several passes.
2. Take care not to touch their clothing, skin, or hair with the smudge stick, and pay attention to ash falling off the stick. They usually burn pretty cleanly, but you don't want to drop ash on someone.
3. Note: You don't need to burn the whole thing at once. A few minutes is usually enough time to make passes through a room and address someone's energy field.
4. To put it out, you can place it smoking-side down in a mason jar or snuff the end out in a bowl.
5. Be sure it is completely done smoking before you put it away.

## Salt Baths

This is my favorite method for clearing out your energy field and doing self-care. It feels indulgent, smells good, and is super relaxing.

Salt draws energy out of your energy field and physical body. It is also a great way to absorb much-needed minerals.

When you perform energetic release techniques, most of the energy you release completely leaves your energy system and physical body, but it's tough to get it all out by doing this sometimes. Think of it as crumbs that are left over. You don't want these crumbs floating around to reincorporate into your energy field and body when you did all that work to release them. Salt draws it out so that doesn't happen.

You can also do emotional releasing techniques while you are in the bath. Emotions are easier to release when you are relaxed, and being in a bath can really help this process. You can combine the use of a salt bath with the element of candles for a more pampering experience. The candles will help to burn up any energy that is drawn out by the bath, and you can use the candle emotional releasing techniques in conjunction if this feels beneficial to you.

## Water Temperature

While I am a fan of a nice hot bath, salt baths are best done in warm water. The skin is a two-way organ. It excretes waste and absorbs things that are on its surface. In a hot bath, your body goes into excretion mode—think sweat. We are not conscious of the fact that we are excreting because we are already wet, but if the bath is too hot, it is happening. When you sit in a warm bath, though, your pores open and absorb whatever goodies you have put in your pampering bath.

## Some Simple Bath Salt Ingredients

While I am not an aromatherapist, I have been making salt bath concoctions for about fifteen years and never tire of them. I use a combination of salts, essential oils, and carrier oils in my bath salts. I channel the recipes for them, but you can make your own using a combination of ingredients on the following pages.

Salts and oils can be used in endless combinations for a unique experience every time. If you are going to use essential oils in your bath, mix them with the salt first! This keeps the oils from sitting on top of the bath water. If you have sensitive skin, dilute the essential oils with a carrier oil, such as sweet almond oil or avocado oil, before you add it to the bath salt.

**Technique 11.5. Basic Salt Bath Ratios**

If you are using the salt bath to draw out a lot of energy, use two cups of salt with two cups of baking soda and soak in the warm water for fifteen to twenty minutes.

Once you start incorporating essential oils, you can use less salt in your bath. Use about fifteen to twenty drops of oil per one cup of salt. This is typically a safe ratio. If you want to use baking soda as well, add half a cup. Soak in it for fifteen to twenty minutes.

If you have sensitive skin, you can dilute the essential oil with carrier oil before you add it to the bath salt. Use a ratio of twenty drops of essential oil to six teaspoons of carrier oil.

It's important to note that if you are allergic to tree nuts, you should not use some carrier oils, such as sweet almond oil, argan oil, or apricot kernel oil.

# Dead Sea Salt

This is my favorite salt for baths. It comes from the Dead Sea, where people have traveled to bathe in it for centuries. It's a good catchall salt and contains twenty-one minerals, including magnesium, calcium, sulfur, bromide, iodine, sodium, zinc, and potassium. It is NOT a food-grade salt and honestly tastes really nasty. However, the minerals in it work wonders for relaxing and detoxifying the body. This is the main salt I use in my salt baths, as it works really well in drawing out stagnant low-vibration energy.

# Himalayan Pink Salt

This is a fun and effective salt to use in your salt baths. The color of the salt comes from its high iron content and is found in the Himalayan Mountains, hence the name. It contains all eighty-four trace elements needed by your body, so it is highly recommended by health experts to use on your food as well.

If you are dealing with negative energy from others or entities, this is a great salt to use. It's also really useful if you have had a particularly intense energy releasing session. The iron in the salt is great at assisting in pulling that energy out and neutralizing it.

# Epsom Salt

This salt is the easiest to come by, as well as the least expensive. It is found in the drug section of the grocery store and is made up of magnesium sulfate. This is not a food-grade salt and in my opinion tastes worse than Dead Sea salt. There are some natural remedies that involve ingesting it, but I am not recommending them here.

Epsom salt is great for sore muscles and cramps. Magnesium is a cofactor in more than three hundred biochemical reactions in our body, and most people are very deficient in this mineral. Taking a bath in Epsom salt is a great way to get this mineral in the body, as it can cause lower digestive issues if you intake too much of it orally.

If you are dealing with depressive states and sadness, this is a great salt to use in your bath.

# Baking Soda

Even though we don't think of it that way, baking soda is a type of salt and it's a great addition to a salt bath. It makes the water feel silkier and can prevent irritation from the other salt in bathwater, if you have really sensitive skin. Energetically speaking, when combined with salt, baking soda ups the releasing and drawing power of the salt in your bath, so it is a good idea to add it if you have it.

It's important to note that if you make a bath salt with oils and plan on storing it, don't add baking soda right away. It can do some funky things to your precious salt blend. While it doesn't hurt the efficacy of your bath salt, the baking soda can cause your mix to become hard. If you are storing it in a jar (preferred), it's super difficult to get out when you want your next relaxing experience, hence making it not so relaxing . . . So mix your salt and oils together, store it in a jar, and then when you go to put the salt in the bath, add the baking soda separately at that time.

# Carrier Oils

While I don't often use these in my bath salt blends, if my skin is particularly dry, it's a nice addition. For some people, it's essential to use a carrier oil if they have sensitive skin. There are many types of carrier oils with different beneficial properties. They can be used alone or to dilute essential oils before adding them to bath salts.

## Sweet Almond Oil

This oil is an excellent emollient that has the ability to soften and recondition the skin. It is nourishing to the skin and contains proteins, linoleic acid, and Vitamin D. It is considered a tree nut.

## Grape Seed Oil

A very light, odorless and virtually colorless oil that is great for carrying essential oil fragrances. It's astringent and toning and is said to have sun-protection benefits.

## Apricot Kernel Oil

Recommended for mature or sensitive skin, it is a mild, moisturizing oil that is easily absorbed into the skin. It is similar to sweet almond oil and is great for use in a salt bath for leaving skin super soft. It is considered a tree nut.

## Avocado Oil

This oil is considered hypoallergenic and is great at hydrating and softening the skin. It is also often recommended as an effective treatment for acne, eczema, and other forms of skin inflammation.

## Argan Oil

It is light and easily absorbed into the skin. It is packed with nutrients that are great for both skin and hair, such as tocopherols and phenols, carotenes, squalene, and fatty acids, which make it a great addition to your bath salts. It is considered a tree nut.

## Jojoba Oil

This oil is very stable because it is actually a wax. It is wonderful for the skin because it has absorption properties that are similar to our skin's own sebum. This makes it a good fit to be used as a face oil but is equally fantastic in a bath salt. It can become solid at cooler room temperatures, but a little warmth turns it back into a liquid.

## Essential Oils

These things are magic in a bath. There are endless combinations of oils that can be used in baths, but in this section are some of the basic ones that are commonly used. In general, it's a good idea to mix essential oils with some carrier oil before you put it on your skin. I have found, however, that when all of the essential oils in this section are mixed with bath salt first, carrier oils aren't really needed.

While essential oils have many benefits, in the descriptions on the following pages, I am focusing on how the oils relate to emotional, mental, and energetic states. I have also listed which emotions they are best used for so you can address your specific needs for emotional releasing.

## Aromatherapy and Memory

Since smell is highly linked to memory, essential oils can actually jog your memory and help you to access things long forgotten. This is one of the advantages in using them when you are working on accessing and releasing emotional states. Even putting a drop or two on the cloth and inhaling it can elicit a renewed focus and access when releasing emotions. Look at the list of emotions associated with each oil to decide which ones to use, and experiment to see which ones work best for you.

## Not All Essential Oils Are Created Equal

Just like any other product out there, some essential oils are better than others. Some of the cheaper oils use harsh chemical extraction methods on the plants. These chemicals wind up in the essential oils. Other oils use a combination of fragrance or perfume oils with a carrier oil and market them as essential oils. These fragrance or perfume oils are made from chemicals, and while they may smell like an essential oil, they do not provide the same benefits as a pure essential oil.

## The Container Matters

Quality essential oils are always found in dark glass bottles, typically amber or blue in color, but can be any dark color. This protects the oil from breaking down due to UV exposure. Pure essential oils are never stored in plastic, because the oil will start to break down the plastic as soon as it comes into contact with it, so if you see essential oils bottled this way, avoid them.

## Residue? It's a No-Go

When you are shopping for essential oils, stores will typically provide little strips of paper for you to drip the oil on to smell it. Try this out. If the oil on the paper doesn't dry without leaving a ring, it is most likely diluted with a carrier oil of some sort. Pure essential oils will not leave a ring when dry.

It's important to note that some of the more expensive essential oils may be diluted in a carrier oil (such as jasmine, rose, or sandalwood), but if they are, it will say that on the bottle. The reason some are sold this way is that due to the cost of the pure oil, it is often too expensive for the average consumer. With a diluted version, you can still receive the benefits of the oil in a more affordable form.

## Leave the Grease

Pure essential oils will not have a greasy or oily feel to them. If they do, they are diluted with a carrier oil. Just rub a drop between your fingers to tell. If it's greasy, take a pass on it, unless it is one of the more expensive oils, as mentioned on the previous pages, and it states that it is diluted on the bottle.

## Still, Use with Caution

Essential oils can be strong. If you know you have very sensitive skin or are allergic to any of the oils listed on the following pages, don't use them. If you have never used them before, I recommend starting with one oil only in a bath to make sure you don't react to it before you start mixing and matching them. This way, if you have an issue with an oil, you will know the culprit right away.

## Peppermint

Peppermint stimulates the mind and increases ability to focus. It's like a rush of fresh energy into your system. It relieves anxiety, preventing it from building up in your body and mind. The relaxing quality of peppermint is great for people who experience mood swings frequently.

Note:
Peppermint oil is stimulating to the mind, so if you are trying to relax before bed, don't use a lot of it, or you could find yourself tossing and turning. A little in a bath salt goes a long way.

It does have a cooling sensation on the skin and should definitely be diluted if you are going to put it directly on the skin. However, it's fine in a bath salt.

Use four to five drops per cup of bath salt.

# Tea Tree

If you are struggling with events that have happened in your life, tea tree oil is your friend. It helps us put things in perspective and see the bigger picture of why things occurred the way that they did. If you are struggling with tolerance, this is a great oil to use. It helps us grow through situations and see the light on the other side.

Note:
Like peppermint, tea tree has a cooling or burning sensation on the skin and should be diluted if used this way, but in a bath salt, it is typically not an issue.

Use up to five drops per cup of bath salt.

# Lavender

Lavender is a "catchall" oil and has been shown to balance the body wherever it is needed. It is great for nurturing us through a variety of stresses, both physical and emotional. If you are struggling with judgment, it can help you to usher in kindness. It's typically thought of as a relaxing oil to use at bedtime, which makes it perfect for a bath.

Note:
In general, lavender oil is safe to be used directly on skin and is perfectly safe to be used in a bath salt. Some people (me included) are actually stimulated by lavender, and I don't personally care for the smell. It is very popular, however, and generally well-tolerated.

Use up to ten drops per cup of bath salt.

# Eucalyptus

If you are lacking confidence and fear trying new things, eucalyptus can help you break through. It's also good for helping you to calmly release resentment without exploding your anger onto someone. Fatigue and exhaustion can be alleviated with this oil as well.

Note:
Just like peppermint and tea tree, eucalyptus can have a cooling or burning effect on the skin, so it is best diluted for this use. It is fine in a bath salt in small amounts.

Use three drops per cup of bath salt.

# Ylang Ylang

This is the happy oil and can be very effective for depression. Ylang ylang can bring joy, harmony, and passion to relationships and is great for balancing sexual energy. It is considered a spiritual oil and nurtures a desire to connect to our souls more deeply, as well as to the Universe. When you are looking to be more emotional, caring, intuitive, and spiritual, ylang ylang can gently guide you in this direction.

Note:
This oil is best diluted with a carrier oil if applied directly to skin but is great for a salt bath. It does tend to ramp up the energy system and physical body, so it is best used at least three hours before bedtime.

Use five drops per cup of bath salt.

# Bergamot

Bergamot is great for releasing deeply held anger and emotional pain. If you are viewed by your friends and family as cheerful, supportive, and being a good listener but are silently suffering, this oil is for you. It helps you dig deep and get to the root of old traumas and combines really well with emotional release techniques.

Note:
Dilute with a carrier oil if applying to skin, but it is safe for use in a salt bath.

Use up to four drops in one cup of bath salt.

# Roman Chamomile (*expensive)

Chamomile is great for calming the body and mind. Roman chamomile is the more expensive form of chamomile, and you may find this with a carrier oil added to reduce the cost. German chamomile is a good oil as well for calming and is less expensive.

Roman chamomile, particularly, smooths the flow of energy in the body and is great at releasing negative emotions that are the root cause of physical ailments. If you are struggling to go with the flow of life, this oil can put you in a state of mind to let the Universe work its magic rather than fighting your circumstances.

Note:
Roman Chamomile can be applied directly to the skin and a popular use is to add a couple of drops to skin moisturizer or shampoo. It is favored to be used in an essential oil diffuser and can be safely used in a salt bath.

Use up to five drops per one cup of bath salt.

# Frankincense

Frankincense is great if you need to get your focus on. It helps carry oxygen and nutrients across the blood/brain barrier, so eat well if you are using it. If you have big changes happening in your life, this oil can help you overcome the fear of it. It is also a very popular oil for meditation and improves our intuition and connection to the Universe/creator.

Note:
Frankincense is a pretty mild oil and is generally well tolerated directly on the skin. If you are particularly sensitive, dilute it first. It is often used in an essential oil diffuser, and it can be safely used in a bath salt.

Use up to four drops of frankincense in one cup of bath salt.

# Patchouli

Patchouli is known for its centering and calming effects. If you are struggling with limiting beliefs, this oil is your friend. It brings balance to the tug of war between your head and your heart and lets the soul lead. Anxiety, fear, and indecision melt away when patchouli is around.

Note:
It is a great oil to pair with citrus notes for the scent and emotional properties. It should be diluted before being applied to the skin. It is safe for use in a bath, but do not use if you are on blood-thinning medications, as it can affect blood clotting.

Use up to eight drops in one cup of bath salt.

# Sandalwood (*expensive)

Pure sandalwood oil is expensive and is often found diluted in a carrier oil. It is energizing and grounding, making it popular in meditation and yoga practices. Sandalwood increases our ability to see inside ourselves and accept what we find. This oil pairs really well with emotional release techniques.

Note:
Personally my favorite oil! This is a popular oil for an essential oil diffuser, and the plant is often used in incense. In general the oil can be applied directly to skin, but dilute with a carrier oil first if you are very sensitive. It is safe for use in a bath salt.

Use up to six drops in one cup of bath salt.

# Rose Absolute (*expensive)

Rose oil is often diluted in carrier oil because of the cost. If you can find it, rose absolute oil is the nondiluted form. Vibrationally speaking, rose is the highest-frequency oil. It helps to really knock loose stuck emotional states and is best to use in an emotional crisis. If you are having trouble moving forward in life, this oil will help you to let go. Strong emotions can fatigue and debilitate the physical body. Rose absolute is great for unraveling those emotions and freeing the body of their grip.

Note:
Rose oil can generally be used directly on the skin, but dilute it with a carrier oil if you are very sensitive. This oil is great for use in a diffuser and works very well in a bath salt.

Use up to six drops of rose absolute in one cup of bath salt. If it is diluted with a carrier oil, you can use up to fifteen drops.

Rose absolute works well on all emotional states and can be used with any emotion listed in this book.

# Crystals and Stones

This is really a subject that warrants its own book, but crystals can be used to energetically enhance a space and create supportive energy for releasing. They can be used for absorbing released emotions as well, but this is usually done when they are laid on the body. For clearing a space, candles and incense are a better fit here.

| Emotion | Peppermint | Tea Tree | Lavender | Eucalyptus | Ylang Ylang | Bergamot | R. Chamomile | Frankincense | Patchouli | Sandalwood | Rose Absolute |
|---|---|---|---|---|---|---|---|---|---|---|---|
| Abandoned | | | x | x | | | | | | x | x |
| Aggressive | x | | | | x | x | | x | | x | x |
| Anger | | | x | x | x | x | | x | | x | x |
| Anxious | x | | x | x | | x | | x | | x | x |
| Betrayed | | x | x | | | | | | | x | x |
| Confused | x | | x | | x | x | x | x | x | | x |
| Controlling | | x | x | | x | x | x | | | x | x |
| Critical | | x | x | | | | | | | x | x |
| Defensive | | | x | | x | x | x | x | x | | x |
| Depressed | x | x | x | x | x | x | x | x | | x | x |
| Detached | x | x | | | x | x | | | x | x | x |
| Discomfort - not phys | x | | x | | x | x | x | | | x | x |
| Disorganized | x | | | | x | x | | | | x | x |
| Distrust | | x | x | | x | x | x | | x | x | x |
| Dramatic | x | x | x | x | x | x | | | x | x | x |
| Embarrassed | x | x | | x | x | x | x | | x | x | x |
| Fearful | x | | x | x | x | | x | x | x | | x |
| Flawed | x | | x | | x | | | x | | x | x |
| Grief | | x | x | | x | x | x | | | | x |
| Guilty | | x | x | | x | x | x | | | | x |
| Hopeless | x | x | x | x | x | x | | | | | x |
| Hyperactive | x | | | | | | x | | | | x |

| Emotion | Peppermint | Tea Tree | Lavender | Eucalyptus | Ylang Ylang | Bergamot | R. Chamomile | Frankincense | Patchouli | Sandalwood | Rose Absolute |
|---|---|---|---|---|---|---|---|---|---|---|---|
| Imbalanced | x | x | x | x | x | x | x | x | x | x | x |
| Imperceptive |  | x |  |  | x |  | x | x | x | x | x |
| Impulsive | x | x | x |  |  |  | x | x | x | x | x |
| Indecisive | x | x | x |  |  |  | x |  | x | x | x |
| Indulgence | x |  | x | x |  |  | x | x |  | x |  |
| Ineffective | x |  | x |  |  | x | x | x | x | x | x |
| Insecure |  | x | x |  |  | x | x | x | x | x | x |
| Jealous |  |  | x | x | x | x |  | x | x | x | x |
| Lonely | x | x |  | x | x |  |  | x | x |  | x |
| Manipulative |  |  | x |  | x |  | x | x | x | x | x |
| Materialistic |  |  | x |  | x |  | x | x | x | x | x |
| Negative (no anger) |  |  | x | x | x | x | x | x |  |  | x |
| Overbearing |  |  | x |  | x |  | x | x |  | x | x |
| Overly independent |  | x |  |  | x |  | x | x |  |  | x |
| Overstimulated | x | x |  | x |  |  | x | x |  | x | x |
| Overwhelmed | x | x | x |  | x | x | x |  | x | x | x |
| Powerless | x |  | x | x | x | x | x | x | x |  | x |
| Rage |  |  |  |  | x |  | x | x | x |  | x |
| Resentful | x |  | x |  | x | x | x | x | x | x | x |
| Sad | x | x | x | x | x | x | x | x | x |  | x |
| Selfish |  | x |  | x | x | x | x | x | x | x | x |
| Sleepless | x | x | x | x |  |  | x | x | x | x | x |

| Emotion | Peppermint | Tea Tree | Lavender | Eucalyptus | Ylang Ylang | Bergamot | R. Chamomile | Frankincense | Patchouli | Sandalwood | Rose Absolute |
|---|---|---|---|---|---|---|---|---|---|---|---|
| Stifled | x | | x | | x | | x | x | x | | x |
| Stressed | x | | x | | x | x | x | | x | | x |
| Suicidal | x | | x | x | x | x | x | x | x | | x |
| Temperamental | x | | x | x | x | x | x | x | x | | x |
| Tired | x | | | x | | | x | x | x | | x |
| Unable to express self | | x | x | | x | x | x | x | x | x | x |
| Unable to speak truth | | x | x | | x | x | x | x | x | x | x |
| Unclear | x | x | | | | x | | x | x | x | x |
| Uncreative | x | x | x | x | | | | x | x | x | x |
| Underwhelmed | x | | x | x | x | x | x | x | x | x | x |
| Unforgiving | | | x | x | x | x | x | x | x | x | x |
| Ungrounded | x | x | x | x | x | x | x | x | x | x | x |
| Unintelligent | x | | | x | x | x | x | | x | x | x |
| Unloved | | | x | | x | x | x | x | | x | x |
| Unmotivated | x | | x | | x | x | x | x | x | x | x |
| Unsafe | x | | x | | x | x | | x | x | x | x |
| Unsuccessful | x | | x | x | x | x | x | x | x | x | x |
| Untruthful | | | x | | x | x | x | | x | x | x |
| Unworthy | x | | x | x | x | x | x | | x | x | x |
| Vulnerable | x | x | x | x | x | x | x | x | x | x | x |
| Weak | x | x | x | x | x | x | x | x | x | x | x |
| Withdrawn | x | x | | | x | x | x | x | x | x | x |

There are many, many different kinds of crystals and stones that have their own unique energetic properties. If you choose to use these, be sure you clear the energy out of them first, especially if you just purchased them. While crystals and stone emit certain energies for healing, they also act like a sponge, soaking up energy. When they get full, they can actually expel energy. If they get full and you use them for energy work or emotional release, it's like squeezing a sponge full of dirt on you.

All stones can be cleared of the energy they have absorbed by laying them in sunlight for several hours. Some can be soaked in salt water, but you have to be careful, as salt water will destroy some types of crystals.

**Technique 11.6. Picking Crystals**

If you have ever been in a rock or crystal shop, all the choices can be a little overwhelming. How do you choose? If you know the type of stone or crystal you are looking for or what attributes you are seeking, this can help narrow it down for you. If all else fails, let the crystal pick you, as they say. When you are shopping for a stone or crystal, you may feel a pull toward a particular stone. Oftentimes, it is not the prettiest one on the shelf (I have some seriously lackluster stones and crystals in my collection), but if you are drawn to it, that is the one for you!

# Bigger Isn't Necessarily Better

Some crystals and stones emit a pretty strong field, so a small stone is enough to get the benefits from it. You don't have to have a huge one for it to help you. In fact, if you get one that is too strong, it can actually aggravate your energy field and your emotional state, throwing you out of balance. So go with the stone that draws you and you will be fine. If you are struggling with what to pick and no one stone in particular draws you in, it probably isn't going to make a difference which one you pick. In other words, you would get the benefit from any of them without a risk of throwing you out of whack.

# A Little Bit Can Go a Long Way

If the crystal or stone is small enough, you can carry it in your pocket or wear it on a necklace or earrings. If you do this, pay attention to how you feel while wearing it. You may feel great for a while and then start to feel agitated or drained. If you start to feel this way, take it off. You have soaked up enough of the energy and need a break. It's a good idea to clear your stone or crystal if this happens. It may have taken on too much low-vibration energy and need to be energetically cleaned.

While there are lots of health claims associated with crystals, the focus here is on the energetic and emotional side of their benefits. Below are a few basic crystals that you can use for working with different emotional states.

# Rose Quartz

This pink quartz is often associated with all aspects of love. It is looked to for restoring love in relationships with others as well as the self. Rose quartz is said to provide calm and comfort in times of grief and encourage respect, trust, and self-worth. It dispels negativity and balances and strengthens the heart chakra.

You can put a stone of rose quartz in your pocket to encourage loving vibes throughout your day. It's also great for holding during emotional healing techniques (you can hold it just in your hands or place it over your heart). Rose quartz can be added to your salt bath to assist in emotional releasing as well (smooth stones are recommended for this use; rough stones can scratch you or the tub).

# Bloodstone

Bloodstone is considered a powerful healing stone. It increases creativity, heightens intuition, and dispels confusion. It's grounding and protective properties increase courage, idealism, and selflessness. Bloodstone helps you to let go and live in the present moment while reducing impatience and aggressiveness.

If you are feeling aggravated or having trouble getting grounded, carrying a bloodstone with you can help you to feel more balanced. It's also great for holding during emotional healing techniques or holding in your lap near your root chakra. Bloodstone can be added to your salt bath to assist in emotional releasing as well (smooth stones recommended for this use; can scratch you or the tub).

# Amethyst

This crystal is good for general balance. It dissolves negativity, dispelling anxiety, rage, fear, and anger. Amethyst assists in releasing sadness and grief and acts as a natural tranquilizer. If you are looking to enhance your intuitive abilities or are working on envisioning, this is the stone for you. It strengthens the third eye chakra (your imagination/envisioning muscle) while encouraging selflessness and spiritual wisdom. It's great for emotional releasing, particularly if you are experiencing emotional pain and stress.

If you are having trouble sleeping or want to enhance your dreams, this is a great stone to put under your pillow. Amethyst is a popular stone to wear as a pendant, or you can carry one in your pocket to chill you out during the day. For added relaxation, you can add a smooth stone or two to your salt bath.

## Smoky Quartz

If you are feeling ungrounded, this stone is a good one to use, because it strengthens the root chakra. Smoky quartz neutralizes bad vibes, bringing positive thoughts while releasing fear and lifting depression. It's a great anxiety reliever, bringing calmness and promoting positive thoughts and actions. Smoky quartz increases concentration and helps with communication difficulties; it is great for use during Mercury retrograde!

Carry this stone around with you if you are prone to anxiety or have a tendency to be ungrounded. It's a great stone to add to your bath for its calming and relaxing effects. Being that it has many general healing effects, it is great to have on your body (anywhere) while doing emotional release techniques.

## Tourmaline

Tourmaline is known for enhancing energy in the body and removing energy blockages, making it great for emotional releasing. It removes fear and allows inspiration and prosperity to enter your life. Tourmaline also increases passion and tolerance while promoting self-confidence.

Tourmaline is a great stone to carry with you if you are headed into a negative environment. Just carry it in your pocket! It's also helpful to have a few pieces in your room or office if conflict tends to take place there. It's a great stone to use for emotional healing techniques. Just hold it in your hands or place it in your lap. DO NOT put it in your bath, as it contains aluminum, and the water will break it down.

| Emotion | Rose Quartz | Blood stone | Amethyst | Smoky Quartz | Tourmaline |
|---|---|---|---|---|---|
| Abandoned | x | x | | x | x |
| Aggressive | x | x | | x | |
| Anger | x | x | x | x | x |
| Anxious | x | x | x | x | x |
| Betrayed | x | | | x | x |
| Confused | x | x | x | x | |
| Controlling | | | x | | |
| Critical | | x | x | | |
| Defensive | | | x | | x |
| Depressed | | x | x | x | x |
| Detached | | x | | x | x |
| Discomfort -not phys | | x | x | x | |
| Disorganized | | x | | x | x |
| Distrust | | x | x | x | x |
| Dramatic | | x | x | x | x |
| Embarrassed | | x | x | | x |
| Fearful | | x | | x | |
| Flawed | x | x | | x | x |
| Grief | x | | x | x | |
| Guilty | x | | x | x | |
| Hopeless | x | | x | x | |
| Hyperactive | | | | x | |
| Imbalanced | | x | | x | |
| Imperceptive | | x | | x | |
| Impulsive | x | x | x | x | |
| Indecisive | x | x | | x | |

| Emotion | Rose Quartz | Blood stone | Amethyst | Smoky Quartz | Tourmaline |
|---|---|---|---|---|---|
| Indulgence | x | x | x | x | |
| Ineffective | x | x | x | x | |
| Insecure | x | x | x | x | |
| Jealous | x | x | x | x | |
| Lonely | x | x | | x | |
| Manipulative | x | x | | x | |
| Materialistic | x | x | | x | x |
| Negative (no anger) | x | x | x | x | x |
| Overbearing | | x | | x | x |
| Overly independent | x | | | x | |
| Overstimulated | | x | | x | x |
| Overwhelmed | x | | x | x | x |
| Powerless | x | x | x | x | x |
| Rage | x | x | x | x | |
| Resentful | x | x | x | x | x |
| Sad | | | | x | x |
| Selfish | x | | x | x | x |
| Sleepless | | | x | x | x |
| Stifled | x | | x | x | x |
| Stressed | x | x | x | x | x |
| Suicidal | x | x | x | x | x |
| Temperamental | x | x | x | x | x |
| Tired | | | x | x | |
| Unable to express self | x | | x | x | |

| Emotion | Rose Quartz | Blood stone | Amethyst | Smoky Quartz | Tourmaline |
|---|---|---|---|---|---|
| Unable to speak truth | x | | x | x | |
| Unclear | | x | x | x | x |
| Uncreative | | x | x | x | x |
| Underwhelmed | | | x | x | x |
| Unforgiving | x | | | x | x |
| Ungrounded | x | | x | x | x |
| Unintelligent | | | x | x | x |
| Unloved | | x | x | x | x |
| Unmotivated | | x | x | x | x |
| Unsafe | | x | x | x | x |
| Unsuccessful | x | x | x | x | x |
| Untruthful | x | x | x | x | x |
| Unworthy | x | x | x | x | x |
| Vulnerable | x | x | x | x | x |
| Weak | x | x | x | x | x |
| Withdrawn | x | x | x | x | |

# Calling in Spirit Guides and Angels

If you are new to the realm of energy, this one might be a little out there for you . . . Crystals might be, too, for that matter. But if you are open to trying something new, try this. When you are releasing particularly heavy emotions, it's nice to have some support. Calling in spirit guides and angels can help in times like these. It's very simple to do, and don't worry, call on them as much as you want. They don't get annoyed, and they aren't too busy for you. It's perfect, really.

**Technique 11.7. Angels and Spirit Guides for Releasing Emotions**

It's not required, but some people feel that lighting a candle when they call on spirit guides and angels helps. You can simply say, "Spirit guides (or angels) in my best and highest good and of pure light, please come help me release these emotions (i.e., fear, anger, sadness) and carry them away. Please clear my space of any residual emotional energy." You can then ask them to take the emotions you release to clear the space.

# Spirit Guides

I don't want to get too deep here (saving it for another book), but I want to talk a little bit about this. Spirit guides are typically beings that have been people; in other words, they have been incarnated at some point. Many people feel that they have loved ones watching over , such as a grandparent, aunt, or spouse that has passed. Some people even feel their crossed-over pets are their guides. You might feel their presence if you are going through a difficult time or on a momentous occasion, such as the birth of a baby. You can also call on them when you are working with emotional releasing, and they can assist you. Just note that some loved ones may be better at it than others. Typically, if that person was good at emotional support during their time on Earth, they keep those gifts when they cross over.

It is possible for your spirit guides to be other people or beings that you have not previously known. They tend to come and go and change throughout your lifetime, kind of like teachers as you move through school. You don't have to know any of your guides' names to call on them for support. Addressing them as a guide is enough.

It's important to note that if you are prone to nightmares or feeling a sense of uneasiness around you on a regular basis, stick with calling on loved ones you know and angels to assist you in your life. You may have energy hanging out that thinks it's your guide and being helpful, when it's actually not. Being specific on asking for help can alleviate the issue of them interfering with your healing work.

# Angels

In general, these are beings that have never been incarnated. I love these guys, but they have no sense of the fact that humans need sleep, food, etc. They are the best ones to call on when in doubt of who to call for help with clearing a space or emotional releasing. Do note that you have to call them, though. They tend not to interfere in our lives in general without being asked. While there are a hierarchy of angels, described below are what are commonly known as ArchAngels and what they specialize in. Try asking for their assistance next time you are doing emotional releasing techniques.

# Archangels

When I first had my awakening years ago, I would make it a discipline to call in and work with different Archangels. It felt like a safe way to explore my gifts and have the ultimate guides in the process. I called on some of the angels more than others. It just depended on what I needed help with at the time. Each of them has their own specialty, so to speak, and believe it or not, they can have different perspectives and advice. Sometimes I would light a candle to call them in, but honestly, there were a lot of times I would just be crying and driving my car, asking for them to fix something. Just note that they are about empowerment, and while they offer help, they really want to give you the tools to fix it yourself. So if you choose to work with them, know that the answers will probably be brought to you in unexpected ways. This requires you to make note of all the little things that get your attention. It's probably them trying to send you a message. I joke that they think we are on a game show or something, so they just leave clues for us, but really, it's about giving you a fishing pole and teaching you to fish rather than giving you all the answers.

Depending on the source, you will find different numbers of Archangels listed. Since angels exist in just about every religious text, the names and numbers of them vary. The ones listed in this section are some of the ones you can find if you do research on the topic. I personally have called on these angels quite a bit when I have been going through my own emotional releasing work, and it helps a great deal, especially if you get really stuck. In addition to the emotions they can help you release, the color associated with them is listed as well. You can light a candle that color to help call the Archangels into your space, but it is not required.

# Michael

This is the guy to call on if you feel like there is not-so-good energy around you. He is really good at clearing the negative vibes out of a space and is known for carrying a sword. If you are dealing with particularly heavy energies, calling on Archangel Michael is your best bet. Michael is also in charge of courage and strength, so if you feel you are lacking these elements in your life, call on him to help usher them in and release anything that is holding you back.

Associated color: Blue

# Gabriel

He is particularly noted as a messenger. If you are looking to derive meaning from things, call on Gabriel for understanding and interpretation. This can be particularly helpful if you are the sort of person who processes emotions by understanding them. Gabriel is in charge of the sense of knowing that you get sometimes in your gut. Ask him to activate this sense when you feel like you can't get a grip on understanding things through your mind. It will help you make sense of what you are experiencing in a new way.

Associated color: White

# Raphael

This angel is associated with healing, and his name literally means "God's doctor." If you are dealing with physical ailments, call on Raphael to be present during your emotional releasing techniques. He can help to unravel the connection between your physical ailments and their emotional roots and help to heal the soul. Abundance and prosperity are his other strong suits. If you are lacking abundance or feel this is blocked for you, call on Raphael to help you release the emotions and energy that are keeping you from the prosperity you desire.

Associated color: Green

# Chamuel

If you are looking to forgive someone, including yourself, call on Chamuel, the Archangel of peaceful relationships. He can help you move through and release emotional states that relate to your relationships with others and with yourself. If you are using rose quartz for emotional releasing, adding Chamuel to the mix is a great idea. He is also helpful if you are looking to heal so that you can attract a healthy, loving relationship, getting energy out of the way that is preventing it from happening.

Associated color: Pink

# Jophiel

Decisions can be tough to make sometimes, so if you are struggling with them, call on Jophiel for clarity. He can help you release anything that is in the way of you being decisive and help dispel any confusing energy that may be influencing you from sources outside of yourself. Jophiel helps to create a distraction-free space so you can sort through things on your own terms. He has a particular affinity for bringing clarity through dreams, so if you are a dreamer, ask him to bring you the answers there.

Associated color: Yellow

# Zadkiel

Emotional releasing is all about having mercy with yourself for where you are and transforming yourself. These are the specialties of Zadkiel. If you have a lot of changes occurring in your life and are having difficulty going with the flow, call on Zadkiel to keep the energy moving so you don't block the flow of transformation for yourself. As you move through these changes, it requires letting go of the past. This requires mercy for yourself and others. If you are struggling with forgiveness or acceptance of what has happened, Zadkiel can help you to release the emotions and traumas that are holding you back from the transformation that is taking place.

Associated color: Purple

# Uriel

If you are having trouble looking into yourself to see the truth, call on Uriel to help you with this process. Looking into ourselves can be, well, not so pretty sometimes. Uriel allows you to look deep inside with an objective view so that you can release what is holding you back in your life without judgment.

Associated color: Red

# Metatron

Thoughts drive our lives, and Metatron helps us to replace negative thoughts with positive ones. When you call on Metatron, he works with you to release the root of the negative thoughts in your subconscious mind so that positive ones can take their place. Most angels were never in human form, but Metatron is one of two exceptions. This gives him a particular connection to people that most other angels don't have. This is why he understands the power of thought so well and how it affects us. If you are looking to release the pattern of negative thoughts, Metatron should be your angel of choice.

Associated colors: Green-and-Pink Stripes or Blue

# Sandalphon

As one of two Archangels that has taken human form at one time, Sandalphon knows the importance of human potential. If you are struggling with finding purpose in your life, Sandalphon can help guide you to it. Call on him if you are working on releasing the ties to your old career, or thoughts or beliefs about what you "should be doing" in the world. Oftentimes these thought patterns and habits are blocking us from achieving what we were put on Earth to do. Sandalphon helps us to release whatever is in the way of us seeking our true purpose. Sandalphon is also said to assist Archangel Michael in protection and can be called on for that purpose.

Associated color: Red

# Barachiel

Success in life is something just about everyone is looking for. Barachiel specializes in helping people achieve success in their pursuits. He helps you release anything standing in your way, especially those things that are trapped in your subconscious, as well as influencing the circumstances in the world around you. Barachiel also helps assist you in marriage and family life. If you are struggling with family patterns or traumas, Barachiel can help to gently shift these into a healthy, new space.

Associated color: Green

| Emotion | Michael | Gabriel | Raphael | Chamuel | Jophiel | Zadkiel | Uriel | Metatron | Sandalphon | Barachiel |
|---|---|---|---|---|---|---|---|---|---|---|
| Abandoned | x | x | | x | | x | x | x | | x |
| Aggressive | | x | | x | | x | x | x | | x |
| Anger | | x | x | x | x | x | x | x | | x |
| Anxious | | x | x | x | | x | x | x | | x |
| Betrayed | x | x | | x | x | x | x | x | | x |
| Confused | x | x | | | | x | x | x | | x |
| Controlling | | x | | | | x | x | x | | x |
| Critical | | x | | | | x | x | x | | x |
| Defensive | x | x | | x | x | x | x | x | | x |
| Depressed | x | x | x | x | x | x | x | x | | x |
| Detached | x | x | | | | x | x | x | | x |
| Discomfort - not phys | x | | x | | | x | x | x | | x |
| Disorganized | x | | | x | | x | x | x | | x |
| Distrust | x | | | x | x | x | x | x | | x |
| Dramatic | x | x | x | x | x | x | x | x | | x |
| Embarrassed | x | x | x | | | x | x | x | | x |
| Fearful | x | x | | | x | x | x | x | | x |
| Flawed | x | | | x | | x | x | x | | x |
| Grief | x | | x | x | x | x | x | x | | x |
| Guilty | x | x | x | x | x | x | x | x | | x |
| Hopeless | x | x | x | x | x | x | x | x | | x |
| Hyperactive | x | | | x | x | x | x | x | | x |

| Emotion | Michael | Gabriel | Raphael | Chamuel | Jophiel | Zadkiel | Uriel | Metatron | Sandalphon | Barachiel |
|---|---|---|---|---|---|---|---|---|---|---|
| Imbalanced | x | | | x | x | x | x | x | | x |
| Imperceptive | x | x | x | x | x | x | x | x | | x |
| Impulsive | x | x | x | x | x | x | x | x | | x |
| Indecisive | x | x | x | | x | x | x | x | | x |
| Indulgence | x | | x | | x | x | x | x | | x |
| Ineffective | x | x | | | | x | x | x | | x |
| Insecure | x | | | | x | x | x | x | | x |
| Jealous | x | | x | x | x | x | x | x | | x |
| Lonely | x | | x | x | x | x | x | x | | x |
| Manipulative | x | x | x | | x | x | x | x | | x |
| Materialistic | x | x | | | x | x | x | x | | x |
| Negative (no anger) | x | | x | x | x | x | x | x | | x |
| Overbearing | x | | | | x | x | x | x | | x |
| Overly independent | x | | | | x | x | x | x | | x |
| Overstimulated | x | | | | x | x | x | x | | x |
| Overwhelmed | x | | x | | x | x | x | x | | x |
| Powerless | x | x | x | x | x | x | x | x | | x |
| Rage | x | x | | x | x | x | x | x | | x |
| Resentful | x | x | | x | x | x | x | x | | x |
| Sad | x | x | x | x | x | x | x | x | | x |
| Selfish | x | x | x | x | | x | x | x | | x |
| Sleepless | x | x | | | x | x | x | x | | x |

| Emotion | Michael | Gabriel | Raphael | Chamuel | Jophiel | Zadkiel | Uriel | Metatron | Sandalphon | Barachiel |
|---|---|---|---|---|---|---|---|---|---|---|
| Stifled | x | x |  | x | x | x | x | x |  | x |
| Stressed | x | x |  |  |  | x | x | x |  | x |
| Suicidal | x |  |  |  |  | x | x | x |  | x |
| Temperamental | x |  | x |  | x | x | x | x |  | x |
| Tired | x | x |  |  | x | x | x | x |  | x |
| Unable to express self | x |  |  |  |  | x | x | x |  | x |
| Unable to speak truth | x |  |  |  | x | x | x | x |  | x |
| Unclear | x | x | x | x |  | x | x | x |  | x |
| Uncreative | x | x |  | x | x | x | x | x |  | x |
| Underwhelmed | x | x |  |  | x | x | x | x |  | x |
| Unforgiving | x | x |  | x | x | x | x | x |  | x |
| Ungrounded | x |  |  |  | x | x | x | x |  | x |
| Unintelligent | x |  |  | x | x | x | x | x |  | x |
| Unloved | x | x |  |  | x | x | x | x |  | x |
| Unmotivated | x | x | x |  | x | x | x | x |  | x |
| Unsafe | x |  |  |  | x | x | x | x |  | x |
| Unsuccessful | x |  |  | x | x | x | x | x |  | x |
| Untruthful | x | x | x | x | x | x | x | x |  | x |
| Unworthy | x | x | x | x | x | x | x | x |  | x |
| Vulnerable | x | x |  | x | x | x | x | x |  | x |
| Weak | x | x |  | x | x | x | x | x |  | x |
| Withdrawn | x | x |  | x | x | x | x | x |  | x |

# What to Do When You Can't Create a Space

If you are in the car, in a meeting, or at your kid's school when emotions strike, you can't exactly bust out your crystals and candles. This is where envisioning comes in. If you find that physical objects really help you to release, it can be stressful when you don't have them with you. If you find yourself in this situation, don't stress out, just envision having them. You can do this with your eyes open or closed. Just envision having that candle lit in front of you or that crystal in your hand and set your intention as you would if you had those objects present. Creating a space in your mind is the next best thing to really being in that space and can tide you over, helping you to release emotions in the moment.

# Eat Color for a Healthy Energy System

A few years ago, "eating the rainbow" became a thing. This means eating fruits and vegetables of various colors to get the full spectrum of nutrients that these foods have to offer. The cool thing is, you can use this same premise to help balance your energy system. Eating foods of certain colors can help you get more of that color present in your physical body and energy system. Refer to the color chart in chapter 5 to identify which colors you need to supplement based on the emotional states you are addressing.

### Foods That Support the Color Red and the Root Chakra

| Vegetables | Fruits | Protein/Fats | Spices | Teas |
|---|---|---|---|---|
| Beets Rutabaga Garlic Ginger Turnips Potatoes Onions Parsnips Carrots Radishes Sweet potatoes | Red apples Watermelon Pomegranates Strawberries Raspberries | Red meat Bone broths Red beans Lentils Eggs Peanut butter Butter | Chives Paprika Black and red pepper Chili powder | Rooibos Hibiscus tea |

## Foods That Support the Color Orange and the Sacral Chakra

| Vegetables | Fruits | Protein/ Fats | Spices | Grains | Sweet- eners | Liquids |
|---|---|---|---|---|---|---|
| Carrots Peppers Squashes | Melons Mangoes Tangerines Oranges Passionfruit Coconut Apricots | Salmon Nuts Sesame seeds | Turmeric Ginger Cumin Cinnamon Vanilla | Oats | Honey | Pure water Broth Tea |

## Foods That Support the Color Yellow and the Solar Plexus Chakra

| Vegeta- bles | Fruits | Digestive Foods | Seeds | Spices | Teas |
|---|---|---|---|---|---|
| Yellow peppers Corn | Lemons Bananas Pineapple | Kefir Kombucha Yogurt (dairy or nondairy) | Flax seed Sunflower seed | Turmeric Cumin Fennel Yellow curry | Chamomile Mint Ginger |

## Foods That Support the Color Green and the Heart Chakra

| Vegetables | Fruits | Protein/Fats | Spices | Teas |
|---|---|---|---|---|
| Leafy & cruciferous Kale Lettuces Spinach Chard Bok choy Collard greens Broccoli Parsley | Limes Green apples Avocados Kiwi | Lima beans Mung beans | Basil Thyme Cilantro Mint | Green tea Matcha |

**Foods That Support the Color Blue and the Throat Chakra**

| Fruits | Beverages |
|---|---|
| Blueberries<br>Apples<br>Peaches<br>Pears<br>Apricots<br>Plums | 100% fruit juices (use sparingly)<br>Herbal teas<br>Coconut water |

**Foods That Support the Color Indigo and the Third Eye Chakra**

| Vegetables | Fruit | Nuts/Seeds | Other |
|---|---|---|---|
| Purple kale<br>Purple cabbage<br>Purple carrots | Goji berries<br>Acai<br>Concord grapes<br>Blackberries<br>Blueberries | Raw walnuts<br>Sprouted almonds<br>Poppy seeds | Mushrooms<br>Cacao |

**Foods That Support the Color Violet and the Crown Chakra**

| Vegetables | Herbs | Essential Oils |
|---|---|---|
| Eat light meals of vegetables | Sage<br>Lavender | Aromatherapy or baths |

## Technique 11.8. How to Drink Color

While juices can provide nutrients, they contain a lot of sugar, too, without the balance of the fiber in the fruit or vegetable to slow the rise in blood sugar. This can mean a lot of extra calories that aren't all that filling and a risk of increasing insulin resistance. If you are trying to get more of a specific color in your diet, try drinking water from a colored cup instead. If you can, let the water sit in the cup for at least ten minutes. Sitting the cup of water in a window to soak up some sunlight is ideal. After about ten minutes, the water takes on the vibration of the color. When you drink it, you get some of that color in your body to help balance it. This may sound a little odd, but I have found that when I have used this method for myself and other clients, I have seen positive results.

## Fish Food, the Miracle Cure

The next time I went into my chiropractor, I couldn't help but have that slimy bag of goop on my mind. Had it helped her? I decided to wait and see if she would say anything.

When I arrived at the office, she heard me walk in and stopped what she was doing with another patient to meet me at the front desk. "I don't know what was in that stuff, but I lay down after my bath and I was out for like three hours. When I woke up, I felt great, and this morning it's like I wasn't even sick. What was in that?"

I looked at her, bewildered. "You wouldn't believe me if I told you," I said.

## Chapter Challenge

Think about your go-to self-care. Is it constructive, like the elements of this chapter, or is it destructive, like eating sugar or drinking caffeine and alcohol?

If it is constructive, what do you like best about the result?

What other elements of self-care in this chapter could you implement that would bring you the results you desire from using physical elements?

## Feel Better Five

- Emotional releasing can be enhanced by using physical elements such as bath salts, essential oils, and candles.
- Physical elements can help you focus in on your intentions and help you to access emotions on a different level.
- The quality of these items matter, as the higher-quality elements are free of toxins, which increases their efficacy and doesn't take a toll on your body.
- Physical elements can be combined to enhance emotional releasing, such as bath salts and essential oils.
- Angels can be called in using physical products such as candles.

## Transform in Five

Technique 11.1. Candles for Emotional Clearing

1. Choose the emotion or emotions you would like to work with.

2. You can choose one emotion or just choose to work with the color associated with its group of emotions.
3. Look at the list of emotions on the color chart in chapter 5 for each color and see if a large number of the emotions under that color (or the one you are wanting to work with) resonate with the emotions you are working on releasing.
4. Light a chosen-color candle.
5. Set your intention: "I choose to release (emotion[s]) and whatever they are attached to."
6. Envision releasing the emotion or emotions into the space around you and watching the emotions burn up in the flame of the candle.

Technique 11.2. Incense for Emotional Clearing

1. Light incense and let it smoke for a few minutes before you begin your emotional clearing techniques. This allows the scent to spread in your space and be present to dispel the low-vibration emotional energy once you start releasing it.
2. It is best to use in a ventilated space so it does not overwhelm you.
3. Be sure to use an incense holder and be mindful of the ash from the burned incense.

Technique 11.3. Using a Smudge Stick in a Room

1. To use in a room, simply light it and then blow it out.
2. When it starts smoking, carry it around the room and let the smoke permeate the space.
3. Go around the edges of the room first and then through the center of the room.
4. If emotional releasing is being done in a certain area of the room, focus on that area with the smoking smudge stick.

Technique 11.4. Smudging a Human Energy Field

1. To use in someone's energy field, simply move the smoking smudge stick slowly around the person, roughly two to ten inches away from their body, starting close to them and moving outward in several passes.
2. Take care not to touch their clothing, skin, or hair with the smudge stick, and pay attention to ash falling off of the stick.

They usually burn pretty cleanly, but you don't want to drop ash on someone.

3. To put it out, you can put it smoking-side down in a mason jar or snuff the end out in a bowl.
4. Be sure it is completely done smoking before you put it away.
5. Note: You don't need to burn the whole thing at once. A few minutes is usually enough time to make passes through a room and address someone's energy field.

Technique 11.5. Basic Salt Bath Ratios

If you are using the salt bath to draw out a lot of energy, use two cups of salt with two cups of baking soda and soak in the warm (not hot) water for fifteen to twenty minutes.

Once you start incorporating essential oils, you can use less salt in your bath. Use about fifteen to twenty drops of oil per one cup of salt. This is typically a safe ratio. If you want to use baking soda as well, add half a cup. Soak in it for fifteen to twenty minutes.

Technique 11.7. Angels and Spirit Guides for Releasing Emotions

It's not required, but some people feel that lighting a candle when they call on spirit guides and angels helps.
You can simply say, "Spirit guides (or angels) in my best and highest good and of pure light, please come help me release (emotions) and carry them away. Please clear my space of any residual emotional energy."
You can then ask them to take the emotions you release to clear the space.

In the next chapter, we put everything you have learned together into protocols that you can implement to feel better right now.

# CHAPTER 12

## Customized Feel-Better Plans

S arah was a client that seemed to have it all together. She walked in decked out. Hair perfect. Makeup perfect. Not a stitch was out of place. It happened to be one of those days that I had woken up late, pulled my hair back, and only managed to get half of my makeup on before the doorbell rang.

After we shared pleasantries, she came in and sat down in my office, firmly clasping her notebook. It just happened to match her purse and her shoes. Despite all of her togetherness, I knew something about Sarah. Even though she was seemingly together on the outside, her life was falling apart. Her marriage was struggling. Her kids were out of control, and her job, which is the first piece of information she gave when talking about herself, was killing her. Sarah was wound as tight as they come, and it was by sheer will that she could even walk upright.

During her first session, she furiously took notes on everything I said. A lot had come through for Sarah as far as how she could manage her emotions and work with her energy. The techniques seemed to resonate with her, and she felt she could do them on her own. My guides even brought her recipes on bath salts she could make to support herself. It was a lot. We also did energy work, and she felt very relaxed when she left.

Today, she was tight again and looked a bit bewildered. She opened her notebook and started flipping through the pages from our session. "There's so much here," she said. "It's great, but what do I do? I mean, there are so many techniques and recipes and . . . I just want to do it *right*."

There is a lot of information in this book, and there are a million ways to use it, but if you don't have any idea of how to put it together, it's really not that helpful. This chapter is about putting it all together for you. It's about giving you some ideas of how to use the techniques in the book, along with the physical elements for your self-care. Of course, these are ideas to get you started. You can use the information in this book to combine any way you wish. So, let's get to it.

## First Rule of Energy: There Is No One Way That Is *Right*

A few years ago, I was invited to a meditation group (not usually my deal) by a new friend. I didn't really dig the meditation, but the woman who was leading it was very kind and grounded. She had been through a great deal of training from a well-known teacher and was in the process of getting the equivalent of her master's in the program.

After the mediation ended, she was showing my new friend and me around her compound. My friend mentioned that she had trouble clearing her mind to meditate. The woman immediately started telling her how she needed to breathe into her chakras to clear her mind. While this is a great technique, I could tell it wasn't landing well with my friend, and it was making her feel inadequate. The woman sensed this as well but persisted, "This is what you have to do if you want to clear out your chakras and your mind."

While I was standing there in the awkwardness, an image came to me of my new friend running. She had her earphones in and her energy was relaxed. So I asked her, "Do you ever run?"
"Yes!" she said. "I feel like it's the only thing that clears my mind."

"That is your meditation, then. There are lots of ways to meditate. Running is yours. You can work into the other way, but it's okay that running is what gets you there."

I didn't think anything about it at the time, but the woman never had me back to her home after that. I don't think she liked my alternative take on meditation. Oops. But the truth was, my friend's energy system wasn't wired, at least at that time, to function the way the woman was proposing.

While there are basic dos and don'ts in working with energy, when it comes to protocols or methods of energy work, there is no one way that works for all. Everyone is different. So, when it comes to the techniques in this book, some of you may be drawn to envisioning and color, while others may resonate more with breathing and grounding. Some of you may love essential oils, while others of you like plain salt baths and candles. There is no right or wrong way to combine things in this book. However, I am going to give you some ideas about what you can combine for certain circumstances that may apply to you.

## How Are You Wired?

In chapter 9 on grounding, I touch on people being wired different ways. Just like our physical body functions in certain ways, our energy system functions in certain ways too. You may have a tendency to be ungrounded, depressed, angry, or have physical ailments. You may be introverted or extroverted. Some of this is how you were wired when you came to the planet, and some are coping mechanisms that are developed over your lifetime. Either way, the protocols in this chapter are grouped for your energetic propensity and personality.

## Take a Baseline

Before you start a protocol, Its a good idea to do the assessment in chapter 3 to get a baseline of where you are right now. Once we start feeling better, we forget where we started from. Repeat the assessment after about a month to see what kind of progress you have made.

## Protocols

In this chapter are five protocols that cover the most common issues I see with clients. They are being ungrounded (experiencing anxiety), depressive states, expressed anger, unexpressed anger, and physical ailments. This is by no means all of them, but these cover most people. These protocols are meant to get you on the right track and get you comfortable working with your energy to release emotions and understand what makes you tick. Really getting to know yourself in a compassionate way helps you to accept where you are now and make progress toward who you truly are inside without all of the traumatic and verbal inhibitory imprints.

If you are struggling with where to start in the book, I encourage you to start with a protocol and then start adding and subtracting things as you try them and see what works for you.

# Invitation

If you are having other specific issues, I want to hear from you. I am always creating new protocols for clients. You are not alone in what you are experiencing, so sharing what you are going through can help others. Send me a message at amandahainline.com, on Instagram @ akhainline, or to Amanda Hainline on Facebook. I will share the protocol I develop around your issue with you and others so they can start Feeling Better in Five Minutes.

When I share the protocol, your name remains anonymous if you so choose.

# Ungrounded Protocol

 If you are the kind of person that experiences anxiety and nervousness, or if you are wound tight like Sarah in the story at the beginning of the chapter, you can really benefit from learning to be grounded. People who are inherently ungrounded tend to do things like put their keys in the freezer or get super frantic over really small things. They don't have their roots in the ground. Without deep roots, it doesn't take much to knock them over and get them in a panicked state. They also tend to have underdeveloped lower chakras in their energy system (the root and sacral chakras) and more highly developed upper chakras (crown and third eye).

While this tendency can be wired into you from the beginning, the repeated need for fleeing situations (such as a volatile home life) when you are young can exacerbate this tendency. People who become ungrounded easily tend to "check out" to escape. They may be called daydreamers by their teachers and parents. It's not their fault. The good news is, you can learn to be inherently grounded. I know. I have done it. The protocol in this Section is one I designed for myself and have used with other clients that struggle with grounding.

# Triggers

When you are inherently ungrounded, you pull your roots up even further when you get triggered. If you get upset, scared, or angry, you probably act a bit like a crazy person or you freeze up and check out. Either way, this protocol can help.

# Your Go-To Emotion

What is the emotion you kind of feel all the time? Is it fear, anxiety, nervousness? Does your mind race constantly in a loop? Choose just one to start with and work on it. Every day, by using envisioning and releasing.

### Technique 12.1. Daily Grounding Preparation

1. Every morning, take a couple of minutes to work on this emotion.
2. While still in bed, close your eyes and relax your body. Say, "I welcome up the (emotion) I am feeling, and I thank it for being here."
3. After a few moments (twenty seconds or so), when you feel it come to the surface, say, "I choose to release all of the (emotion) that I am feeling and *whatever it is attached to.*"
4. Envision it floating up out of your body and out of your space (out a window is preferable).

This prepares your energy system to ground much more easily during the second technique, focusing on your roots. Since you are inherently ungrounded, you need to retrain your energy system to be grounded.

### Technique 12.2. Training Your Roots to Ground

1. First thing in the morning, after you release your go-to emotion, ground yourself. Most people who are inherently ungrounded have the innate ability to envision.
2. You can be lying down, or you can stand with your feet on the floor.
3. Envision roots coming out of your feet and going deep into the ground.
4. Next, breathe up through your feet and envision the grounded energy coming up into your body and filling you up.
5. Do this a few times until you feel calm and centered.

This may take a few minutes the first few times you do it, but it gets easier. After some practice, you can give the energy a color. In general, red and orange (the color of your underdeveloped chakras: root and sacral) are good colors to breathe in through your feet. If you are quick to anger, use pink instead.

Do this technique several times a day if you can. If you are in public, you can do the envisioning part of driving your roots into the ground and bringing the energy up into your body without the deep breathing.

You can also do this technique while driving, just don't close your eyes, obviously.

Doing this technique repeatedly will help to retrain your energy system to be grounded. Be patient; it takes time. As you work on releasing the energy in your emotional imprints, this technique will get easier, too, and you will be more grounded as a result.

## Carry a Crystal

If you can, an easy thing to do for support on a daily basis is to carry either a small smoky quartz crystal or a bloodstone (or both) in your pocket. These are both great grounding stones.

## Use Sandalwood

Put a dab of sandalwood oil on your wrists or on your neck. Dilute it first with a carrier oil if you are sensitive. This will help you stay grounded.

## Grounding Bath

Bath salts
1 cup of Epsom salt
1 cup of Himalayan pink salt if you have it (if not, use 2 cups Epsom salt)

Essential oils
6 drops lavender
8 drops sandalwood
12 drops patchouli
3 drops bergamot
8 drops eucalyptus
6 drops frankincense

1. Mix salt and oils well together in a bowl.
2. Dump into the warm bath and soak yourself for fifteen to twenty minutes.
3. You can add smoky quartz and bloodstone to the bath as well for extra support. Take this bath a couple of times a week or whenever you feel really frazzled.
4. Lighting a red or orange candle while you soak in your bath brings in these colors for support as well.

## Eat Grounding Foods

Pretty much any foods that grow in the ground are grounding foods. Focus on the foods that are listed for the root and sacral chakras in chapter 10, such as potatoes and sweet potatoes, onions, carrots, strawberries, red meat, eggs, butter, nuts, and ginger (see chapter 10 for full list). Avoid foods that tend to be ungrounding, such as caffeine, sugar, any foods you are allergic to (try to avoid foods with gluten, dairy, soy, and corn, as these are common allergens).

# Pessimistic, Depressed, Negative Thought Patterns Protocol

 People that struggle with negative thought patterns have a tendency toward depression and pessimism and even suicidal thoughts. This can be a really serious issue, and if you are in a deep state of depression, by all means, seek help.

If you have a tendency toward these states, you probably have a very depleted energy system. The flow of energy coming into your body is all but shut off. You aren't getting nourished energetically, or any other way, for that matter. The lives of people with these patterns often feel futile and everything seems to go wrong all the time. When things in your life feel this way, it can be hard to shift out of it. The truth is, all you can control is how you react to your life. Most people try to start by shifting their mindset. While it seems like a great place to start, it isn't. The arrested energy system is the root of it all, and starting by addressing this will automatically make any mindset changes you try infinitely easier.

Honestly, this protocol could be an entire book. There is so much to this state of mind and set of emotions, but trying the protocol in this Section is a good start.

## You're Probably an Empath

Most people with this type of energy system tend to soak up the energy around them in their environments. This is one of the symptoms of being an empath. Oftentimes, their environments are very negative; whether in their job or their family, the people around them tend to hold bad vibes. Since their vibration is low, it is easier for them to pick up other low-vibration energy around them. It's no different than having a weak immune system. People with weak immune systems tend to get sick more often. The same is true for people with depressed energy systems. It's easier for them to pick up negative energy in their environment. So, if you are struggling with depression, check your environment. What kind of people are you around? Are they nice and kind?

Some (or all) of the reasons you feel bad may just be what you are picking up from others. It's hard to tell sometimes where your emotions end and another person's start if you are already feeling bad or are overly sensitive to other people's energy.

Not all empaths are depressed or feel bad, but since they generally have weak energetic boundaries, it can be hard for them to stay strong when others around them are negative. The best way to alleviate this issue is to distance yourself from people who are negative, if at all possible. I have been through this myself and know the power of changing who the people are in your life. It absolutely transformed my life for the better. If you know you need to do this, start by working on yourself first so you can differentiate your emotions from others. Shifting your energy system and emotional states will help you see your situation with more clarity. Use this protocol as a starting point.

# Get Moving

People with this energetic pattern tend not to do much because they feel so bad all the time. Since the energy system is in such a stuck state, it makes them physically and mentally tired. Although I don't have a separate section for this anywhere else in the book, it's important for people with this energy system to move their bodies.

**Technique 12.3. Stretching Out the Blahs**

Stretching is a fantastic way to start. If you haven't exercised in a while, this is a great way to get moving again. This series of exercises is simple and easy.

Take a deep breath and reach up to the sky with both hands and really stretch. Go up on your tiptoes, even.

As you bring your arms down, breathe all the way out.

1. Repeat this five times.
2. Next, put your arms straight out to your sides and gently twist from side to side six times. Take deep breaths as you do so.
3. Take one arm and reach it up high while the other arm rests on your opposite hip.
4. Now take your upstretched arm and bend to your opposite side.
5. Take deep breaths as you do so. Repeat with the opposite side. Do this three times on each side.
6. Lastly, stand with your legs shoulder-width apart.
7. Reach your arms up high and take a deep breath.
8. As you breath out, bend forward and reach toward the ground. Breathe in as you stand up.
9. Repeat two to five times.

These techniques will get the energy and blood in your body moving. You will be able to feel a difference.

Also try going for short walks to start, even down one side of your block and back home. Do these things daily to start shifting your life.

# Breathing in Light

Getting circulation back into your energy system is the most important thing you can do to start shifting to a more positive place. Breathing in light is a simple yet powerful technique that starts to break up the really stuck energy in your energy system. Breathing deeply also increases blood flow and oxygen in your body, which gives you more physical energy.

### Technique 12.4. Increasing Energy System Circulation

1. First, envision a cloud of white light in front of you.
2. Now take a deep breath in, breathing in as much of the white light as you can.
3. Envision it moving through your body, breaking loose the stuck energy.
4. Now blow out your breath forcefully, breathing out all of the stuck energy that broke loose from the light.

5. Repeat this technique at least five times.
6. Next, envision the cloud of white light over your head.
7. Breathe in, but this time envision breathing in the white light through the top of your head and envision the light going as far down your body as it can go.
8. Hold your breath for five seconds, envisioning the light breaking up all of the stuck energy.
9. Now, breathe out and envision the stuck energy exiting through the top of your head.
10. Each time you breathe in, pull the light down farther and farther until you breathe it in through the top of your head and it can reach your toes.
11. Blow it out the top of your head.

This technique clears out your main energy channel and allows you to start getting nourished from the energy in your environment.

Repeat these light breathing techniques a couple of times a day for about a week and see how you feel. Continue doing them on a daily basis for energy system health and clearing.

## Positivity bath

2 cups Epsom, Dead Sea salt or Himalayan pink salt
2 cups baking soda

Essential oils
6 drops peppermint
3 drops tea tree
10 drops ylang ylang
11 drops bergamot
10 drops Roman chamomile
8 drops patchouli
6 drops sandalwood
12 drops rose absolute

1. Mix salt and essential oils together in a bowl.
2. Add baking soda and mix.
3. Add the entire mixture to a warm bath and soak for fifteen to twenty minutes.
4. You can add rose quartz to the bath and light a white candle for extra support.

# Emotional Release Technique

While most protocols begin with releasing a specific emotion, this protocol works on breaking up energy in a very arrested system. Most people with this state have trouble identifying an emotion to start with. They just feel bad. After you work with the first sets of techniques for about one week, you can add in the basic emotional release technique.

## Your Go-To Emotion

What is the emotion you kind of feel all the time? Is it depression, negativity, fear of bad things happening, apathy? Choose just one to start with and work on it. Every day. It can change from day to day. Just pick one to work with.

This technique is good to do after you have done your light breathing technique. This way, it will be easier to identify which emotion is most present for you.

### Technique 12.5. Daily Depressive Emotion Release

1. Every morning, take a couple of minutes to work on this emotion.
2. While still in bed, close your eyes and relax your body. Say, "I welcome up the (emotion) I am feeling, and I thank it for being here."
3. After a few moments (twenty seconds or so), when you feel it come to the surface, say, "I choose to release all of the (emotion) that I am feeling and *whatever it is attached to.*"
4. Envision it floating up out of your body and your space (out a window is preferable).
5. Give it some time to flow out. Because your energy tends to be thick, it may take some time for the emotions that are on the surface to leave your body.

Repeat this technique at night after you do your light breathing technique. Also, don't forget to keep up your stretching daily!

## Releasing the Emotions of Other People

When I started on my journey of healing, I didn't really understand how much other people's energy impacted me. I just knew that I was a hot mess and was totally consumed in processing my own stuff. At the time, I was working at a daycare center. I had a coteacher that worked in the same room with me. While she was good with the children, she had a very serious demeanor and had a habit of really getting stuck in negative thought patterns and self-talk.

One morning we had a cold front blow in. The class had to go outside, and I was wearing a short-sleeved shirt. My coworker had brought a jacket but also had on long sleeves. She offered me her jacket and I was happy to put it on, but within the hour, something strange started to happen. I became really negative and was snapping at everyone. I could just see the worst in everything and was making negative comments at every turn. I really wasn't even conscious of it while it was occurring. I just thought, I hate it here and I want to go home.

At the end of the day, I couldn't wait to leave and almost left with her jacket on. She stopped me on the way out the door. I took it off and handed it back to her. In less than five minutes, I felt noticeably different. My energy lightened and my mood shifted completely. It was then that I realized I had been wearing her energy all day! When I put her jacket on, it was carrying all of her negativity, and my energy system took it in and made it my own.

Like we talked about above, if you struggle with depressive states or negative thought patterns, part of your issue is most likely that you are picking up the energy of other people. This can happen with people you know and don't know; it doesn't matter. The reason this happens is that, when it comes to energy, like attracts like. If you are carrying a particular emotion and you come into contact with someone else that is carrying it too, you can very easily take on more of the same energy. When this happens, it heightens the emotion or vibrational pattern inside of you, making you feel worse, and if you aren't trained to recognize it, you will think it's your own. The good news is, you can use this "like attracts like" principle to your advantage. While it isn't fun to feel worse, you can actually turn it around to make you feel *better*.

**Technique 12.6. Releasing Other People's Emotions**

When vibrational states of energy or emotions come into contact with one another, they stick and become indistinguishable from each other. While you can set the intention to just release the other person's energy you picked up, some of it will naturally stay with you due to the vibrational similarity. So instead, set the intention to release all of it.

1. Say, "I welcome up the (emotion), and I thank it for being here."
2. After you feel it, say, "I choose to release the (emotion) from other people (or you can call out a name if it helps you) and anything it is attached to."
3. Envision the energy floating up and out of your space.

Keeping it general by saying "other people" in your intention grabs more of the energy, since you probably have picked up similar things from more than one person. It can be helpful, though, to call out a person by name if you have an idea of where you got it from, because you are adding another level of processing of that energy for yourself. This can be helpful for you in distinguishing where the other energy is coming from if you are working to fine-tune your intuitive skills.

When you are first starting out, though, being general is a good thing. Most likely, you have years and years of other people's emotional energy you are carrying with you, and you just need to start unloading it!

## Watching Your Thought Patterns

As you start clearing out your energetic imprints, you can't help but change. Energy is the basis of everything, and as you shift your vibration through emotional releasing, you will probably start to notice changes. This is why it's a good idea to get a baseline assessment in chapter 3 before you start the work.

It's a common practice to start with positive affirmations to change your mindset, but this is kind of like cleaning up a school cafeteria with a toothbrush. It's going to take A LONG TIME. I'm not saying that energy work is instantaneous, but doing it will automatically shift your mindset so you are not putting in a ton of grunt work and getting frustrated. After a couple of weeks of working on your energy every day, you may find yourself automatically doing new things and thinking differently. Maybe you have more energy to cook dinner or work out. You might just have a more positive take on a situation or find yourself smiling more. This is when adding affirmations is a great idea. You have to have enough of the gunk out of your energy system so the affirmations have somewhere to stick. Something really positive is not vibrationally going to take hold in a really low-vibration place. It's just not possible. So, when you find yourself starting to change, give it a boost with affirmations.

## Setting Up Affirmations

It's pretty easy, and you have already done the work IF you did the self-assessment in chapter 3. If you haven't done it already, do it now (the self-assessment from chapter 3 is given below). If you have already done your assessment, refer back to your notes from chapter 3.

1.  Close your eyes and imagine you are looking at yourself in the mirror (or actually do it). What do you look like?

    -   This question goes beyond physical characteristics, but you can definitely write those down. Describe yourself: your face, your expression, posture, etc. What kind of vibe do you put off? Be as detailed or as general as you want.
    -   Do you describe yourself generally in a positive or negative way?
    -   If you described your "perfect self" what would you say?

2.  Imagine that you are having a conversation. What kinds of things do you say about yourself?

    -   What are your "go-to statements"?
    -   Are they positive or negative?

3.  What are your relationships like?

    -   If you struggle with your relationships, how do you struggle?
    -   If you had perfect relationships, what would they look like?

4.  Describe how you feel about your job.

    -   If you struggle with your job, how do you struggle?
    -   If you had the perfect job, what would that look like?

By looking at where you are now and what you would describe as perfect right now, you will be able to tell where you feel like you are falling short. That may be in one category, or it may be every category. If it's every category, don't worry. I have been there myself. It just means that when you start making changes and clearing out your imprints, your life will change that much for the better.

I find that when we describe where we are and what we think is perfect, it does a few things:

- It helps us realize where we stand in our life now and what we value.
- It gives us a perspective of what we spend time subconsciously thinking about.
- It helps us understand how much societal pressures of perfection impact us.

After you write down your answers, you will have the basis for your affirmations. Start with your physical appearance and work your way down. Don't overwhelm yourself with a ton of affirmations at once. Pick three to work with to start.

## Technique 12.7. Creating Healthy Affirmations

If you feel that you are overweight and wrote that down as a descriptor, you could make an affirmation of something like, "I love my body at this healthy weight." If you tend to anger quickly, you could make an affirmation such as, "I enjoy staying calm and centered when things frustrate me."

1. It's important to construct your affirmations with the acceptance of where you are but also encompassing where you want to be and to say it as if it has already happened.
2. Remember, it doesn't matter if you believe them or not right now. They will stick over time, especially if you keep doing your emotional releasing work.

Other examples to use could be:

- I am whole and full of self-love.
- My relationships are healthy and loving.
- My job/career is fulfilling, and my coworkers are supportive.

3. You can modify these depending on what you struggle with and what you view as perfect.
4. Just remember, love and accept where you are now and address where you want to be as if it has already happened.

Do these affirmations after you do your emotional clearing in the morning and at night before bed. Doing them twice, and especially at night, allows those thoughts to be present close to a time when your subconscious is highly engaged in your sleep state. This allows the energy work and affirmations to work double duty, as outside stimulus is removed and your body is in a restorative state.

### Technique 12.8. Mirror Work

Mirror work is a powerful technique that activates the brain in multiple ways and has a strong energetic impact as well. It supercharges your intentions. By watching yourself declare your intentions, you empower yourself at a higher level and hold yourself accountable in new ways.

1. Put your affirmations on a sticky note on your bathroom mirror and look at yourself as you say them.
2. Use a color of sticky note that corresponds to the emotions you are working with (see chapter 5).
3. As you say your intentions, pay attention to your body language. Are you slouching? Are you smiling? Are you confident or withdrawn?
4. Adjust your posture to be straight, have a confident, strong voice, and look yourself in the eye.
5. Repeat the affirmations four times and with focused intention.
6. Notice how you change over time.

### Technique 12.9. Asking Angels to Take Depressive Emotions

When you are dealing with heavy emotional states, working with angels is a great way to get some extra support. There is no set way to talk to angels. One way is just to simply hand over your burdens.

1. Say, "Angels, please take the burdens/emotions/worries that are heavy and causing me to feel (emotion)."
2. You can be more specific and vent what is bothering you to them and ask them to take it as well.

# Angels That Help with Depressive States

You can call on any angel, but these specifically deal with certain aspects of life that may be contributing to how you feel. Lighting a candle can help focus the energy to call in a particular angel. It's not required to use a certain color candle. If all you have is white, that's fine too.

Michael
Candle color: Blue
Specialty: Clearing very heavy or dark energy (in your environment and from others), protection, courage, strength

Raphael
Candle color: Green
Specialty: Physical ailments and emotions related to physical ailments

Chamuel
Candle color: Pink
Specialty: Forgiveness of self and others; relationships

Zadkiel
Candle color: Purple
Specialty: Mercy with self and transformation

Metatron
Candle colors: Green-and-Pink Stripes or Blue
Specialty: Replace negative thoughts with positive ones

# Eat Supportive Foods

What you eat makes a big difference in how you feel. Years ago, I struggled with depressive states. No matter what I did, I couldn't seem to shake it, until I changed up my diet. It turns out I was highly sensitive to a few foods, and removing them made all the difference. It was like a fog lifted after that. While I still needed to make changes (like removing negative people from my life—I did this later), I felt stable more regularly and could deal with my day-to-day life better.

When you are depressed, you tend to not eat well. Turning to food for comfort can be detrimental because you are most likely eating things that are making your situation worse. Grabbing a bag of chips, fast food, or sweets to fill yourself up actually causes greater imbalances in the body. So be kind to yourself. We're working on a little self-love here, remember? Even a few small changes in your diet can make a big difference.

## What Are You Drinking?

Drinking pure water is the best thing you can do, but for some people, they just can't stand it. The next best thing are waters with a little bit of flavor added to them. Take a look at products like Hint brand water. These are just water and natural flavor, plain and simple. Drinking something like this can help you get off of sodas, which can wreak havoc on your body.

## What to Eat

Most of us don't get enough good fats. Your brain is made of over 60-percent fat and will uptake any fats that you put into your body, regardless of what type of fat it is. The problem is, the fats we most commonly eat, found in fried and highly processed foods, can actually keep our brains from working correctly. They interfere with the connections between the brain cells and slow down our brain activity.

If you are struggling with depressive moods, eating good fats, such as avocados, coconut oil, grass-fed butter, and raw nuts is a great way to add healthy fats to your diet. These fats actually help our brains work better and improve our moods.

Since people with depressive moods have very stuck energy systems, eating vegetables is a good way to get the energy flowing again. Eating a variety of vegetables (try cooked and raw) can be a good way to jump-start your body into letting the energy flow again and can increase your physical energy.

If you aren't a regular vegetable eater, start slow. Starting to eat a lot of vegetables at once can cause your body to start dumping all of the toxins it has stored up, and this can actually make you feel worse. Start off with one serving a day and work your way up to several. If you literally can't stand vegetables and you know there is no way you can ever stand to eat them, there are tastier ways to get them. Products like Amazing Grass green superfood in the chocolate variety are a great way to get your veggies in, and you can put it in milk (dairy or dairy-free).

Lean meats and wild-caught fish are great sources of protein, which is needed for a strong body and brain. If you can afford organic, it's definitely recommended. Regular commercial meats can contain antibiotics and hormones that aggravate depressive states, so paying a little more is better than eating something that makes you feel worse. If you're going to the trouble to cook it, it might as well be good for you!

# What to Wear

Color can really influence how you feel. In general, adding the colors of red, orange, or yellow to your wardrobe or to your environment can enrich your energy system with colors it is lacking. It doesn't have to be a lot of these colors. A little bit can go a long way.

# Anger

When we think of an angry person, we generally imagine someone who flies off the handle at the smallest thing or maybe someone who broods, sucking the life out of a room. While these people exhibit anger on the outside, there are a whole other group of people who are angry and you would never know it. These are the people that stuff their anger deep down and never let it out. They typically cry when they are angry, so it gets mistaken for another emotion, such as depression or sadness, and the anger gets missed. It may not feel safe for them to express their anger, or they may be afraid of hurting others' feelings. Oftentimes, the person doesn't even realize that they have anger or are suppressing it. This is the most self-destructive kind of anger and can often end up manifesting into physical ailments. In this Section, we are going to address both types of anger, expressed and unexpressed anger.

# Expressed Anger

This is the textbook type of anger, where a person gets angry easily or has specific triggers that incite anger. It's important to note that it's perfectly normal to experience the emotion of anger at times. Expressed anger is really referring to people with the go-to emotion of anger through outbursts, cutting words, or inciting drama. These tend to be their responses if even small things happen in their life that are an inconvenience, such as spilling food or getting cut off in traffic. It's understandable to be a little frustrated when things like this happen, but angry people tend to have a greater than natural response to the situation. It is also common for people with expressed anger to not even realize that they are reacting this way. It is a blind spot for them. However, it is a trigger for them to see other people respond in anger, and they tend to "point the finger" at that person by responding in anger or commenting about how "off" that person is. As they start to let go of the deep-rooted anger that makes them express it, they can start to react more naturally to situations. This can greatly increase their quality of life and improve relationships across the board.

## Unexpressed Anger

There are a lot of people with unexpressed anger that don't even realize they have it. While people with the go-to emotion of expressed anger let it out regardless of who is around, people with unexpressed anger tend to keep it to themselves most of the time. If they do let anger out, they are typically alone, like at home or in the car. Oftentimes, the anger is directed inward at themselves. This is the reason that this type of anger is so destructive. It can be highly damaging to the energy system, since the emotion of anger is being used as a self-inflicted attack. By the time clients with this type of anger come to me, they often have some type of physical ailment, and it is often autoimmune in nature. This is where the body attacks itself. By attacking yourself with your anger and "beating yourself up," you are training your energy system to perform this act, and it's only a matter of time before your physical body follows suit.

## How Do You Know If You Have Unexpressed Anger?

Unexpressed anger is something I have dealt with most of my life. My reasoning was that if I was hard enough on myself, other people wouldn't have to be as hard on me. I despised conflict, and this was a way of heading it off at the pass. If they saw how hard I was on me, they were less likely to confront me about things I had done wrong or punish me in some way. I realize that may sound a little crazy, but that is how I thought about things. I once got over-the-moon angry with myself in my twenties for forgetting to wash the conditioner out of my hair before I went to work and proceeded to beat myself up verbally for about two hours in front of my bewildered coworkers.

I now know after lots of energy work that the roots of this thinking went all the way back to being in utero, where energetic patterns developed from my environment, as well as other traumas over my lifetime. The past few years, I have unraveled this web of traumatic and verbal inhibitory imprints that created the tendency for me to revisit this emotion time and time again. This is no longer my go-to emotion, but it has been a combination of emotional releasing, energy work, and changing my mindset to get there. Now if I happened to forget to wash the conditioner out of my hair, it would be something to laugh about rather than a barrage of self-destruction.

When angry, do you:

- "Beat yourself up" on a regular basis internally (mentally) or physically (like cutting)?
- Think you are stupid or engage in other negative self-talk?
- Suffer from ailments like headaches, intestinal issues, or autoimmune diseases?
- Get quiet or shut down (without brooding)? This is often mistaken by others as compliance or agreement.
- Cry?
- Make excuses when you are angry (saying things like "I am just tired" when asked by others)?
- Engage in excessive work or exercise?

## Groundedness and Anger

Being ungrounded and expressing anger outwardly or inwardly often go hand in hand. When anger is the go-to emotion, this often manifests from triggers, when people pull up their energetic roots first. Part of the fight-or-flight response is energetic in that the person becomes ungrounded, causing them to overreact to a situation with anger. If you have a tendency toward anger, it's a good idea to practice the grounding protocols as well. Especially if your actions leave you saying, "What was I thinking?" The answer is, your emotional imprints were doing the thinking for you. That's why it's so important to work on them.

There are exceptions to these being linked, however. When someone has a brooding anger that sucks the life out of a room or if they tend to exhibit calculated sociopathic behavior, this is typically very grounded anger and can be much more formidable. These types of people can be very destructive to others, intentionally or unintentionally. Of these two types of anger, brooding anger can be dealt with more easily than sociopathic anger. Brooding anger is a primal learned defense mechanism. Sociopaths have a lot more going on than just being angry and are out of the scope of this book.

# Expressed Anger Protocol

 Before we start, it's important to understand that expressing anger is natural, and if you are outwardly expressing it, this is healthier than holding it in. The focus of this protocol is to help you get to the bottom of your anger so that you can start releasing the emotions from the traumatic and verbal inhibitory imprints that are causing you to overexpress or inappropriately express your anger so that you can have a happier life.

No one wants to be angry or overreact, including you. It's a defense mechanism that has developed over time. It is often modeled to you by someone highly influential in your life, like a parent or caregiver. Sometimes it may be the only way you feel you can get what you want, or you feel that it is essential for your survival. Other people turn to anger when they feel they are not being seen, heard, or understood. For each of these situations, the root of the issue is different, but the results are the same. Regardless of the root cause, this protocol can help you unravel and release the emotions and energy that make anger your go-to response.

# In-the-Moment Relief

Anger can come on quickly, and to change the pattern of exploding is going to take some time. But small, immediate changes can make a big difference. To start, you can take a breath to prevent collateral damage.

### Technique 12.10. Pause and Breathe

The simple act of pausing to take a few deep breaths can let off some steam and prevent you from doing something you will regret. The reactivity you have in the moment takes your power from you. It makes you unable to control your reaction. Your actions or words often hurt you or someone else. When you pause to take a breath, it allows your energy system to let out some of the emotional energy that is boiling over. It's kind of like lifting the lid off a boiling pot. When you lift the lid, the boiling immediately calms down. While it is still boiling, it's not running all over your stove and leaving a mess for you to clean up later. The same goes for your reaction.

1. Lift the lid off your anger by pausing and breathing.
2. Set the intention to breathe out your emotions in the moment.

3. Envision that ball of red-hot anger coming up and out of your mouth through your breath (preferably not directed at anyone).
4. As you do this practice, pay attention to how many breaths it takes you to get to a manageable level.
5. Write this down and put it in your assessment.

As you start to work on your anger-related traumatic and verbal inhibitory imprints, the number of breaths you have to take should go down over time. This is because you have released the underlying emotions that caused the pattern in the first place.

## Is This Really a Big Deal?

After you take a few deep breaths, you are going to have better access to the reasoning part of your brain and energy system. Ask yourself a simple question . . .

How big of a deal is this issue that I am angry about? The answer may be that it IS a big deal to you right now, which is fine. If it is, ask yourself will this matter five minutes from now, tomorrow, or next week? If the answer is that it really isn't a big deal, then you can act more appropriately in the moment. If it is a big deal, taking a pause and breathing can allow you to calm down enough to problem-solve, turning your usually reactive response into a proactive one.

## How to Dig Deeper to Find the Root

After things calm down, reflect on the situation a bit so that you can start digging into the underlying patterns.

News flash: What you are angry about isn't actually what you are angry about.

Hear me out on this one. It will make sense after I explain it. When situations arise in our lives and we get angry, most of the time, the root of the anger has absolutely nothing to do with what we are angry about. Our reaction of anger is caused by something completely different from the actual event. Here's an example from something that literally just happened and fueled me to write this part of the book, which I have been blocked on for several days.

My husband and I went to a late breakfast and I told him I had a client call at 12:30. While we were driving around afterward, he said he wanted to go get one of our cars sold today, like, right now. I told him I didn't think we had time, and he was certain we did. I objected kindly, but he was insistent and then got on another business call in the car as we were driving back to the house. I was absolutely livid. For me, my anger is mostly a quiet anger, or repressed, but I never get a free lunch on it, because he can tell. After his call, he point-blank called me on it and told me why he thought I was angry. I smiled and told him he was right on. I was stressed because I didn't feel like there was enough time to get that done. I had a client call I needed to be home for, and it was too tight a timeline.

After we got home, I got the information together, and he decided we were low on time and it was too stressful to try and do it right then. You would think that would have been the end of me being ticked, but it wasn't. I was still boiling mad. "REALLY??" I thought. "It's over. What's the deal?" That's when I started to dig in and ask myself the questions above. Is it a big deal? Part of me understood it wasn't, but part of me was stomping my foot, saying that it was. So, then, what was that angry part of me so mad about??

It turns out it didn't have anything to do with getting the car sold. It had everything to do with feeling like my time and priorities weren't important to him. Most of my life, I have spent my time in response to what everyone else wanted to do, but now I am in a time when I have a lot I want- and need-to-dos. I feel like my boundaries and priorities deserve respect and consideration.

After I addressed the root cause and released the immediate emotion, the anger went away. I was able to articulate why I was angry to my husband. He said, "Oh, that's not how I feel at all. What you have to do is important. I'm sorry it came across that way. I just really want to get the car thing done."

I felt silly, but my emotions were triggered from a place of not feeling valued or seen, heard, and understood. They were old patterns that got lit on fire from the immediate circumstances. It could have been any situation that triggered the anger, but it just happened to be selling the car that did it.

## Finding the Root Cause of Your Anger

If you have repeated bouts of expressed anger, chances are you have an underlying root cause that keeps getting triggered that you may not even be aware of. To get a better idea of where your anger may be coming from, ask yourself the questions given in the following technique (12.11).

**Technique 12.11. Finding the Root of Anger**

Currently

- What was the last situation you really got angry over?
- How did you react?

Past history

- Does that reaction remind you of anyone in your life (parent, caregiver)?
- Growing up, were you understood by your parents, teachers, and peers?
- Did people listen to what you had to say and value your opinion?
- Were you disregarded, abandoned, or ignored?
- Did someone in your life betray you on a deep level?
- Were you abused?
- Did you turn to anger to keep you safe in a hostile environment, having to fight back for physical and emotional survival?

Connect the dots

- When you think about the last thing you got really angry over and you review the questions above about your history, what stands out to you?
- Is there a connection between your last blow up and historically how you were treated?

Thinking about the answers to these questions can help to open up and understand where your anger comes from. This is the first step to managing it.

# Using Color for Managing and Clearing Anger

Anger is often associated with the color red. People who are angry do tend to have an inflamed color of red in their energy system. That is not to be confused with the presence of red that is found in the root chakra and denotes being grounded. Anger red is "hot-looking," generally very bright red, and often has globs of black mixed into it because it can burn out or arrest the energy system in spots where it is present for a long time. To calm the red of anger, use blue in the moment.

### Technique 12.12. Breathing In Blue

You can use color to calm anger in the moment as well as use it to release anger on a deeper level.

1. Envision a cloud of calm blue in front of you.
2. Take a deep breath in, breathing in the blue cloud of energy.
3. Repeat this as many times as you need to.

This works like pouring water on a fire. It will calm the anger down more quickly than just taking breaths without envisioning the color blue. By simply breathing it into your energy system, the color blue goes to where it is needed and squelches the energetic inflammation that is going on.

## Find the Anger Where It Hides

In the physical body, certain areas are more prone to holding anger than others. The liver/gallbladder and pancreas typically house expressed and repressed anger.

When you are calm, you can work on your stored anger, which will help to release the deeper emotions and energy in your traumatic and verbal inhibitory imprints.

### Technique 12.13. Breathing Blue In to Hidden Anger

1. Start by setting an intention: "I choose to release this anger and whatever it is attached to."
2. Place your hands over your liver/gallbladder area or your pancreas and breathe into them while you are envisioning the color blue.
3. Do this between five and ten times for each area.

## Going Deeper

As you are using the color blue to dig deeper into your stored anger, refer to the questions you answered on the previous page regarding your history.

What did you answer yes to?
Do you see patterns in situations that have made you angry?
Is there a recurring theme?

What is the earliest instance of not being valued, being abandoned, etc., that you remember?

### Technique 12.14. Addressing the Beginning of Anger

1. After you have the earliest situation you can remember in mind, set your intention: "I choose to release the emotions related to this situation and whatever it is attached to."
2. Envision the emotion(s) from this verbal inhibitory or traumatic imprint rising up to the surface and out of your body.
3. Envision it leaving through a window or out of your space.
4. To help it along, especially if it triggers you deeply, breathe in a calm color of blue to help push the emotion(s) out of your energy field.
5. Repeat this breathing until you feel like it has left your body.

As you address the first imprint, other situations may come to mind that are the roots of your anger. This means they are on the same emotional string of beads. By repeating the process of the technique above, you can start to more deeply unravel the roots of your anger and begin to lead a happier life.

## Salt Bath for Expressed Anger

2 cups Epsom salt
2 cups baking soda

Essential oils
6 drops lavender
4 drops eucalyptus
5 drops ylang ylang
14 drops bergamot
6 drops Roman chamomile
3 drops patchouli
6 drops sandalwood
10 drops rose absolute

Use two cups of mixture per bath.

1. Mix Epsom salt and oils together well. You can store what you don't use in a glass jar.
2. When you have a bath, add equal parts of baking soda and the salt mixture to your bath, as in one cup of salt and essential oil mix and one cup of baking soda.

Note: You can mix the baking soda in the salt mixture and store it that way, but it's a gamble. If the salt's moisture content is too high, your mixture will become really hard and be difficult to get out of the jar. This situation doesn't exactly help your anger. That's why I recommend adding the baking soda right before your bath.

## Taking on Other People's Anger

To illustrate my point, here I have to give you a little more detail on the story of me getting so angry about selling the car. The night before, we'd gone to dinner with my two sons and my father-in-law. My older son, who doesn't live with me, got angry with me, my husband, and the son that lives with me over some things that were said at dinner. He was fuming mad. I didn't think much about it at the time, but the next day when I got so over-the-top angry about selling the car, I remembered what had occurred the night before. That level of anger was really out of character for me, and I couldn't seem to shake it. On the way to sell the car, after I had been really angry for a couple of hours, I was like, "Oooohhhh, yeahhhh, now this makes sense." By the time we got to the dealership, the anger I had been experiencing was gone, since I ran through techniques to release it over and over again and then let the rest go by setting an intention to let go of this anger that wasn't mine. However, my poor husband had spent the last couple of hours with me, and when he got out of the other car at the dealership (we had to follow each other), *he* was fuming and angry. I could feel it on him, and he commented about how he felt. I told him what I had discovered, and he suddenly understood what he had to do to let it all go.

Just like being around people that are in depressive states can cause you to feel that way, being around angry people can make you feel that way too. Really, you can pick up anyone else's stuff, no matter what emotion it is. You can even pick up energetic signatures of memories from other people and dream about them, but that nugget is a tangent to be discussed another time.

It's important to remember, though, that picking these things up from other people is actually a gift. It agitates your own deep-seated energy that is similar and allows you to let go of the emotions you picked up, along with your own. It's often energy that you couldn't get to any other way. That's why the Universe provided you with a way to release it. Be grateful, even if it is uncomfortable.

### Technique 12.15. Releasing Anger from Other People

Just as we talked about with depressive states, when vibrational states of energy or emotions come into contact with one another, they stick and become indistinguishable from one another. While you can set the intention to just release the other person's energy you picked up, some of it will naturally stay with you due to the vibrational similarity. So instead, set the intention to release all of it.

1. Say, "I welcome up the anger (note that any emotion can be used here), and I thank it for being here."
2. After you feel it, say, "I choose to release the anger from other people (you can call out a name if it helps you) and anything it is attached to."
3. Envision the energy floating up and out of your space.

## Angels That Can Help You Release Anger

Angels deal with anger on the regular. Depending on why you have anger, the best angel for helping you release it will vary, but all of the ones listed in this section deal with an aspect of life that may be part of the source of your anger. You can call on the angels individually or all at once. There is no set way to talk to angels.

### Technique 12.16. Angels for Releasing Anger

One way is just to simply hand over your burdens.

Say, "Angels, please take the energy that is heavy inside of me and causing me to feel anger."
You can be more specific and vent what is bothering you to them and ask them to take that as well.
Talking it out can help you release it more effectively.

Lighting a candle can help focus the energy to call in a particular angel. It's not required to use a certain color candle. If all you have is white, that's fine too.

Michael
Candle color: Blue
Specialty: Clearing very heavy or dark energy (in your environment and from others), protection, courage, strength

Gabriel
Candle color: White
Specialty: Helping you process why things have happened; helps with understanding and interpretation; shifts your perspective

Raphael
Candle color: Green
Specialty: Physical ailments and emotions related to physical ailments

Chamuel
Candle color: Pink
Specialty: Forgiveness of self and others, especially in relationships

Metatron
Candle colors: Green-and-Pink Stripes or Blue
Specialty: Replace negative thoughts with positive ones

# Eat Supportive Foods

Cool foods such as yogurt (dairy or nondairy), salads, or other green vegetables are supportive of squelching anger. Blue foods such as blueberries, blueberry tea, or plums are also helpful.

Avoid spicy, red, and orange foods, as these can stir up anger. Spicy peppers; spices such as turmeric, cinnamon, or ginger; and red foods such as beets, strawberries, mangoes, and carrots should be avoided. See the full list of these foods in chapter 10. Of course, not all of these foods will cause an issue for you and stir up anger. It's important to observe how your body handles them and whether they elicit an emotional response for you.

In addition to the foods above, stimulants such as coffee (caffeine), sugar, and allergenic foods can overstimulate you and make your anger trigger more sensitive. Just pay attention to what is an issue for you and avoid it or use those items in moderation.

# Use the Right Color

If anger is something you are working on, avoid wearing bright, bold colors or having those colors in your environment. Bright, strong colors like red, orange, and even yellow can agitate the state of anger, putting too much of that color into your energy system. It's really no different from picking up someone else's anger. The colors cause an imbalance. Instead, look to tones of blue and green to help keep the anger at a chill level. Paint your walls with them and wear them. It will truly make a difference in how you feel.

## Repressed Anger Protocol

 Driving down the road after dropping my kids off at school, I felt a pit in my stomach. This hard lump was all too familiar. "Crap," I thought, "am I ever going to be through this?" The lump started to rise up through me. It hurt, like swallowing a giant horse pill in reverse, only instead of being some kind of medicine or nutrient, it was a ball of emotions: anger, rage, despair. I didn't know what all the ball contained yet, I just knew the next little bit here was going to be interesting. And hopefully I wouldn't hurt myself too badly in the process. My mouth started to salivate and I felt nauseous. "What is it this time?" I thought. "What am I going to let go of now?"

This scene had become pretty much a daily thing for me. If I was lucky, I would have two or three days in between these episodes, but it was definitely a regular occurrence. I stepped on the gas to make it home before it started. I was grateful the kids were at school and my husband was at work, and thank God animals can't talk and don't judge.

I got home, slammed the car door, ran into the house, and burst into tears. The lump was in my throat now and I couldn't breathe. "Get to the closet. Get to the closet." This is the safest place for me to have these meltdowns. I made it. As soon as I stepped in, my legs gave out. Now I screamed. I beat my hands on the wall and the floor like a crazy person. I was separate from my body and didn't have any control over what I was doing. Memory after memory flashed before my eyes. Situations I wanted to cry about, be angry about, and speak up for myself about but couldn't at the time they happened. It wasn't safe or compliant. Reacting would mean I wasn't a good girl. Instead, I would just turn myself off, like flipping a switch. But now I was making up for it.

One of the things that is most vivid to me about my kundalini awakening was realizing how much repressed anger I had been packing away. Even though I didn't really understand what was happening to me, I did know one thing: this stuff was coming out, whether I wanted it to or not. Up until that point in my life, I wasn't really allowed to express anger. Doing that would mean conflict and putting myself in a situation that I would most definitely be sorry for later.

The process of getting out my explosive repressed anger took about six months to get under control. I got used to having a spiraling rage fit, cleaning up my face, putting on a smile, and going to make dinner. It was a way to manage and not end up in a mental hospital.

Dealing with repressed anger is trickier than dealing with expressed anger in that lots of people don't even realize they have it. They are, in many cases, so dissociated from it that the mere suggestion of it makes them laugh. The trick is to bring up the anger in a safe way to move it out of the traumatic and verbal inhibitory imprints. Since it is repressed, it may take some work to get to it, but once you do, you will be able to let it go more easily.

Start by asking yourself these questions about your history:

- Growing up, did you have a volatile home environment?
- Were you bullied at home or at school?
- Did you have an angry parent or caregiver that you were afraid of?
- Were you allowed to speak up for yourself or have an opinion?
- Were you allowed to be angry?
- Did it feel safe to be angry and express it?
- Did/do people say things to you like, "Wow you never get mad/angry"?
- Did/do people say things to you like, "You're cute when you're mad," causing you to shut down?
- Do you freeze up when conflict arises in your life or someone is yelling at you?

## The Wisdom Cloak

Chances are if you answered yes to a few of these questions, you are the one people come to for advice. You've seen or been through a lot and it makes you much more aware of other people. You tend to develop an innate sense of what to do in all types of situations. You're probably a great listener and come off as empathetic, compassionate, and wise. All super cool things. The only problem is, you most likely have paid a price for the heightening of those traits.

Being in a tough environment calls on you to develop any skill you possibly can to survive it. One of those is repressing anger to get along with those around you. You probably rationalize their behavior and "put the shoe on the other foot" when it comes to trying to understand why they would behave that way toward you or other people. It's a way of avoiding anger yourself and dissociating it from something to be angry about. In the moment, it's survival. In the long run, though, it's detrimental. If not addressed, any type of repressed emotion can lead to physical and mental ailments. That's why it's important to recognize your anger and get it out.

# Popping the Cork

If you answered yes to a few of the questions on the previous page, you probably have some repressed anger hiding in you. Like I said, most people aren't even aware of it. At the time you probably felt fear, sadness, or numbness or just froze. Anger often isn't felt in the moment if you have a habit of repressing it.

I lovingly call this section "Popping the Cork" for a reason. That's exactly what it is. You're allowing yourself to feel the anger, in many cases, for the first time. I will say it can be a little alarming when you do these techniques, because your reactions may be really out of character for you. It doesn't mean you are going to lose control forever or that you are a terrible person. You might even feel shame for the thoughts that come into your head or the words that come out of your mouth. It's important to remember that these are pent-up energy and emotions. It's not going to be smooth. Think of popping a champagne cork. Everyone in the room is wondering where that sucker is going to end up. And then the champagne comes boiling out of the top of the bottle. It's messy and chaotic. If you've ever opened champagne, you know it's not a bad idea to do it over a sink or outside. You don't want it to get everywhere. That's why in the "popping the cork" techniques, you are in a relatively controlled space. So, allow yourself to let loose. You've earned it.

# Shout It All Out

This is pretty basic but effective. It gets the ball rolling without feeling too out of control.

Get somewhere by yourself. Try the car (parked in a parking lot), your house when no one is home, or far out in nature somewhere. Worst case, you can scream into a pillow at home. Just be sure to leave some room in front of your face for everything to come out. If other people are home, it's best if it's just adults and that they are aware of what you are doing. Kids get a little freaked out (I might be speaking from experience here), so do it while they are gone.

It's also a good idea to have something nearby you can physically let out your anger on, like a pillow or mattress. A little arm flailing and fist pounding may be had. That's a good thing. You just want to make sure you don't break a hand or something. You don't want to negatively reinforce releasing anger by causing yourself pain.

### Technique 12.17. Popping the Cork

1. Think of a situation when you feel that you might have repressed anger. Remember, you might have just felt fear or sadness in the moment. Look at it this way: if you saw what happened to you occurring to someone else, would you be angry about it? If the answer is yes, there's probably some anger nuggets there for you.
2. When you access the memory, you will most likely feel other emotions first, such as the ones that you felt when the situation was occurring.
3. Set the intention to release what you are feeling first: "I choose to release the (emotion) that I am feeling and anything that it is attached to."
4. Envision the emotions rising up out of your body and floating off.
5. Repeat this until you don't feel those emotions anymore.
6. Ask your energy system for access to your anger about the situation: "I choose to access the anger I repressed in this situation."
7. If this isn't enough to let you touch the anger, start to think about what elements would make you angry if you were observing them. Verbalize it even if you don't feel it. "I was angry when (that person) broke my toy." "I was angry when (that person) called me (a name).
8. When you start to feel the anger, DON'T shove it back down. You are working on breaking that pattern.
9. Envision it coming to the surface to be released.
10. Now yell. Like, as loud as you can. Dig down really deep and scream the anger out. It may feel like all you can do is make a faint sound at first. Keep going. It may take a few tries. You may feel silly, but don't judge yourself.
11. Think about the situation again to bring it up, and yell. It's perfectly normal to start crying or having body tremors when

this is going on. The more your body reacts, the more you are letting go of. GREAT JOB. KEEP GOING. You may need to hit that pillow or mattress nearby. It may last thirty seconds or a few minutes. You will probably feel exhausted afterward if you have a good release.

12. Take a few deep breaths and give yourself a big love hug. You just gave yourself a voice for the first time.

13. Continue to take some deep breaths and envision the anger floating up and out of you. Be sure you are in a space where it can float off and out.

14. If you did this technique in the car, roll the windows down when you are done for a while to let the energy of the anger out.

15. If you are at home, it's a good idea to smudge the area with a cedar or sage smudge stick. Smudge the pillow and run the smudge stick over the mattress, too, taking care not to drop ash on it.

16. If you can, go for a walk or do some stretching after your release. This will help you process what you just did and stabilize your physical body and energy system.

17. If you feel shaky, this is normal.

18. Envision sinking your roots deep into the ground and take a few deep breaths up through them to ground yourself.

## Smash Therapy

Another option is to go to a smash therapy room. These are found all over the US. In the UK they are called rage rooms or wreck rooms. It's probably a good idea to practice alone first with the technique above before you go public if you are not used to expressing your anger, but these rooms can be fun. You get to smash things like plates and glasses with various tools like crowbars and hammers. It can be a great way to get some exercise and let go of some pent-up frustration. The best part is, you are expected to lose it a little. That's what the room is for. Letting your anger out has never been more kosher. Hop on Google and see if there is one in your area.

## After You Pop the Cork

While you may need to return to the Popping the Cork technique on the regular for a while, chances are you will need it less and less. Eventually, you will get comfortable with feeling anger, admitting you have it, and releasing it. It doesn't have to be some dramatic thing. If you have dealt with repressed anger, blowing up probably isn't your style. You can let go of it just like any other emotion. The techniques from the expressed anger section are actually really helpful here too. You just have to get the ball rolling first by feeling it. (The following section is similar to the expressed anger section.)

## Using Color for Managing and Clearing Anger

Anger is often associated with the color red. People who have repressed anger do tend to have an inflamed color of red in their energy system. That is not to be confused with the presence of red that is found in the root chakra and denotes being grounded. Anger red is "hot-looking," generally very bright red, and often has globs of black mixed into it because it can burn out or arrest the energy system in spots where it is present for a long time. This is especially the case with repressed anger.

## Use Blue in the Moment

Once you give yourself permission to feel anger, you may feel it more in the moment than you used to. That's not a bad thing, but you want to have tools to manage it. You can use color to calm anger in the moment as well as use it to release anger on a deeper level.

**Technique 12.18. Letting Blue Cure the Anger**

In the moment, take some deep breaths and visualize breathing in a calm, blue color. This works like pouring water on fire. It will calm the anger down more quickly than just taking breaths without envisioning the color blue. By simply breathing it into your energy system, you allow the color blue to go to where it is needed and squelch the energetic inflammation that is going on without repressing it. Green can also be used to access similar vibrations of anger. Simply repeat the technique and envision green instead of blue.

## Find the Anger Where It Hides

In the physical body, certain areas are more prone to holding anger than others. The liver/gallbladder and pancreas typically house expressed and repressed anger. The throat holds repressed anger.

When you are calm, you can work on your stored anger, which will help to release the deeper emotions and energy in your traumatic and verbal inhibitory imprints.

**Technique 12.19. Releasing Stored Anger**

1. Be sure that you have done the Pop the Cork exercise at least once before starting to work on your stored anger. There is often a strong emotional charge that you need to release before working on stored anger.
2. Start by setting an intention: "I choose to release this anger and whatever it is attached to."
3. Place your hands over your liver/gallbladder area or your pancreas and breathe into them while you are envisioning the color blue.
4. Do this between five and ten times for each area.

# Going Deeper

As you are using the color blue to dig deeper into your repressed anger, refer to the questions you answered regarding your history.

What did you answer yes to?
Do you see patterns in situations that have made you angry?
Is there a recurring theme?
What is the earliest instance of not being valued, being abandoned, bullied, scared, etc., that you remember?

**Technique 12.20. Finding the Root of Repressed Anger**

1. After you have the earliest situation you can remember in mind, set your intention: "I choose to release the (emotion[s]) related to this situation and whatever it is attached to."
2. Envision the emotion(s) from this verbal inhibitory or traumatic imprint rising up to the surface and out of your body.
3. Envision it leaving through a window or out of your space.
4. Be sure to give it some time to come up and process out of you. It has been stuck for a long time.
5. To help it along, especially if it triggers you deeply, breathe in a calm color of blue or green to help push it out of your energy field. Repeat this breathing until you feel like it has left your body.

As you address the first imprint, other situations may come to mind that are roots of your repressed anger. This means they are on the same emotional string of beads. By repeating the process of the technique on the previous page, you can start to more deeply unravel the roots of your repressed anger and begin to lead a happier life.

**Technique 12.21. Releasing Anger You Picked Up from Other People**

Just as we talked about with depressive states, when vibrational states of energy or emotions come into contact with one another, they stick and become indistinguishable from one another. This can occur even with states of repressed anger, and it can actually allow you to access it easier to release it. While you can set the intention to just release the other person's energy you picked up, some of it will naturally stay with you due to the vibrational similarity. So instead, set the intention to release all of it.

1. Say, "I welcome up the anger, and I thank it for being here."
2. After you feel it, say, "I choose to release the anger I took on from other people (you can call out a name if it helps you) and anything it is attached to."
3. Envision the energy floating up and out of your space.

# Salt Bath for Repressed Anger

This salt bath gives you access to the anger to release it without turning down the emotion or exacerbating it.

Bath salts
1½ cups Dead Sea salt
½ cup Himalayan pink salt

Essential oils
3 drops peppermint
6–13 drops tea tree
3 drops eucalyptus
6–12 drops bergamot
3 drops Roman chamomile
6 drops frankincense
2–4 drops sandalwood

Use one cup of mixture per bath.

1. Mix bath salts and oils together well.
2. You can store what you don't use in a glass jar.

## 12.22. Angels for Releasing Anger

Depending on why you have anger, the best angel for helping you release it will vary, but all of the ones listed below deal with an aspect of life that may be part of the source of your anger. You can call on them individually or all at once. There is no set way to talk to angels. One way is just to simply hand over your burdens.

1. Say, "Angels, please take the energy that is heavy inside of me and causing me to feel anger (note that you can use this for other emotions as well)."
2. You can be more specific and vent what is bothering you to them and ask them to take it as well.
3. Voicing what you are feeling to angels can give you a voice in a different way and allow you to more easily process your emotions.

Lighting a candle can help focus the energy to call in a particular angel. It's not required to use a certain color candle. If all you have is white, that's fine too.

Michael
Candle color: Blue
Specialty: Clearing very heavy or dark energy (in your environment and from others), protection, courage, strength

Gabriel
Candle color: White
Specialty: Helping you process why things have happened; helps with understanding and interpretation; shifts your perspective

Raphael
Candle color: Green
Specialty: Physical ailments and emotions related to physical ailments

Chamuel
Candle color: Pink
Specialty: Forgiveness of self and others, especially in relationships

Jophiel
Candle color: Yellow
Specialty: Decisions, allowing you to sort through things on your own terms without outside influence

Zadkiel
Candle color: Purple
Specialty: Transformation and forgiveness; helps you let go of the past; keeps energy moving so you don't block yourself from change.

Metatron
Candle colors: Green-and-Pink Stripes or Blue
Specialty: Replace negative thoughts with positive ones

# Eat Supportive Foods

When you are dealing with repressed anger, the support of foods is twofold. In the first phase of dealing with repressed anger, you want to actually increase your intake of foods that can help access the anger so that you can release it. These are good foods to eat before you perform the Pop the Cork technique, although being on a fairly empty stomach may be preferable.

Spicy, red, and orange foods can stir up anger, including spicy peppers; spices such as turmeric, cinnamon, or ginger; and red foods such as beets, strawberries, mangoes, and carrots. See the full list of these foods in chapter 10 under foods that support the root chakra and sacral chakra. Of course, not all of these foods will stir up anger. It's important to observe how your body handles them and whether they elicit an emotional response for you.

While stimulants such as coffee (caffeine), sugar, and allergenic foods can overstimulate you and make your anger trigger more sensitive, they can also cause you to be ungrounded. If you have repressed anger, this is something you probably have a propensity toward and want to avoid. Just pay attention to what is an issue for you and avoid or use those items in moderation.

After you get good at allowing anger to be experienced and you need to calm yourself down, cool foods such as yogurt (dairy or nondairy), salads, or other green vegetables are supportive of squelching anger. Blue foods such as blueberries, blueberry tea, or plums are also good. Remember, though, don't turn to these foods in the beginning of working on your repressed anger. It can block access to it.

# Use the Right Color

If repressed anger is something you are working on, wearing bright, bold colors or having those colors in your environment is a great idea. If you experience repressed anger, these colors are most likely depleted in your energy system to begin with, and you may be drawn to them for that reason. Replenishing them can help you to bring nourishment to your energy system, helping you to feel better and allowing you access to your anger so that you can release it.

When you find yourself shying away from these colors, you probably have enough of them in your system and can access your anger more easily to release it. At this point, the colors of orange and red can cause an imbalance. Instead, look to tones of blue and green to help keep the anger at a chill level if it is an issue. Paint your walls with them and wear them. It's important to note this preference change may take years.

## Physical Ailments Protocol

 My friend Fiona called me out of the blue one day and started telling me she had been having health issues. She expressed how frustrated she had been for months with her doctors, who kept dismissing her symptoms, and called to tell me she finally had a diagnosis. "Turns out it's cancer," she said.

I got quiet and just said, "I'm so sorry. You're so strong, you can beat it, though." We talked for another couple of minutes about what her next steps were and hung up. As I said goodbye to her, I heard so clearly from my guides, "She's going to die, and there's nothing you can do about it."

I didn't believe them, but they were right.

Each person has their own path on this planet. We do what we can to help each other, but our destiny is truly our own. Every person has come here to work on certain things in their lives, and they do it in a myriad of ways. Some people struggle with addiction, others with relationships and money, and still others with physical ailments. We work out our stuff as best we can. Our energy system and emotional states heavily influence our physical being. Everything physical we experience, from ailments to accidents, starts in the energy system first, shows up as emotional states, and if not addressed eventually manifests in the physical body.

In the case of Fiona, I could clearly see then, and even more clearly now, where her physical ailments stemmed from. She was the youngest of three girls and the quietest of the three. While her parents were well-meaning, the older two children got a lot more attention than she did. Fiona would just keep to herself and became very self-reliant. When she expressed that she didn't feel well to her parents, she was casual, not wanting to make a big deal out of it, and because of this, her parents didn't take her seriously. As a child, she had an ear infection that landed her in the hospital because it had gotten so bad, the infection leaked into her blood. When she was twenty, she suffered a stroke from a thyroid disorder, and her parents didn't believe her about it until she had the doctor call them. She didn't feel that expressing her emotions would do any good, so she never did. Several years later, she developed Celiac disease, Hashimoto's disease, and eventually cancer.

While there are several factors that go into all of these things, such as environment, foods, and genetics, we are going to talk about the one thing that rarely gets taken into account: the role the energy system and emotions play in physical health. This protocol is designed to help you start releasing the emotions at the root of your physical ailments and get you on a track back to health.

## Acute Illness versus Chronic Illness

As we discussed in chapter 6, acute illness often has something to do with issues that are immediately occurring in your life. For example, if you are having problems speaking up for yourself at work lately, you might develop a sore throat. (For the relationship between organs and emotions, see the chart on page 77.) If the pattern of not speaking up for yourself becomes persistent, over time it may lead to the development of a thyroid disorder, like Fiona had.

Chronic conditions take years to develop and are preceded by trauma or repeated energetic and emotional patterns that inflame, restrict, or shut down the energy system. The lives of people with chronic physical ailments often feel futile. When things in your life feel this way, it can be hard to think about anything else. The good news is that as you perform the techniques in this Section, you can start to gain a more positive perspective and possibly make gains in your physical health.

# Emotions as They Relate to Physical Organs

Although we address this at length in chapter 6, the techniques from that chapter with a little twist are perfect for this protocol. If you are having issues with a particular organ in your body, look at the chart on page 77 PAGE FOR FIG 9 ORGAN CHART to see what emotions tend to gravitate toward that organ and apply them to the techniques below. If you have an ailment that affects more than one organ, be sure to address it.

### Technique 12.23. Releasing Emotions from Several Organs

1. Start by choosing an emotion to work on. Let's use the example of anger.
2. Locate all of the organs anger is found in on the chart on page 77. (It is found in the throat, liver/gallbladder, and pancreas.)
3. You can set the intention to release this emotion by saying, "I choose to release anger from my throat, liver, gallbladder, and pancreas."
4. If you want to dig deeper, add the ending of "and whatever it's attached to." Such as: "I choose to release anger from my throat, liver, gallbladder, and pancreas *and whatever it's attached to.*"
5. Envision the emotion floating up and out of your body, directing the energy out of your space.

### Technique 12.24. Releasing Emotions from a Particular Organ

1. Start by choosing an organ to work on. Let's use the example of lungs.
2. You can set the intention to release the emotions located in the lungs by saying, "I choose to release all of the low-vibration emotions from my lungs."
3. If you want to dig deeper, add the ending of "and whatever it's attached to." Such as: "I choose to release all of the low-vibration emotions from my lungs *and whatever they are attached to.*"
4. Place your hands over your lungs (or whatever organ you are working with) and take a deep breath.
5. As you breathe in, envision breathing in white light, directing the light to the organ you are releasing the emotions from.
6. As you breathe out, exhale the energy and emotions that were stuck in that organ.
7. Repeat until you feel that the organ is clear.

8. In addition, when you breathe light into the organ, you can also set the intention for the congested emotions to leave your body in a cloud and exit your space.

### Technique 12.25. Releasing One or a Few Emotions from a Particular Organ

1. Start by choosing an organ on the chart on pages 78-80 and an emotion or emotions that are found in that organ.
2. You can set the intention for an organ by simply saying, *"I choose to release (the emotion) from (the organ)."* Example: "I choose to release anxiety from my stomach."
3. If you feel that you need to release more than one emotion related to the organ, you can simply add it on to the statement, such as: "I choose to release anxiety and fear of new things from my stomach."
4. If you want to dig deeper, add the ending of "and whatever it's attached to." Such as: "I choose to release anxiety and fear of new things from my stomach *and whatever they are attached to.*"
5. Envision the emotions floating up out of your body and leaving your space.
6. In addition, you can place your hand over the organ and breathe white light into the organ.
7. When you breathe out, breathe out the congested energy from that organ.
8. In addition, when you breathe light into the organ, you can also set the intention for the congested emotions to leave your body in a cloud and exit your space.
9. If you feel you have the base technique down, you can look up what colors correspond to the emotions you are releasing and breathe those colors into the organ to help clear the emotions.

# Ailments That Are Systemic

For ailments that involve the whole body, such as ailments of the blood or some autoimmune disorders, addressing organs isn't the way to go. If there is a systemic disorder that originated in an organ (such as diabetes in the pancreas, or Hashimoto's in the thyroid) that is affecting you systemically, address both the organ of origin and the entire body.

For systemic ailments, you need to address the whole body rather than just one part. Just as in depressive states, if a physical condition is systemic, the energy system depletion and arrest is systemic too. Use the protocol given here to the extent you are able. Some of the physical techniques may not be possible depending on your condition. Use your discretion.

# Get Moving

People with this energetic pattern tend not to do much because they feel unwell. Since the energy system is in such a stuck state, it makes them physically and mentally tired. If they are in pain, this further exacerbates the issue. While there may be physical limitations, it's important for people with this energy system to move their bodies.

### Technique 12.26. Stretching for Systemic Ailments

1. Stretching is a fantastic way to start moving your body.
2. Take a deep breath and reach up to the sky with both hands and really stretch.
3. Go up on your tiptoes if you are able.
4. As you bring your arms down, breathe all the way out.
5. Repeat this five times.
6. Next, put your arms straight out to your sides and gently twist from side to side.
7. Take deep breaths as you do so.
8. You can also simply put your hands on your hips and twist side to side slowly.
9. Do this six times.
10. Next take one arm and reach it up high while the other arm rests on your opposite hip.
11. Now take your upstretched arm and bend to your opposite side.
12. Take deep breaths as you do so.
13. Repeat with the opposite side.
14. Do this three times on each side.
15. Put your hands on your hips.
16. Move your hips slowly in a circle like you are hula-hooping
17. Do this movement counterclockwise five times and then clockwise five times.
18. Sit on the ground with your legs extended out in front of you.
19. Make your legs as straight as you can and make your spine as straight as you can.
20. Reach forward with your arms and try to touch your toes.

21. Hold for three seconds and release.
22. Do this five times.
23. As a challenge, see if you can reach a little farther each time.

These techniques will get the energy and blood in your body moving. You will be able to feel a difference.

Try going for short walks; even down one side of your block and back home is a great start.

### Technique 12.27. Breathing In White Light for Physical Ailments

Getting circulation back into your energy system is the most important thing you can do to start shifting to a more positive place. Breathing in light is a simple yet powerful technique that starts to break up the really stuck energy in your energy system. Breathing deeply also increases blood flow and oxygen in your body, which gives you more physical energy.

1. First, envision a cloud of white light in front of you.
2. Now take a deep breath in, breathing in as much of the white light as you can.
3. Envision it moving through your body, breaking loose the stuck energy.
4. Now blow out your breath forcefully, breathing out all of the stuck energy that broke loose from the light.
5. Repeat this technique at least ten times.
6. If you get tired, just do it however many times you are able and work up to ten times.

### Technique 12.28. Breathing In through Your Crown

1. Envision the cloud of white light over your head.
2. Breathe in, but this time envision breathing in the white light through the top of your head and envision the light going as far down your body as it can go.
3. Hold your breath for five seconds, envisioning the light breaking up all of the stuck energy.
4. Now, breathe out and envision the stuck energy exiting through the top of your head.
5. Each time you breathe in, pull the light down farther and farther until you breathe it in through the top of your head and it can reach your toes.

6. Blow it out the top of your head.
7. Envision the energy you breathe out floating out of your space.

This technique clears out your main energy channel and allows you to start getting nourished from the energy in your environment.

### Technique 12.29. Using Color to Clear Organs

1. For a more focused approach, choose which emotion or emotions you want to address.
2. Next look at the color chart on page 62 to see which colors correspond to clearing each emotion.
3. Use the light breathing techniques on the previous page, substituting the appropriate color for white.
4. Repeat these light breathing techniques a couple of times a day. In about a week, you should see some improvement.

### Technique 12.30. Breathing In Light for Relieving Pain and Discomfort

One of the unfortunate sides of ailments is that they often come with pain and discomfort. This technique can help to alleviate pain by directing light into the area.

1. Place your hands over where you want to direct the light.
2. After you place your hands over your area of discomfort, say your intention: "I choose to release this emotion and anything that it is attached to."
3. You can also use a variation of this to make the statement more general: "I choose to release this (discomfort, pain, nausea, etc.) and anything it is attached to."
4. With your hand over the area, breathe light in through your crown. Envision it traveling through your heart and down your arm to your hand, entering the area of discomfort.
5. As you hold your breath for five to ten seconds, envision the light filling up the area and breaking free all of the energy stored there that is causing the discomfort.
6. Exhale it out fully through your mouth.
7. Since you are dealing with the physical body, it may take some time to alleviate the discomfort.
8. If you feel up to it, look up that body organ or area and see what emotions might be present that could be affecting you.

9. You can call out these emotions specifically with an intention and work through the technique if you feel that the general technique is not enough.

# Talk to Your Body

When you start having physical ailments, your body has been trying to get your attention for a while. Since you didn't notice that energy and emotions were affecting it, your body had to take more severe measures to get your attention. This technique is about letting your body speak for itself. While this takes at least a little intuition, it is worth a shot, especially if it helps you feel better.

**Technique 12.31. Talking to Your Body**

1. To start, we are going to simply envision what you are wanting to open up a dialog with.

Let's say you are having gallbladder issues, such as gallbladder attacks or gallstones. The gallbladder and liver are intimately linked, and the liver typically houses anger, frustration, and rage. Maybe you have already worked on this using techniques from earlier in the book. That's great! This is a different way of addressing it that can shed more light on the emotions and energy that is trapped there by giving it a chance to directly have a voice.

Imagine for a second that something was wrong and you needed to get someone's attention.

Has this ever happened to you? You are trying desperately to get someone to listen to you, but whatever you try doesn't work. Now imagine all of a sudden you got to let it all out and speak your mind after years of being silenced. In this case, that's what you are doing for your liver and gall bladder. You are giving it a voice. You are allowing it to tell you what's wrong.

2. So let's envision your liver with your gallbladder right underneath it.

For other areas of discomfort or ailments, see the body diagram on the following page to help you envision it.

3. Now hold the image of that in your mind.

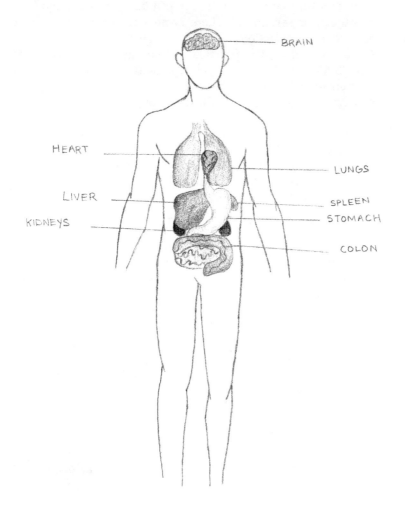

BRAIN

HEART

LUNGS

LIVER

SPLEEN

KIDNEYS

STOMACH

COLON

4.  Next envision a cord that is connected to your liver and gallbladder. This cord allows for the transmission of information, such as visions and pictures, emotions, and words, to all travel between the liver/gallbladder and your mind. This cord allows you to understand what the liver and gallbladder are saying so that you can give it voice.

5.  For the sake of this technique, you will be journaling what you see, feel, hear, and know. The information could come to you in a variety of ways.

6. At first, just write down whatever comes into your mind from that translation cord. It may just be images or memories, emotions, or sensations. There is no right or wrong way to receive the information.

7. Once you get a little practice of tapping into the liver and gallbladder in this way, you will start to have more of a conversational flow with it.

8. You can ask questions directly to it, like:

   - What do you want to say?
   - What is making you ill?
   - What emotional imprints are you storing?
   - What emotions do you need to release?
   - What can I do to help you?
   - What foods do you need me to eat for you to be healthy?

9. You can repeat this process with any ailment, organ in your body, or body system and even cells.

Whatever you are having an issue with, you can give a voice to. Giving your body a chance to speak up can also shift your mindset about your body in general. Your illness is your body trying to communicate with you. It is not against you and is not your enemy. It's trying to tell you, Hey, you need to pay attention to me. It's like a puppy chewing up your shoes. It just wants attention. Once you give it that, things can truly shift for the better.

# Salt Bath

This formula is for helping unlock the emotional states that are affecting you physically. There are other protocols for particular organs, but this general one is good to use in conjunction with emotional releasing for physical ailments. Do not take baths if you have been directed not to by your physician.

2 cups Dead Sea salt
1 cup Epsom salt
3 cups baking soda

Essential oils
10 drops tea tree
15 drops lavender
6 drops ylang ylang

15 drops bergamot
10 drops Roman chamomile
16 drops frankincense
10 drops rose absolute

1. Mix salts and oils together well.
2. You can store what you don't use in a glass jar.
3. When you have a bath, add equal parts baking soda and the salt mixture to your bath, as in 1 cup of salt and essential oil mix and 1 cup of baking soda.

Note: You can mix the baking soda in the salt mixture and store it that way, but it's a gamble. If the salt's moisture content is too high, your mixture will become really hard and be difficult to get out of the jar. That's why I recommend adding the baking soda right before your bath.

### Technique 12.32. Angels That Can Help You Release Emotions for Physical Ailments

Depending on why you have your ailment, the best angel for helping you release it will vary, but all of the ones listed in this section deal with an aspect of life that may be part of the source of your ailment. You can call them in individually or all at once. There is no set way to talk to angels.

1. One way is just to simply hand over your burdens. Say, "Angels, please take the energy/emotion(s) that is/are heavy inside of me and causing me to have (ailment or pain)."
2. You can be more specific and vent what is bothering you to them and ask them to take it as well.
3. You can even write down notes of things to say before you engage with them if that is easier for you.

Angels are there to listen and empower you. All you have to do is ask.

Lighting a candle can also help focus the energy to call in a particular angel. It's not required to use a certain color candle. If all you have is white, that's fine too.

Michael
Candle color: Blue
Specialty: Clearing very heavy or dark energy (in your environment and from others), protection, courage, strength

Gabriel
Candle color: White
Specialty: Helping you process why things have happened; helps
with understanding and interpretation; shifts your perspective

Raphael
Candle color: Green
Specialty: Releasing emotions related to physical ailments, and
physical ailments themselves

Chamuel
Candle color: Pink
Specialty: Forgiveness of self and others, especially in relationships

Jophiel
Candle color: Yellow
Specialty: Decisions; allowing you to sort through things on your own
terms without outside influence

Zadkiel
Candle color: Purple
Specialty: Transformation and forgiveness; helps you let go of the
past; keeps energy moving so you don't block yourself from change.

Uriel
Candle color: Red
Specialty: Helps you look inside to see the truth and release what is
holding you back without judgment

Metatron
Candle color: Green-and-Pink Stripes or Blue
Specialty: Replace negative thoughts with positive ones

# Eat Supportive Foods

This is a very general recommendation, as different physical ailments
have foods you should and should not eat.

Eat nutrient-dense foods that help the body to heal. Bone broths and
stocks are excellent to drink, as they are nutrient-packed and easy on
the body. Add a little Himalayan pink salt if you want. Vegetables
are essential for a healing diet. Many people have trouble digesting
raw vegetables because the state of their gut is compromised. Instead,
consume cooked vegetables. Lower-starch vegetables such as yellow

and zucchini squash, collard greens, broccoli, and cauliflower are easier on the gut and don't contain too much sugar. Lean organic meats are a good choice for protein, such as bison, beef, and chicken. Wild-caught fish, such as salmon, are also good choices. If you want to step it up a bit, get organic, grass-fed meats when available.

Avoid anything with gluten, dairy, grains, sugar, corn, soy, or caffeine. All of these are known to exacerbate chronic conditions, especially autoimmune.

## Use the Right Color

Your color needs are varied, so instead of recommending a set color to use or avoid, I recommend surrounding yourself with the colors that feel good to you if you have a systemic, chronic ailment. For acute ailments, look at the organ chart on pages 78-80 and color chart pages 62-64 to see which colors would support you the most. For instance, if you have a sore throat, putting a blue scarf around your neck is a good choice.

## Fiona Waited Too Long

I approached Fiona several times and asked her if she would like help processing her stuck emotional states. She always told me she wanted to wait until she felt better to do it. She never got the chance.

This was obviously the right path for Fiona, and it was her decision to make. I think of her often and use her story as a motivation to do my own emotional releasing work every day. The great thing about emotional releasing is that it gives you your power back. If you feel helpless or hopeless, it allows you to take control of your life in a new way. The tools in this book can save you a lifetime of pain and suffering. They have done that for me.

## Chapter Challenge

Read through the five protocols for feeling ungrounded (anxiety), negative thought patterns (depression), expressed anger, unexpressed anger, and physical ailments.

Do these protocols apply to you? Why or why not?

Take a baseline for where you are now, then try the protocol for a couple of weeks and see how you feel.

Are you seeing things differently? Do you feel different?

If it's helping, keep going, even if it's just a small improvement.

## Feel Better Five

- Having a Feel Better Plan ahead of time is helpful to clear emotional states when they arise.
- Most people can use one of the protocols in this chapter (or portions of it) for their plan.
- Emotional clearing techniques can be tailored to suit your needs.
- Emotional clearing and physical elements can be combined to increase success of techniques.
- Don't wait to start working on yourself.

## Transform in Five (or Ten)

This chapter is pretty much all techniques, so I will not revisit them here. There are five protocols or sets of techniques and physical elements, given in this chapter. Check out the one you feel applies and try it out.

Ungrounded (for anxiety), pages 218-221

Negative thought patterns (depression), pages 221-233

Expressed anger, pages 236–245

Unexpressed or repressed anger, pages 245-255

Physical ailments, pages 255-266

In the next chapter, you are the master of your own domain. Now that you have an idea of how to form a protocol, you are going to learn the formula for coming up with your own so you can take control and feel better fast on your terms.

# CHAPTER 13

# Design Your Own Feel Better Plan

 I still remember standing backstage in that scratchy purple dress. I'm not even sure why I signed up to be there. I was a tomboy, after all, and it was normally an act of God to get me to wear anything but jeans. But here I was, waiting to go onstage in a beauty pageant.

All of my soccer friends were in it too.

I'm not sure whose idea it was first, but we all followed suit. At soccer practice, our moms sat us all in a circle as we filled out the information for the pageant. My mom must have asked me eighty times if I was sure I wanted to do it.

"You know you have to wear a dress, right?" I nodded. She proceeded to fill out the card with my name, age, and school.

She stopped her pencil and paused, reading the next question. "What do you want to be when you grow up?"

My friend Katie yelled, "Say you want to be a soccer player!" from across the circle.

"Or a ballerina" another friend urged. Wear a dress for a living? No thanks.

I looked up at my mom, "Soccer player!"

"You sure?"

"Yeah!"

My mom proceeded to write it down.

Fast forward one month. As I gracefully stomped onto the stage, everyone clapped politely. I plopped in my seat, legs sprawled out in front of me. The man with the microphone was reading off a card.

"So, you are seven years old, is that right?"

He stuck the microphone in my face. "Yeah, uh-huh."

"Okay, and you go to Clyde Elementary School?"

"Yeah."

"And I see here that you want to be a soccer player when you grow up?"

"No."

The man looked confused. "But don't you want to be a soccer player?"

"No," I said matter-of-factly. "I want to be an artist and live on a farm."

Needless to say, I didn't win the pageant.

Sometimes, you just have to make your own plan. If the protocols in the last chapter didn't really speak to you, that's okay. They aren't for everyone. Making your own plan may be the way to go. It's best to stay simple when doing this, however, otherwise you may get a little overwhelmed by all of the information in this book. So here is a basic way you can make up your own plan easily.

1. Go back through the book and check out the techniques.
2. Highlight the ones that you feel helped you when you tried them out.
3. Pick one or two from each of chapters 4–10. You can rate them 1–5 if that helps you narrow it down. This is your list of favorite techniques.
4. If there is a chapter that didn't really speak to you, for instance, if you are pretty grounded, skip those techniques. If the color thing isn't your jam, don't use it. Remember, this is YOUR plan. Just like you don't put everything at a buffet on your plate, you get to choose the things that you like here, too, and leave the rest.

| Favorite Techniques | | | | When to use | | |
|---|---|---|---|---|---|---|
| Technique # | Technique name | Pg # | Rate 1-5 | In Moment | FB in 5 | FB in 10 |
| | | | | | | |
| | | | | | | |
| | | | | | | |
| | | | | | | |
| | | | | | | |
| | | | | | | |
| | | | | | | |
| | | | | | | |
| | | | | | | |
| | | | | | | |
| | | | | | | |
| | | | | | | |
| | | | | | | |
| Favorite Physical Elements | | | | | | |
| | | | | | | |
| | | | | | | |
| | | | | | | |
| | | | | | | |
| | | | | | | |

| Triggers | |
|---|---|
| Rating | Situation |
| | |
| | |
| | |
| | |
| | |

Biggest Trigger: _____

| Trigger Protocols (refer to list in master chart and pick techniques) | | | | |
|---|---|---|---|---|
| Category | Technique name | Technique # | Page # | Notes |
| In Moment | | | | |
| | | | | |
| | | | | |
| | | | | |
| FB in 5 | | | | |
| | | | | |
| | | | | |
| | | | | |
| FB in 10 | | | | |
| | | | | |
| | | | | |
| | | | | |

| Physical elements | | | | |
|---|---|---|---|---|
| Category | Element name | Technique # | Page # | Notes |
| In Moment | | | | |
| | | | | |
| | | | | |
| FB in 5 | | | | |
| | | | | |
| FB in 10 | | | | |
| | | | | |
| | | | | |

5. Thumb through chapter 11 and see which physical elements you feel benefit you the most.

6. Next, make a list of the techniques with their numbers, for example, "Technique 7.5. Feeling and Releasing a Stuck Emotion." Note the page number from the book for easy reference, or see the reference section.

7. Combine your list of favorite techniques with your favorite physical elements (see chapter 11), and—ta da!—you have your own customized master protocol!

8. Next, look at your master protocol and ask yourself, "What's my biggest trigger?" Is it when you are driving; dealing with your kids, spouse, or boss; taking a test? Rate your triggers on a scale of 1–5. Make a protocol for the biggest trigger first.

9. Now look at your list and break them down into three categories: In the Moment, Feel Better in Five, and Feel Better in Ten.

10. Identify one or more exercises to use in the moment for each situation. You may have one exercise for each of your triggers, or you may have a few. Pick what's right for you.

11. Now choose a few exercises that each take about five minutes. After you practice a bit, you may find you can do two or three of them in your five minutes.
12. Next, make a list of the exercises that take more time. This is where you would put the Feel Better in Ten techniques, such as journaling or taking a salt bath.

By the end, you should have at least four protocols that you can use in your daily life to make it easier.

## Changing It Up Is a Great Idea

When you process emotions and energy, your body can get used to one way of doing things, and after a while, it may not feel as effective. Just like our body needs a variety of exercises and foods to stay optimally strong and healthy, your energy system needs different ways to process out emotional states too. So, this is where you get to use the intuition you have been developing.

If your protocol starts to feel a bit stale or ineffective, try adding in or deleting a technique. Maybe try calling in angels while you take a bath or throw in a grounding technique instead of breathing in color. Play with it. That's why there are so many techniques in the book.

## Chapter Challenge

Set up your own protocol that works for your life and start using it.

Note what you feel is working. Does your protocol work in every situation, or do you need to add and subtract some things?

## Feel Better Five

Making your own protocol allows you to customize your healing process to suit your needs.
Creating a master protocol helps to simplify the process of creating other protocols.
Taking control of your energetic health can be simple and fun.

Changing up your emotional clearing protocol is necessary, just as changing up your diet or exercise is.

Keep an open mind and be creative when crafting your protocol.

# Transform in Five (or Ten)

Use the techniques you grouped together to create protocols for at least two weeks and see how you feel. Don't forget to take a baseline beforehand using the chapter 3 assessment you completed.

Drop me a line at www.amandahainline.com and tell me what protocols you have developed! I'm excited to see how you are using the book.

Keep it going! The next chapter is a reminder that this is a process. You are taking charge. Doesn't it feel good??

CHAPTER 14

# You Got This

I had a session with a lovely college student named June. She came to me because she had severe anxiety and had tried natural means of managing it for years but was at a point where she was considering going on medication. My heart went out to her. I know what that is like and how scary that can be. It's where I was after my awakening and before I learned how to process and release my emotions. We discussed her life situations a great deal, and I offered her some new perspectives on things. This was helpful for her to understand where her anxiety had been coming from. We then worked on releasing her emotions from the traumatic imprints she had in her energy system. I taught her some envisioning and grounding techniques. We went through them several times until she got the hang of them. It helped tremendously.

She later texted me that she had no anxiety whatsoever. This had not happened in years. She was ecstatic.

I was glad to hear this, but I also knew that we had just begun her journey. A few days later, she texted me to tell me her anxiety was back. She was worried that what we did hadn't worked.

When you are working with the energy system and emotions, you have to remember that just as you did not get into the emotional state that you are overnight, it cannot be reversed overnight, either, unfortunately. Releasing emotions from your traumatic and verbal inhibitory imprints is a process. There are often many layers to them and many connections between them. Healing takes time and slowly reveals the true you underneath all of the emotions you have been carrying for so long. But it's important to remember that you aren't broken. There is nothing wrong with YOU. There are just emotions that need to be released from your energy system that are causing you to not be all of who you are: a brilliantly beautiful being with endless potential.

This is precisely what I told June when I texted her back. This is a process, but the fact she felt better after the first session showed she was on the right track.

We scheduled another session and talked through more things she had anxiety about. When we found emotional triggers, I talked her through releasing the emotions, and at times we addressed the imprints directly so that she could learn that technique as well. Again, after the session, she reported being free of anxiety, and now she understands that this is a process. Her beautiful soul is starting to shine.

Hey, I know that life can be tough sometimes. It can downright suck. Carrying emotions around with us that are weighing us down can make it way harder. You weren't meant to carry that mountain. You were meant to climb it. So let go. Release those emotions that are holding you back. When you do, nothing in this world can stop you from being everything you were meant to be. By doing the techniques in this book, you are light-years ahead of everyone else. You are finally taking control of your life.

Here's to you Feeling Better in Five Minutes.

# Congratulations

 I would love to hear what you think of this book. Send me a message at amandahainline.com, on Instagram @ akhainline, or to Amanda Hainline on Facebook.

 If you loved the book, it helped you, and want to show some love, you are the best human ever! Click on this QR code to write an Amazon review. I appreciate you!

# Reference Section

 In this section, you will find each emotion listed with a brief narrative on how the emotion may show up in your life and what part of your energy system can be affected. It also gives you an idea of where to start working with the emotion to release it and lists related emotions for you to explore that may be related. In addition, the related colors to use, organs, essential oils, crystals, and archangels for each emotion are compiled here from all of the charts in the book so that you can refer to them all in one place. It prevents you from having to flip through the whole book to figure it out. Note that when looking at a chart, you can mix and match the items in each category. For instance, when looking at the first chart for Abandoned, you **do not** have to use everything on one row such as Red, Pancreas, Lavender, Rose quartz and Michael. You can use the color Red with any organ, such as Adrenal, any Essential oil such as Eucalyptus, any Crystal/Stone such as Tourmaline or any Archangel such as Michael.

It is also not necessary to use one item for each category if you do not want to. You can choose to just work with a color and an essential oil for example. The combinations are flexible and endless. Use what works for you.

The idea is that you can create a customized mini protocol for working with one particular emotion.

## How to create a protocol for one emotion

- Pick one emotion to work on, such as Abandoned.
- Choose your favorite emotional release technique or techniques in the book.
- If these are techniques that require a color, organ or Archangel be used, refer to the chart under your chosen emotion to complete the technique. (For example, if it is the technique 8.4, Breathing in Color, you would refer to the chart and use one of the colors listed. For Abandoned, you would use either Red or Orange in the technique.)
- Next, look at the list of items in each column on the chart under the emotion you chose and pick the physical elements items you feel would help you. Refer to each physical element in Chapter 11 on how to best utilize the element.

This section is meant to be a reference to help you figure out which emotions may be driving your life (or someone else's) that you don't even realize. So check it out and see what resonates with you.

# Abandoned

When we think of abandonment, we often think of being physically abandoned, but one can be emotionally abandoned as well. This can occur if a parent or caregiver is emotionally unavailable. Maybe they are too busy or depressed. Abandonment can even occur in utero if a child is an unwanted pregnancy or if the mother has had other miscarriages before the baby and detaches to emotionally protect herself. The mother can energetically and emotionally detach from the child during pregnancy. This sets up energetic patterns of abandonment in the baby and causes the inherent wiring of the baby being ungrounded. Abandonment is one of the trickier emotions to deal with, because the fear of being rejected often causes someone with this imprint to isolate themselves from others or push others away to avoid being abandoned. Patterns of self-sabotage in relationships are very common with this emotion. Working on the related traumatic and verbal inhibitory imprints is necessary to move through this emotion and change the pattern. Other emotions that may be present in the imprint are fearful, flawed, sad, unworthy, unloved, ungrounded, and unsafe.

| Colors to Use | Organs | Essential Oils | Crystals/ Stones | Archangels |
|---|---|---|---|---|
| Red Orange | Pancreas Bladder/ Kidney/ Adrenal Brain/ Head | Lavender Eucalyptus Sandalwood Rose absolute | Rose quartz Bloodstone Smoky quartz Tourmaline | Michael Gabriel Chamuel Zadkiel Uriel Metatron Sandalphon Barachiel |

# Aggressive

Aggressive can mean acts of physical aggression, such as physical abuse, but often means acts of verbal aggression. People that carry this emotion long-term tend to seek out conflict. It might have been modeled to them as a child by a parent, or they may have been bullied early on. When modeled by a parent, the person with this emotion probably has it transposed with love. In their energy system and mind, love and conflict go hand in hand. This causes problems in relationships with those closest to them.

Aggression can also come from a place of survival. Having this emotion may have been the only way they knew to stay alive or to get ahead. Other people tend to be wired like this from the start, even if it is not modeled to them. In this case, it is most likely carried over energetically from another family member, such as a grandparent, aunt, or uncle.

If it was modeled to them, thinking about the earliest instances of these events can help to isolate the imprints in which the energy exists. If it is something that is carried over from another family member and not modeled, this can be a little trickier. Asking your energy system to release the energy and emotions you have taken on from other people is the best approach. Related emotions to aggression are anger, controlling, critical, defensive, distrust, rage, sad, and unworthy.

| Colors to Use | Organs | Essential Oils | Crystals/ Stones | Archangels |
|---|---|---|---|---|
| Blue Green | Liver/Gall-bladder Pancreas Heart | Peppermint Ylang ylang Bergamot Frankincense Sandalwood Rose absolute | Rose quartz Bloodstone Smoky quartz | Gabriel Chamuel Zadkiel Uriel Metatron Sandalphon Barachiel |

# Anger

Similar to aggression, anger is often a learned behavior. One can also have a propensity to anger easily. When this is combined with having a parent that models anger, this emotion and its responses can be very deeply ingrained, since anger and love are then transposed together. This can make close relationships difficult. Working on the related traumatic and verbal inhibitory imprints can help to shift this behavior. Releasing energy that has been taken on from other people is also helpful, particularly those related to aggression and anger. Related emotions are aggression, betrayed, controlling, critical, defensive, fearful, and ungrounded.

| Colors to Use | Organs | Essential Oils | Crystals/ Stones | Archangels |
|---|---|---|---|---|
| Blue Green | Liver/ Gallbladder Throat Pancreas | Lavender Eucalyptus Ylang ylang Bergamot Frankincense Sandalwood Rose abso- lute | Rose quartz Bloodstone Amethyst Smoky quartz Tourmaline | Gabriel Raphael Chamuel Jophiel Zadkiel Uriel Metatron Sandalphon Barachiel |

## Anxious

Anxiousness is often coupled with some type of abandonment at some point in a person's life. People with anxiety tend to live in their head, trying to process all of their energy with their upper chakras, since their lower chakras are in a state of arrest. This inherently ungrounded state leads to overthinking, with very little resolve. Through working on grounding, the energy in their system can gain balance, creating greater emotional stability and a clearer mind to problem-solve with. Exploring the imprints related to anxiety and releasing the emotions from them can start to alleviate the chronic feeling that things will go wrong all the time. Related emotions can be confusion, controlling, dramatic, fearful, hopeless, insecure, negative, overstimulated, and sad.

| Colors to Use | Organs | Essential Oils | Crystals/ Stones | Archangels |
|---|---|---|---|---|
| Blue Green | Liver/Gall- bladder Stomach Feet Bladder/ Kidney/ Adrenal Intestines | Peppermint Lavender Eucalyptus Bergamot Frankincense Sandalwood Rose absolute | Rose quartz Bloodstone Amethyst Smoky quartz Tourmaline | Gabriel Raphael Chamuel Zadkiel Uriel Metatron Sandalphon Barachiel |

## Betrayed

Experiencing betrayal can make trust difficult. Betrayal can take many forms, such as being cheated on in a relationship or someone taking advantage of you in some way. Betrayal can also occur in conjunction with abandonment if a child is left by a parent or if one parent cheats on the other parent. The child may feel betrayed by the cheating parent. People who experience betrayal of some sort early in life (such as one parent cheats on the other) have a higher likelihood of experiencing betrayal in their intimate relationships as adults. It's important to note that betrayal is very much an emotion that plays into the victim consciousness, which can make it tricky to release. Calling out and releasing the victim consciousness when working with the emotion of betrayal can help unravel this emotion from the imprints in the energy system. Related emotions are anger, distrust, embarrassed, grief, insecurity, powerless, rage, resentful, sad, and unsafe.

| Colors to Use | Organs | Essential Oils | Crystals/ Stones | Archangels |
|---|---|---|---|---|
| Green Light Pink | Liver/Gall-bladder Heart Pancreas | Lavender Tea tree Sandalwood Rose absolute | Rose quartz Smoky quartz Tourmaline | Michael Gabriel Chamuel Jophiel Zadkiel Uriel Metatron Barachiel |

# Confused

Some people have trouble operating in the world. They spend a lot of their time trying to figure out the environment they are in and the people around them. These people tend to be wired differently from other people and just don't seem to "click" with others. They struggle to relate and are confused a lot of the time.

Confusion can also be a state of mind when one has trouble making decisions. This often occurs when one has too many people trying to give them advice on what to do in a situation. It can also occur when your head is telling you one thing and your heart is telling you another. This is where tapping into your soul and journaling can be really helpful. For people that struggle to operate in the world, this can just be how they are wired, but working on grounding can help, as well as working on the emotions related to confusion. If making decisions is the issue, weak boundaries can be a big contributor. The person is a people pleaser, and choosing one person's advice over another can be stressful, since they want to avoid conflict. Working on their traumatic and verbal inhibitory imprints that deal with people-pleasing, such as imprints that involve appeasing a volatile parent, is a good start. Related emotions are abandoned, anxious, embarrassed, fearful, guilt, imperceptive, overwhelmed, and unclear.

| Colors to Use | Organs | Essential Oils | Crystals/ Stones | Archangels |
|---|---|---|---|---|
| Blue Yellow Indigo | Brain/Head Stomach Bladder/Kidney/Adrenal | Peppermint Lavender Ylang ylang Bergamot Rom. chamomile Frankincense Patchouli Rose absolute | Rose quartz Bloodstone Amethyst Smoky quartz | Michael Gabriel Zadkiel Uriel Metatron Barachiel |

# Controlling

When one is controlling, it is often coupled with other emotions, causing it to manifest. Some people feel the need for control because they have underlying anxiety or nervousness running the show. Others tend to feel out of control inside themselves and therefore try to control others and the world around them to feel at peace. This is sometimes taken a step further and gets combined with narcissism. While not really discussed in this book, narcissists can be extremely controlling, to the point of complete detriment to those that are close to them in their lives.

Those that experience underlying nervousness, fear, or anxiety can learn to repattern themselves by releasing the underlying imprints and emotions in conjunction with control. Related emotions are abandoned, anger, anxious, betrayed, critical, fearful, hopeless, jealous, overbearing, powerless, and stress.

| Colors to Use | Organs | Essential Oils | Crystals/ Stones | Archangels |
|---|---|---|---|---|
| Indigo | Liver/Gallbladder Throat Knees | Tea tree Lavender Ylang ylang Bergamot Rom. chamomile Sandalwood Rose absolute | Amethyst | Gabriel Zadkiel Uriel Metatron Barachiel |

# Critical

People with a critical nature tend to judge others with overreaching opinions. A critical nature is one that is overly harsh and usually stems from that person being very hard on themselves inwardly. Critical people are uncomfortable inside, so they tend to project that judgment harshly onto others. This is not to be confused with giving someone constructive criticism to help them improve something, such as a theatrical performance or an essay, for example. A critical person doesn't offer ways to improve anything; it is just a practice of tearing others down. To address this, the critical person needs to work on the deep wounds that are underlying this tendency. Being critical can be a defense mechanism that is often coupled with imprints of abandonment and other types of abuse. It can also be the way the person is wired, and life events have exacerbated the tendency. Related emotions can be abandoned, anger, controlling, fearful, insecure, rage, selfish, unforgiving, and unloved.

| Colors to Use | Organs | Essential Oils | Crystals/ Stones | Archangels |
|---|---|---|---|---|
| Green | Brain/Head Heart Liver/Gall- bladder Pancreas Bladder/ Kidney/ Adrenal Spleen Feet | Tea tree Lavender Sandalwood Rose absolute | Amethyst | Gabriel Zadkiel Uriel Metatron Sandalphon Barachiel |

# Defensive

Defensiveness and being critical often go hand in hand and are not mutually exclusive. People who are defensive have a soft underbelly, and their feelings are hurt easily. They often feel as if they are being attacked, even if a person is not ill-meaning toward them. Just as anxiety is a side product of being ungrounded, defensiveness falls in the same category. When people are triggered into a defensive place, they pull up their roots and attack back, defend, or overexplain themselves. A common misconception a defensive person has is that they are being yelled at, when the other person has not even raised their voice. This misconception often comes from verbal trauma the person has experienced in their life, and this emotion is often found in people with anxiety. It can also come from traumatic imprints in the person's energy system. Releasing defensiveness and related emotions can help to shift the pattern of defensiveness and help them to communicate better. Related emotions are critical, dramatic, fearful, flawed, manipulative, overwhelmed, ungrounded, unsafe, and unworthy.

| Colors to Use | Organs | Essential Oils | Crystals/ Stones | Archangels |
|---|---|---|---|---|
| Green | Brain/Head Heart Liver/Gall-bladder Pancreas Bladder/ Kidney/ Adrenal Spleen | Lavender Ylang ylang Bergamot Rom. chamo-mile Frankincense Patchouli Rose absolute | Amethyst Tourmaline | Michael Gabriel Chamuel Jophiel Zadkiel Uriel Metatron Sandalphon Barachiel |

# Depressed

Depression is a complicated emotion with many facets. Depression is often misunderstood as a feeling of just sadness, but it is more than that. People with depression experience high levels of apathy. They often think, "What's the point?" as in, what's the point of getting dressed, seeing people, going to work, etc.? It's like they are in a dark hole and can't see anything but how they feel. Oftentimes they "have a great life" and are confused by the way they feel and are ashamed, which further arrests the body and energy system. To the outside observer, the person looks lazy, selfish, and self-loathing. It can be frustrating for the person living with the depressed person because it can be hard to understand them.

There is a chemical component to depression that is often addressed with medication, but oftentimes there are other crucial components that are missed. Diet and gut health can play a large role in depression. Eating things that are high in sugar feeds bad bacteria, viruses, and fungus in the gut that exacerbate anxiety and depression. Ninety-five percent of the hormone serotonin, which regulates your mood and happiness, is produced in your gut. Eating healthy and taking probiotics increases the presence of this hormone in your body and brain. This change can boost mood significantly.

In addition, energetic health is a huge component that is not addressed. In a depressed person, there is a high level of energy system arrest.

Nothing is moving. This shutdown can start from traumas and verbal abuse when the person is young and gets exacerbated over the lifetime. Depression often runs in families, so there can be genetic predispositions, as well as learned behavior components. By addressing the energy system and getting things moving, depression can start to shift on a fundamental level, making lifestyle changes easier. Starting with simple stretches and breathing in light to release energetic congestion is a gentle way to begin. After the person feels a bit better, they can move on to addressing their energetic imprints that caused the energetic arrest. Working on related emotions is also key to lifting depression. Some of them are abandoned, angry, grief, guilt, hopeless, lonely, overwhelmed, sad, unloved, and unworthy.

| Colors to Use | Organs | Essential Oils | Crystals/ Stones | Archan- gels |
|---|---|---|---|---|
| Yellow | Brain/Head Throat Heart Liver/Gall- bladder Lungs Bladder/ Kidney/ Adrenal Stomach Knees | Peppermint Tea tree Lavender Eucalyptus Ylang ylang Bergamot Rom. chamomile Frankincense Sandalwood Rose absolute | Bloodstone Amethyst Smoky quartz Tourmaline | Michael Gabriel Raphael Chamuel Jophiel Zadkiel Uriel Metatron Sandal- phon Barachiel |

# Detached

This emotion can go hand in hand with depression, but it can exist on its own in a person's energy system. While being detached to a degree is actually a healthy thing, such as the ability to not try to control everything in your life, the detachment we are talking about can actually be detrimental. Overly detached people are ungrounded by nature and tend to "float away" rather than deal with things in their life. They tend to let bills go unpaid, neglect fixing things such as car repairs, and avoid conflict at all costs. When things get tough, they check out. Energetically, people with detachment have developed this defense mechanism because they are not fully in their bodies. They originally had a wiring of being ungrounded, and traumas over their lifetime caused them to develop the habit of "checking out." They freeze or glaze over instead of losing control. This type of person often has a great deal of repressed anger and doesn't even realize it. By training themselves to be grounded and clearing out the repressed anger and other stuffed emotions, they can start to lead a more productive life. Related emotions can be anger, anxious, depressed, fearful, hopeless, indecisive, overwhelmed, powerless, and stifled .

| Colors to Use | Organs | Essential Oils | Crystals/ Stones | Archangels |
|---|---|---|---|---|
| Red Orange Yellow | Lungs Intestines Pancreas Bladder/ Kidney/ Adrenal | Peppermint Tea tree Ylang ylang Bergamot Patchouli Sandalwood Rose absolute | Bloodstone Smoky quartz Tourmaline | Michael Gabriel Zadkiel Uriel Metatron Sandalphon Barachiel |

# Discomfort (Not Physical)

While there are levels of physical discomfort, some people are just not comfortable in general. This is usually due to their sensitivity, both emotionally and energetically. They may have a great deal of things in their life that make them uncomfortable, whether that be conflict, noise, lights, or fabric. There are physical components to these, but there are energetic and emotional components as well. The discomfort they feel can be part of their empathic ability or the fact that their physical body is not a comfortable place for them on an energetic level. Their energy system most likely contains a great deal of stuck emotions that get triggered easily. They usually have difficulty being grounded, but oftentimes, working on grounding makes them more uncomfortable. This is when working on the other stored emotions is key. Digging in and addressing emotions such as anger, anxious, fearful, overstimulated, overwhelmed, and unworthy can help them get to the point that they are more comfortable and grounding is possible.

| Colors to Use | Organs | Essential Oils | Crystals/ Stones | Archangels |
|---|---|---|---|---|
| Green Orange | Heart Lungs Bladder/ Kidney/ Adrenal | Peppermint Lavender Ylang ylang Bergamot Rom. chamomile Sandalwood Rose absolute | Bloodstone Amethyst Smoky quartz | Michael Raphael Zadkiel Uriel Metatron Sandalphon Barachiel |

# Disorganized

Being disorganized is often misunderstood as being messy, sloppy, or lazy. Oftentimes, people who are disorganized really want to be organized, but while their intentions are good, in the long run, they end up with a mess again. Disorganization may have been modeled to them growing up, or they might be inherently wired that way. Trying to change this can bring a great deal of shame and frustration to them.

While some systems of organization can be effective, starting with a system is a long road.

When someone is disorganized, they tend to be ungrounded as well. Their lower chakras (root and sacral) are not highly developed in most cases, leaving all of the functions in their life to the upper chakras, which are meant more for mental tasks and divine connection. This is where addressing groundedness can really help. Being more grounded helps to develop the lower chakras, and it is easier for them to put systems in place to be organized. Other emotions that can arrest the lower chakras, such as abandoned, fearful, flawed, hopeless, insecure, overwhelmed, and unclear, should be addressed, along with the traumatic and verbal inhibitory imprints that are blocking those chakras.

| Colors to Use | Organs | Essential Oils | Crystals/ Stones | Archangels |
|---|---|---|---|---|
| Blue | Brain/Head Throat Bladder/ Kidney/ Adrenal Pancreas | Peppermint Ylang ylang Bergamot Sandalwood Rose absolute | Bloodstone Smoky quartz Tourmaline | Michael Chamuel Zadkiel Uriel Metatron Barachiel |

# Distrust

Distrust is generally a learned behavior and not one that is inherently wired into someone. It comes from life experience where a person, place, or thing brought some sort of harm or discomfort to the person and that experience has become an imprint. People who are distrusting tend to generalize their distrust, such as "All roller coasters are dangerous" or "All men are no good." This generalization is where their experience that created the distrust really starts to cripple their life. By addressing the emotions accompanying distrust, one can start to release this emotion and shift their life. Distrust is usually accompanied by other emotions such as abandoned, anger, betrayed, critical, fearful, flawed, and resentful.

| Colors to Use | Organs | Essential Oils | Crystals/ Stones | Archangels |
|---|---|---|---|---|
| Blue Green | Heart Intestines Stomach Liver/Gall-bladder Pancreas Bladder/ Kidney/ Adrenal Feet | Tea tree Lavender Ylang ylang Bergamot Rom. chamo-mile Patchouli Sandalwood Rose absolute | Bloodstone Amethyst Smoky quartz Tourmaline | Michael Chamuel Jophiel Zadkiel Uriel Metatron Barachiel |

# Dramatic

Being dramatic tends to be a trait that is hardwired but can be exacerbated by life events. Like tends to attract like, and with the emotion of drama, one tends to create or attract it into their life if they are carrying this vibration. In general, people who are dramatic are inherently ungrounded, with underdeveloped lower chakras. They tend to overreact to situations. The drama can manifest as fear, anxiety, anger, crying, or overly harsh self-criticism. People who are overly dramatic do not feel good about themselves. They tend to feel like they don't fit in or have been cast aside. The drama helps to draw attention to them, which can feel good. These actions are often subconscious in nature. People who carry drama often had trauma early on, such as abandonment. By addressing the underlying imprints and practicing being grounded, one can move through and release the emotion of drama. Related emotions are abandoned, aggressive, anger, betrayed, controlling, critical, distrust, fearful, grief, and hyperactive.

| Colors to Use | Organs | Essential Oils | Crystals/Stones | Archangels |
|---|---|---|---|---|
| Blue<br>Green | Brain/Head<br>Lungs<br>Stomach<br>Intestines<br>Liver/Gall-<br>bladder<br>Pancreas<br>Spleen<br>Bladder/<br>Kidney/<br>Adrenal<br>Knees<br>Feet | Peppermint<br>Tea tree<br>Lavender<br>Eucalyptus<br>Ylang ylang<br>Bergamot<br>Patchouli<br>Sandalwood<br>Rose absolute | Bloodstone<br>Amethyst<br>Smoky<br>quartz<br>Tourmaline | Michael<br>Gabriel<br>Raphael<br>Chamuel<br>Jophiel<br>Zadkiel<br>Uriel<br>Metatron<br>Sandalphon<br>Barachiel |

# Embarrassed

Being embarrassed is usually a fleeting emotion, but for some people, it can be something they carry around all the time. This usually occurs when they are uncomfortable with themselves or something in their life. Maybe they do not like the way they look, or they feel embarrassed about their lifestyle, income level, or people they know or are related to. Releasing the emotion of embarrassment and coming to a place of acceptance of where you are brings all of your power to the present so that you can start to change their circumstances. The belief and emotion of embarrassment can be powerful and crippling. Loving and accepting yourself and others allows you to move through and release embarrassment and the accompanying emotions. This emotion is often accompanied by flawed, hopeless, overwhelmed, powerless, shame, or withdrawn.

| Colors to Use | Organs | Essential Oils | Crystals/Stones | Archangels |
|---|---|---|---|---|
| Indigo | Stomach<br>Bladder/<br>Kidney/<br>Adrenal | Peppermint<br>Tea tree<br>Eucalyptus<br>Ylang ylang<br>Bergamot<br>Rom. chamo-<br>mile<br>Patchouli<br>Sandalwood<br>Rose absolute | Bloodstone<br>Amethyst<br>Tourmaline | Michael<br>Gabriel<br>Raphael<br>Jophiel<br>Zadkiel<br>Uriel<br>Metatron<br>Sandalphon<br>Barachiel |

# Fearful

This is one of the most common emotions people experience and can be the most crippling, since it can arrest just about any part of the energy system. It can occur in conjunction with pretty much any other emotion, so whatever emotion you are working on releasing, tacking on "I choose to release the fear of (emotion)" when you are doing emotional release work is the key to letting go of all of it. Fear occurs for a variety of reasons. It can be based on past life experiences or things that we see other people experience. It can also be an inherent fear that is passed down.

We can have fear of failure, and we can have fear of success, fear of spiders and heights and fear of losing a loved one. It can take many forms, and biologically speaking, it exists to keep us safe. But all in all, fear is generally limiting. Our fears set us up to be stuck where we are and prevent us from moving forward. By releasing fear, we can move into new spaces in our lives. The truth is, most of what we are afraid of never happens, and if it does, it isn't nearly as bad as we thought it would be.

| Colors to Use | Organs | Essential Oils | Crystals/ Stones | Archangels |
|---|---|---|---|---|
| Red Orange Violet | Brain/Head Heart Intestines Stomach Bladder/ Kidney/ Adrenals Knees Feet | Peppermint Lavender Eucalyptus Ylang ylang Rom. chamo- mile Frankincense Patchouli Rose absolute | Bloodstone Smoky quartz | Michael Gabriel Jophiel Zadkiel Uriel Metatron Sandalphon Barachiel |

# Flawed

Us humans can be hard on ourselves. The feeling of being flawed is akin to not feeling good enough. This belief can come from our habit of comparing ourselves to others, but if we carry this emotion, it most often stems from childhood. Feeling flawed can arrest the energy system in several places, just like fear does. By remembering the first instances of feeling flawed and working on the imprints of that feeling, one can start shifting to a better place. If you are working on this emotion, also consider working on abandoned, controlling, fearful, defensive, insecure, lonely, and unloved. These emotions often accompany feeling flawed. Releasing these emotions can help you come to a place of self-love and acceptance.

| Colors to Use | Organs | Essential Oils | Crystals/ Stones | Archangels |
|---|---|---|---|---|
| Indigo | Stomach Bladder/ Kidney/ Adrenal | Peppermint Tea tree Eucalyptus Ylang ylang Bergamot Rom. chamomile Patchouli Sandalwood Rose absolute | Bloodstone Amethyst Tourmaline | Michael Gabriel Raphael Jophiel Zadkiel Uriel Metatron Sandalphon Barachiel |

# Grief

Grief is a complicated emotion with many stages and layers. The basic stages are denial, anger, bargaining, depression, and acceptance. A person doesn't necessarily experience the emotions in that order and can bounce back and forth between different emotional states even after the stage of acceptance is reached. We most often associate grief with the loss of a loved one, but stages of grief can be experienced for any type of loss. Loss of a relationship or job, moving to a new place, or shedding old layers of ourselves. With all of these losses, there is a portion of our identities that are wrapped up in each of these. This can feel like we are losing a part of ourselves, so it is a double grieving process. Energetically, the connections we have to what we have lost get severed and have to be dissolved or transmuted (changed) for us to move to a place of acceptance. This takes time, but releasing emotions as they come up can help us to get there faster and with less heartache. Related emotions to grief are abandoned, anger, anxious, confused, depressed, fearful, guilt, hopeless, overwhelmed, and sad.

| Colors to Use | Organs | Essential Oils | Crystals/ Stones | Archangels |
|---|---|---|---|---|
| White | Lungs<br>Throat<br>Heart<br>Stomach<br>Pancreas | Tea tree<br>Lavender<br>Ylang ylang<br>Bergamot<br>Rom. chamo-<br>mile<br>Rose absolute | Rose quartz<br>Amethyst<br>Smoky<br>quartz | Michael<br>Raphael<br>Chamuel<br>Jophiel<br>Zadkiel<br>Uriel<br>Metatron<br>Sandalphon<br>Barachiel |

## Guilt

Feeling guilty can be a heavy load to bear. Guilt happens when we feel responsible for bringing harm to someone (including ourselves) or something else in some way. This emotion is one that does not hide quietly. Guilt is usually one that resurfaces frequently and replays often in the conscious and subconscious mind. It tends to gnaw at us until we resolve it and can cause physical illness or injury in rather short order if it goes unaddressed. If guilt can be resolved by talking something out with the person we feel we have wronged, this can be a way to release this emotion and start the process of forgiveness, both for ourselves and from the person we wronged. Sometimes, though, it is not possible, such as if someone passed away before we had a chance to talk things over with them. In this case, guilt can be resolved by talking or saying a prayer to the person we wronged and asking for forgiveness. They can still hear us even if they are not incarnate anymore. Next, we have to work on releasing the emotion from ourselves by using the techniques in the book and by also releasing related emotions such as anger, anxious, grief, resentful, sad, and shame. Next, we need to call in forgiveness to take its place. Most of us don't mean to hurt someone else. It's important to forgive ourselves when this happens.

| Colors to Use | Organs | Essential Oils | Crystals/ Stones | Archangels |
|---|---|---|---|---|
| Green | Heart Stomach Liver/Gall-bladder | Tea tree Lavender Ylang ylang Rom. chamo-mile Rose absolute | Rose quartz Amethyst Smoky quartz | Michael Gabriel Raphael Chamuel Jophiel Zadkiel Uriel Metatron Barachiel |

# Hopeless

While some people are wired for depressive states like this, hopelessness tends to be the emotion that takes place when we feel that we have no other options in a situation. We may have thought through everything and don't see another way out. Typically, there is a block in our energy system located near our crown or third eye chakra that is keeping us from seeing the solution. By releasing hopelessness and related emotions that may apply, such as anxious, betrayed, confusion, depressed, fearful, and powerless, one can start to remove the blocks that are keeping you from seeing other solutions to the problem.

| Colors to Use | Organs | Essential Oils | Crystals/ Stones | Archangels |
|---|---|---|---|---|
| Green Orange | Heart Lungs Bladder/ Kidney/ Adrenal Knees | Peppermint Tea tree Lavender Eucalyptus Ylang ylang Bergamot Sandalwood Rose absolute | Rose quartz Amethyst Smoky quartz | Michael Gabriel Raphael Chamuel Jophiel Zadkiel Uriel Metatron Sandalphon Barachiel |

# Hyperactive

When we think of hyperactive, we may think of kids bouncing off the walls, but adults can have hyperactivity too. In general, by the time adulthood comes around, the person has learned to have control of their bodies more, and they are mainly hyperactive in their mind.

Hyperactivity can be caused by a few things, and one of those is diet. If the person has a diet high in carbohydrates, sugars, caffeine, and other food additives, this can exacerbate the condition. Eating foods that are lower in carbohydrates and eating good fats, such as avocados, coconut oil, and animal protein, can help to regulate the physical body and energy system to keep the hyperactivity at a lower level. For people with hyperactivity, grounding is very important. They tend to hold their energy in their heads, causing their minds to overload. By practicing grounding, all of the energy they have can be channeled throughout the body instead, allowing it to nourish all of the chakras and balancing their function. Children who are taught to ground or allowed to get their energy moving by running around and exercising can listen for longer periods of time because the energy they are using to focus can be distributed evenly versus being crammed into their heads with nowhere to go.

When working on releasing the emotion of hyperactivity, also consider working with the emotions of abandoned, aggressive, anger, discomfort, disorganized, dramatic, flawed, imbalance, impulsive, and overstimulated.

| Colors to Use | Organs | Essential Oils | Crystals/ Stones | Archangels |
|---|---|---|---|---|
| Blue Indigo Violet | Brain/Head Throat Spleen Intestines Liver/Gall-bladder Pancreas Bladder/ Kidney/ Adrenal | Peppermint Rom. chamo-mile Rose absolute | Smoky quartz | Chamuel Jophiel Zadkiel Uriel Metatron Barachiel |

# Imbalanced

The feeling of imbalance can be nutritional, but in this case, we are talking about the energy system. Sometimes, you just feel off or out of whack. If there are other emotions that need to be released, those can be worked on directly first, as this is usually the reason for this feeling.

If you can tell where you feel imbalance, you can breathe white light into the area to clear out the congested energy there, setting the intention to let go of any imbalance that you have.

Another reason for the feeling of imbalance is when we put too much energy into one thing, such as too much energy into our jobs. When we focus too much on one area of our lives, other areas suffer. This sort of imbalance can happen without us realizing it. New moms tend to neglect the nurture of themselves and their unique expression. This can leave them feeling depressed. If you find yourself in a bad mood often and are stressed out, think about the balance you have in areas of your life. Was this imbalance modeled to you in some way by a parent or by society? If so, think about these occurrences and work on the related emotional imprints. Other emotions that can accompany imbalance are anger, guilt, hopeless, indecisive, overstimulated, overwhelmed, resentful, sad, unable to express self, and ungrounded.

| Colors to Use | Organs | Essential Oils | Crystals/ Stones | Archangels |
|---|---|---|---|---|
| Green Indigo | Throat Lungs Pancreas Bladder/ Kidney/ Adrenal Knees | Peppermint Tea tree Lavender Eucalyptus Ylang ylang Bergamot Rom. chamomile Frankincense Patchouli Sandalwood Rose absolute | Rose quartz Bloodstone Smoky quartz | Michael Chamuel Jophiel Zadkiel Uriel Metatron Barachiel |

# Imperceptive

Being imperceptive is not a negative emotion per se, but being wired this way can be frustrating and limiting. When a person is imperceptive, it can make it difficult to read other people's body language or read between the lines in conversation or written communication. Things get missed, and the person that is imperceptive may be perceived as airheaded or awkward. People that are diagnosed with spectrum disorders (autism, ADHD, or sensory disorders) often struggle with this dynamic. It can lead to them being taken advantage of or left on the outside of things.

From an energetic perspective, one can work on being more perceptive by working on grounding. This can help you to clue in more to your surroundings. In addition, releasing emotions that are a result of being imperceptive, such as anger, confused, embarrassed, overwhelmed, and sad, can help to gain a level of acceptance for oneself, and in turn this enables you to be more grounded. Being more perceptive can be learned through taking classes on reading body language and a mere openness to learn the nuances of how other people operate. When the judgment of self is removed, one can open up to understanding that this is a skill to be learned, just like math.

| Colors to Use | Organs | Essential Oils | Crystals/ Stones | Archangels |
|---|---|---|---|---|
| Indigo | Brain/Head Bladder/ Kidney/ Adrenal | Tea tree Ylang ylang Rom. chamo- mile Frankincense Patchouli Sandalwood Rose absolute | Bloodstone Smoky quartz | Michael Gabriel Raphael Chamuel Jophiel Zadkiel Uriel Metatron Barachiel |

# Impulsive

General impulsivity often goes hand in hand with hyperactivity, but it can exist alone. Someone who is impulsive tends to act without thinking or being highly reactive to situations. Working on grounding is very helpful for people who are impulsive, as well as limiting caffeine, sugar, or other stimulants, since this keeps you in an ungrounded state.

People who are impulsive across the board are generally just wired that way, while others may only be impulsive in certain situations. If the impulsivity is situational and is set off by a trigger, one needs to explore where the trigger comes from and address the root imprint of the trigger, as well as the emotions that are housed there. Grounding is super helpful for situational impulsivity, too, as being triggered causes the energy system to pull up its roots in a fight-or-flight response. Emotions that may be related to impulsivity are abandoned, anger, anxious, defensive, fearful, hyperactive, overwhelmed, stressed, ungrounded, and unsafe.

| Colors to Use | Organs | Essential Oils | Crystals/ Stones | Archangels |
|---|---|---|---|---|
| Green Blue | Brain/Head Heart Stomach Intestines Liver/Gall-bladder Pancreas Knees | Peppermint Tea tree Lavender Rom. chamo-mile Frankincense Patchouli Sandalwood Rose absolute | Rose quartz Bloodstone Amethyst Smoky quartz | Michael Gabriel Raphael Chamuel Jophiel Zadkiel Uriel Metatron Sandalphon Barachiel |

# Indecisive

All of us have trouble making decisions sometimes, but some people have a chronic issue with being indecisive. At their core, they do not trust themselves to make good choices and have weak boundaries energetically. These people are often people pleasers and want to avoid conflict at all costs. They tend to hold their decisions with an absolute finality, as if they can't change their mind once they have decided on something. This can cripple them into making no decision at all. In another light, some indecisive people tend to be perfectionists, which in itself is crippling. Since they want to do everything perfectly and are afraid of making mistakes, it often keeps them from moving forward in life. Changing this pattern takes time, but it starts by focusing inward and getting in touch with the self. Learning to trust that you know what is best for you can start you on the path to being more decisive. Working on releasing the emotion of indecisiveness, as well as related emotions of anxious, confusion, critical, embarrassed, fearful, flawed, overwhelmed, and powerless, can help to set one on the track to overcoming indecisiveness.

| Colors to Use | Organs | Essential Oils | Crystals/ Stones | Archangels |
|---|---|---|---|---|
| Blue Orange Yellow | Brain/Head Heart Lungs Stomach Bladder/ Kidney/ Adrenal Feet | Peppermint Tea tree Lavender Rom. chamo-mile Patchouli Sandalwood Rose absolute | Rose quartz Bloodstone Smoky quartz | Michael Gabriel Raphael Jophiel Zadkiel Uriel Metatron Barachiel |

# Indulgence

We all want to indulge once in a while, but some people have a habit of doing it too often. They do things in excess on the regular, like, eat, shop, or binge on sugar, alcohol, or drugs. This isn't necessarily addiction but can still be detrimental. When someone is overindulgent, it is because they are feeling empty inside. "Treating themselves" to make themselves feel better is a way of coping with other things in their life that aren't working. This could be a difficult relationship or job, or they could just feel empty and bad inside and are trying to shift themselves. The indulgence often backfires, though, leaving them in a worse place than before they started.

This person needs to take stock and see what is causing this pattern for them, such as a situation or person in their life. It could also be a coping mechanism they learned as a child, like eating ice cream to make you feel better. If it is from an emptiness in life, this is due to an energetic leak in their energy system caused by traumatic and verbal inhibitory imprints. By working on these imprints and the related emotions, such as abandoned, anger, anxious, betrayed, depressed, discomfort, grief, impulsive, lonely, sad, selfish, and ungrounded, one can start to shift this pattern and start to feel whole. This will automatically change the behavior of overindulgence over time.

| Colors to Use | Organs | Essential Oils | Crystals/ Stones | Archangels |
|---|---|---|---|---|
| Blue | Heart Stomach Feet | Peppermint Lavender Eucalyptus Rom. chamomile Frankincense Sandalwood Rose absolute | Rose quartz Bloodstone Amethyst Smoky quartz | Michael Raphael Jophiel Zadkiel Uriel Metatron Sandalphon Barachiel |

# Ineffective

When one feels ineffective, they can feel as if they are not accomplishing what they want to in life. There can be many reasons for this feeling. Some people just have trouble focusing to get things done. If this is the case, working on grounding is very helpful. Being grounded makes one more effective overall in life and increases focus and emotional stability. Sometimes the feeling of being ineffective is due to lack of action from being a perfectionist. The belief that everything you do has to be perfect prevents you from doing anything at all. Related emotions, such as fear of failure and being critical of yourself, should be addressed, as well as any related emotional verbal and inhibitory imprints, if perfection is an issue. Lastly, sometimes we feel ineffective if we are comparing ourselves to others. Remember that your path is different from theirs. While it is great to use others to inspire you, comparing yourself and feeling inadequate as a result is limiting and damaging. If this is why you feel inadequate, address any imprints and the emotions housed in them that relate to comparing yourself. Basic related emotions would be critical, embarrassed, fearful, flawed, hopeless, sad, and uncreative. Release these if they apply to start getting to the root of your ineffective emotion.

| Colors to Use | Organs | Essential Oils | Crystals/ Stones | Archangels |
|---|---|---|---|---|
| Violet Orange Indigo | Heart Lungs Spleen Stomach Liver/Gall- bladder Pancreas Bladder/ Kidney/ Adrenal Knees | Peppermint Lavender Bergamot Rom. chamo- mile Frankincense Patchouli Sandalwood Rose absolute | Rose quartz Bloodstone Amethyst Smoky quartz | Michael Gabriel Zadkiel Uriel Metatron Sandalphon Barachiel |

# Insecure

While we all have moments of insecurity from time to time, people who carry the feeling of insecurity all the time can be greatly affected by it. Feeling like they are not good enough leads people in one of two directions: either they become withdrawn, feel the need to explain themselves all the time, and are awkward, or they are over the top, putting themselves out there in a big way, which often involves putting others down. Regardless of the manifestation, the root is the same. Insecurity creates a soft underbelly, stemming from a feeling of inadequacy that often has its beginnings in childhood. Most of the time, something is said to the person, often repeatedly, that makes them question themselves. As a result, their actions start to reflect that new belief. They either withdraw, becoming an awkward wallflower, or deflect, becoming critical and cutting. One can overcome insecurity by working on the related imprints and accompanying emotions. Common ones are abandoned, anger, betrayed, fearful, guilt, rage, sad, and shame.

| Colors to Use | Organs | Essential Oils | Crystals/ Stones | Archangels |
|---|---|---|---|---|
| Red Green | Throat Heart Lungs Intestines Feet | Tea tree Lavender Bergamot Rom. chamomile Frankincense Patchouli Sandalwood Rose absolute | Rose quartz Bloodstone Amethyst Smoky quartz | Michael Jophiel Zadkiel Uriel Metatron Sandalphon Barachiel |

# Jealous

People who have issues with jealousy cropping up on a regular basis usually have emotional imprints with some sort of abandonment. This can be physical or emotional, but in general the person gets jealous because they are afraid of losing someone or something in their life. This is often coupled with the emotion of betrayal, such as being cheated on in a relationship or stabbed in the back by a friend or coworker. Imprints with these emotions tend to highly distort a person's perception of reality, making them highly sensitive to attention being taken off of them in some way. This can make them highly reactive, causing them to lash out even when the other person is not ill-meaning. Working on related emotions of abandoned, anger, betrayed, insecurity, powerless, and rage are helpful to release the feeling of jealousy.

There are other circumstances, though, where the jealousy is warranted, so to speak. If a person is not usually jealous but is feeling that emotion, it is probably your intuition telling you that something is up. Pay attention. Ask questions. And most of all, trust yourself.

| Colors to Use | Organs | Essential Oils | Crystals/ Stones | Archangels |
|---|---|---|---|---|
| White | Liver/Gall-bladder Pancreas | Lavender Eucalyptus Ylang ylang Bergamot Frankincense Patchouli Sandalwood Rose absolute | Rose quartz Bloodstone Amethyst Smoky quartz | Michael Raphael Chamuel Jophiel Zadkiel Uriel Metatron Sandalphon Barachiel |

# Lonely

There are a couple kinds of loneliness. One is when one is actually lacking interaction with others. At times there are extenuating circumstances that prevent interaction, but other times the loneliness is self-inflicted. The person may have imprints of abandonment or insecurity, which causes them to withdraw from others. This can also be caused by high levels of social anxiety. If this is the case, working on grounding, as well as addressing the root imprint of the social anxiety, is key.

In other cases, one can be surrounded by people and still feel alone. These people often put on a happy face, but inside they are struggling. They feel misunderstood or feel that if people knew the skeletons in their closet, they would be abandoned. The person energetically cuts themselves off from others, and this is what feeds the feeling. This type of loneliness can lead to depression or suicide and is often a huge shock to everyone that knows them.

If you are experiencing this type of loneliness, it can help to talk to someone about how you are feeling, as well as to start releasing the accompanying emotions, such as abandoned, anger, betrayed, depressed, fearful, hopeless, and sad. If you have traumas in your past, working on these imprints directly can help to heal your energy system so that you feel safe to connect with others again.

| Colors to Use | Organs | Essential Oils | Crystals/Stones | Archangels |
|---|---|---|---|---|
| Red Indigo | Heart | Peppermint Tea tree Eucalyptus Ylang ylang Frankincense Patchouli Rose absolute | Rose quartz Bloodstone Smoky quartz | Michael Raphael Chamuel Jophiel Zadkiel Uriel Metatron Sandalphon Barachiel |

# Manipulative

While this can be a learned behavior, it is usually how someone is wired, although life circumstances can cause the person to further develop this habit. People who manipulate tend to do it to get ahead in life and to get their way. It may have been necessary to develop their manipulation for survival, either emotional or physical. They often don't even realize they are doing it, and most of the time, it is not meant to hurt anyone. It is easy, however, for people with the tendency to manipulate to operate in shades of gray, so to speak, blurring the lines of what is socially and morally acceptable. They tend to rationalize their behavior, to themselves and others, to justify what they do and how they do it.

Most people have the ability to manipulate and have done it at one time or another. The advantage of knowing how is that you have the ability to spot it when it is happening to you. Takes one to know one, as they say.

If a person has the habit of manipulating to get ahead at the expense of others, it's a good idea to look at the underlying imprints that led to that behavior. What traumas or verbal inhibitory imprints are present that set the pattern? It's also important to look at the other emotions present in the imprint and start releasing those emotions as well. Some that may be present in the imprints are abandoned, anger, betrayed, guilt, rage, and sad.

| Colors to Use | Organs | Essential Oils | Crystals/ Stones | Archangels |
|---|---|---|---|---|
| Blue Indigo | Brain/Head Throat Heart Lungs Spleen Liver/Gall-bladder Feet | Lavender Ylang ylang Rom. chamomile Frankincense Patchouli Sandalwood Rose absolute | Rose quartz Bloodstone Smoky quartz | Michael Gabriel Raphael Jophiel Zadkiel Uriel Metatron Sandalphon Barachiel |

# Materialistic

While we like nice things, people with an underlying emotion of materialism tend to place this value above everything else. They have equated love, success, and fulfillment with objects or money. This is usually the way someone is wired, but it can be exacerbated by life events, especially the values of parents or caregivers.

People that carry this emotion at a high level often try to fill themselves up with material things to feel better. Oftentimes they reach a point in life where they realize that things don't make them happy. They feel lost and lonely as a result. Looking at the verbal and traumatic imprints that hold this emotion are the key to releasing it. Other emotions that often accompany materialistic are abandoned, betrayed, flawed, insecure, lonely, and unloved.

| Colors to Use | Organs | Essential Oils | Crystals/ Stones | Archangels |
|---|---|---|---|---|
| Green Indigo | Heart Spleen Intestines Liver/Gall-bladder Pancreas Knees | Lavender Ylang ylang Rom. chamomile Frankincense Patchouli Sandalwood Rose absolute | Rose quartz Bloodstone Smoky quartz Tourmaline | Michael Gabriel Jophiel Zadkiel Uriel Metatron Sandalphon Barachiel |

# Negative (With No Anger)

Having a go-to emotion of negativity can be wired, learned, or both. People who are predominantly negative have a heavy energy about them, and their energy system is arrested in several places and moves slowly in general. In order for negative people to change, they have to address the emotion of negativity, as well as related emotions such as anxious, depressed, fearful, and hopeless. In addition, working directly on one's mindset, using positive affirmations, can help to rewire them into a more positive place. Sometimes the behavior is modeled to them growing up. If this is the case, working on mindset combined with the related traumatic and verbal inhibitory imprints is necessary.

| Colors to Use | Organs | Essential Oils | Crystals/ Stones | Archangels |
|---|---|---|---|---|
| Red Orange Yellow | Throat Heart Spleen Stomach Intestines Liver/Gall-bladder Pancreas Bladder/ Kidney/ Adrenals Feet | Lavender Eucalyptus Ylang ylang Bergamot Rom. chamo-mile Frankincense Rose absolute | Rose quartz Bloodstone Amethyst Smoky quartz Tourmaline | Michael Raphael Chamuel Jophiel Zadkiel Uriel Metatron Sandalphon Barachiel |

# Overstimulated

Lights, noise, and motion are something that we get desensitized to, but a person who is overstimulated can get overwhelmed by any one of these things. These people are also energetically sensitive and are usually empathic. This is an aspect that oftentimes the person themselves isn't even aware of. It can be very frustrating to the person with sensitivity, because they just want to be "normal." But overstimulation can sometimes lead to anxiety attacks, crying fits, hyperventilation, headaches, and anger fits.

People who get overstimulated easily can help themselves out by learning how to ground. When the upper chakras are more developed than the lower chakras, it can result in an energetic imbalance, causing a lot of energy to stay in the head. Grounding can balance the energy load and help to prevent overstimulation, or at the very least temper the over reactivity that can come with this emotion.

| Colors to Use | Organs | Essential Oils | Crystals/ Stones | Archangels |
|---|---|---|---|---|
| Blue | Brain/Head Throat Spleen Stomach Intestines Bladder/ Kidney/ Adrenals Feet | Peppermint Tea tree Eucalyptus Rom. chamo-mile Frankincense Sandalwood Rose absolute | Bloodstone Smoky quartz Tourmaline | Michael Jophiel Zadkiel Uriel Metatron Sandalphon Barachiel |

# Overbearing

Overbearing is an emotion that is associated with control. People who are overbearing tend to feel that they can't control something in their lives and compensate by trying to create things around them the way that they want them. Parents are typically a regular culprit of this behavior with their children. While they rationalize that they are coming from a place of love, there is always fear mixed in, and this is what is driving their behavior. Being overbearing with kids is a no-sum game. Since these children aren't allowed to explore as they grow up and don't have permission to make mistakes, they often "go off the rails," so to speak, after leaving home, if not before. The normal process of emotional and behavioral modulation that would have normally been learned is absent in their development, and this can have detrimental consequences.

Anyone with a controlling nature can benefit from looking at where this emotion of being overbearing comes from. What events led to this behavior? Where in life does one feel out of control? Address the emotion of being overbearing along with related emotions such as aggressive, anger, anxious, controlling, critical, grief, guilt, hopeless, and powerless.

| Colors to Use | Organs | Essential Oils | Crystals/ Stones | Archangels |
|---|---|---|---|---|
| Blue Green Indigo | Throat Spleen Stomach Liver/Gall-bladder Pancreas Knees Feet | Lavender Ylang ylang Rom. chamo-mile Frankincense Sandalwood Rose absolute | Bloodstone Smoky quartz Tourmaline | Michael Jophiel Zadkiel Uriel Metatron Sandalphon Barachiel |

# Overly Independent

Being independent is a good thing, but being overly independent can lead to an imbalance in the sacral chakra. This is typically seen in women but can exist in men as well. Moms are a classic example of overly independent. They often learn this behavior from their own mothers. Overly independent people don't ask for help. They feel that they have to carry the load themselves and therefore are constantly giving to others and never to themselves. This is what causes the imbalance in the sacral chakra. Regaining that balance requires the person to receive. This can be receiving help with tasks or nurturing themselves.

Another form of being overly independent is when you feel that no one else can do something like you can. While this may be true, is that a big deal? Maybe you are the best dishwasher loader in the house, but that doesn't mean someone else can't do it from time to time. Learning to let go of controlling everything is essential if this is part of why you are overly independent.

If you struggle with this emotion, ask yourself who modeled this behavior to you. Next, look at the verbal inhibitory imprints behind it. Oftentimes we are programmed with sayings from childhood that we adopt as truth. Addressing these imprints is the key to relinquishing control and starting to put yourself as a priority for a change. Related emotions are abandoned, anger, anxious, controlling, critical, dramatic, hopeless, imbalanced, impulsive, overbearing, and resentful.

| Colors to Use | Organs | Essential Oils | Crystals/ Stones | Archangels |
|---|---|---|---|---|
| Violet | Brain/Head<br>Throat<br>Heart<br>Lungs<br>Intestines<br>Pancreas<br>Bladder/<br>Kidney/<br>Adrenals<br>Feet | Tea tree<br>Ylang ylang<br>Rom. chamo-<br>mile<br>Frankincense<br>Rose absolute | Rose quartz<br>Smoky<br>quartz | Michael<br>Jophiel<br>Zadkiel<br>Uriel<br>Metatron<br>Sandalphon<br>Barachiel |

# Overwhelmed

Being overwhelmed is a common emotion if you have a lot going on. It is also a common emotion for people who are inherently ungrounded or those that have a lot of traumas they need to process. These people may feel emotionally full all the time, and it doesn't take a lot for overwhelm to set in. People who have issues with being controlling or overly independent often struggle with overwhelm. If you have too much on your plate, delegate some things off of it—even if you have to hire some help.

Another common occurrence of overwhelm is when a person is being flooded energetically from Source. They may have so much energy coming in, with so many ideas and inspirations, that the pipeline gets clogged. It's like putting too much in a funnel and expecting it to go through quickly. Using the rod exercise in chapter 9 to clear this energy can be helpful if this is the case.

For people who get overwhelmed easily in life, looking at the traumatic imprints that lead to these triggers is key. Releasing the related emotions, such as anger, anxious, confused, controlling, fearful, hopeless, overstimulated, and ungrounded, can help to prevent overwhelm and even enable you to more easily see solutions in the moment.

| Colors to Use | Organs | Essential Oils | Crystals/ Stones | Archangels |
|---|---|---|---|---|
| Green | Lungs Stomach | Peppermint Tea tree Lavender Ylang ylang Rom. chamomile Patchouli Sandalwood Rose absolute | Rose quartz Amethyst Smoky quartz Tourmaline | Michael Raphael Jophiel Zadkiel Uriel Metatron Barachiel |

# Powerless

People who feel powerless have often experienced situations or interactions in their lives in which they feel as though they have no control. The emotion of powerlessness is all about perspective and attachment. When we are attached to an outcome and it doesn't go the way that we want, this can bring on an emotion of powerlessness. Traumatic situations can bring that emotion on strongly. The key is to not hold on to the emotion after the situation has passed.

For people with a general feeling of powerlessness that is pervasive, shifting the perspective and letting go can return your power to you. Sometimes there is truly nothing you can do about a situation. Letting go releases you from the energetic grip and energy of whatever it is that is happening. This can return you to a state of calm. If you are feeling powerless, look at releasing related emotions, such as abandoned, anger, controlling, frustration, hopeless, overbearing, and sad.

| Colors to Use | Organs | Essential Oils | Crystals/ Stones | Archangels |
|---|---|---|---|---|
| Red Orange Yellow | Heart Lungs Intestines Pancreas Knees | Peppermint Lavender Eucalyptus Ylang ylang Bergamot Rom. chamomile Frankincense Patchouli Rose absolute | Rose quartz Bloodstone Amethyst Smoky quartz Tourmaline | Michael Gabriel Raphael Chamuel Jophiel Zadkiel Uriel Metatron Barachiel |

# Rage

Rage is anger at a whole other level. People with rage often have violent outbursts. It can be uncontrolled anger. For some people, rage can be an out-of-body experience, where they realize what they are doing but they are disassociated from the act while it is happening. This is dangerous, because they have no control. This behavior is driven by traumatic and verbal inhibitory imprints, sometimes of extreme nature. Working on these imprints is very important in shifting this behavior and releasing the energy behind it. If you are prone to dissociative outbursts, it may be wise to seek help as you are working through your traumas. If you are fairly self-controlled, looking at the imprints as well as accompanying emotions to release will help release the rage. The emotions of abandoned, anger, anxious, betrayed, distrust, guilt, and overbearing can often be found with rage.

| Colors to Use | Organs | Essential Oils | Crystals/ Stones | Archangels |
|---|---|---|---|---|
| Indigo | Brain/Head | Peppermint | Rose quartz | Michael |
| Blue | Throat | Lavender | Bloodstone | Gabriel |
| Green | Heart | Eucalyptus | Amethyst | Raphael |
| | Lungs | Ylang ylang | Smoky | Chamuel |
| | Liver/Gall- | Bergamot | quartz | Jophiel |
| | bladder | Rom. chamo- | Tourmaline | Zadkiel |
| | Pancreas | mile | | Uriel |
| | Knees | Frankincense | | Metatron |
| | | Patchouli | | Barachiel |
| | | Rose absolute | | |

# Resentful

The emotion of resentfulness can take many forms but often stems from not speaking up for oneself. People who tend to get resentful are those that say yes too much, overwhelming themselves. Their perception is that others are not doing their fair share, but they don't feel as if they can speak up and ask for help or delegate. This emotion often goes hand in hand with being controlling and overly independent. Resentful people are often passive-aggressive in nature, which can make others uncomfortable. Most of the time, the other person doesn't know what is wrong and the resentful person won't tell them, even if asked.

Being resentful is often a learned behavior that is seated in being controlling or the feeling that one must shoulder a burden alone. Looking at the root imprint for these emotions can help to get to the bottom of resentfulness and its related emotions, such as anger, controlling, frustration, guilt, overbearing, overly independent, overwhelmed, and unable to speak up.

| Colors to Use | Organs | Essential Oils | Crystals/ Stones | Archangels |
|---|---|---|---|---|
| Green | Heart Spleen Intestines Liver/Gall-bladder Pancreas Knees | Peppermint Lavender Ylang ylang Bergamot Rom. chamomile Frankincense Patchouli Sandalwood Rose absolute | Rose quartz Bloodstone Amethyst Smoky quartz Tourmaline | Michael Gabriel Chamuel Jophiel Zadkiel Uriel Metatron Sandalphon Barachiel |

## Sad

While sadness can be related to depression, it is often independent of it. Sadness is typically a situational emotion but can be carried long-term. It often has its root in some sort of trauma, so thinking about and addressing the related imprints is important. Related emotions can be abandoned, betrayed, depressed, grief, guilt, and lonely.

| Colors to Use | Organs | Essential Oils | Crystals/ Stones | Archangels |
|---|---|---|---|---|
| Yellow | Brain/Head Heart Lungs Intestines Pancreas Knees | Peppermint Tea tree Lavender Eucalyptus Ylang ylang Bergamot Rom. chamomile Frankincense Patchouli Rose absolute | Smoky quartz Tourmaline | Michael Gabriel Raphael Chamuel Jophiel Zadkiel Uriel Metatron Sandalphon Barachiel |

# Selfish

Everyone should have a little of this emotion. It's healthy to look after yourself and put yourself first. However, people who do this at the detriment of others have an imbalance of selfishness. They have a blind spot for the needs of others and put little or no value on them. This can be wired into them from the beginning, but it is often exacerbated over time. Selfishness can come from not being taught to look at and address the needs of others. As children, these people are often catered to, waited on, and bought for without any bounds. They don't know any different. On the other hand, some people turn to imbalanced selfishness as a defense mechanism. They may have had to do this for survival growing up or fear that they cannot think of the needs of others and get ahead in life themselves. Imbalanced selfishness tends to contain a belief that there is not enough to go around. To address this emotion, look at when this behavior comes and tie it back to your imprints. Related emotions are abandoned, anger, controlling, critical fearful, imperceptive, manipulative, and materialistic.

| Colors to Use | Organs | Essential Oils | Crystals/ Stones | Archangels |
|---|---|---|---|---|
| Green | Throat Heart Intestines Pancreas Bladder/ Kidney/ Adrenals Knees | Tea tree Eucalyptus Ylang ylang Bergamot Rom. chamomile Frankincense Patchouli Sandalwood Rose absolute | Rose quartz Amethyst Smoky quartz Tourmaline | Michael Gabriel Raphael Chamuel Zadkiel Uriel Metatron Sandalphon Barachiel |

# Sleepless

Being sleepless can be caused by biological processes, but we are going to talk here about energetic ones. Typically, people who struggle with sleeplessness keep a lot of energy in their heads. They are ungrounded by nature, and their upper chakras are overdeveloped, causing an energetic imbalance. Doing grounding exercises right before bed can help to balance this energy.

If you tend to worry a lot, practicing letting go is also very helpful. Working on releasing emotions such as anxious, controlling, fearful, hopeless, and overwhelmed, which exacerbate being ungrounded, can relax your physical body and mind so you sleep better.

| Colors to Use | Organs | Essential Oils | Crystals/ Stones | Archangels |
|---|---|---|---|---|
| Blue | Brain/Head Lungs Spleen Intestines Stomach Bladder/ Kidney/ Adrenals | Peppermint Tea tree Lavender Eucalyptus Bergamot Rom. chamomile Frankincense Patchouli Sandalwood Rose absolute | Amethyst Smoky quartz Tourmaline | Michael Gabriel Chamuel Jophiel Zadkiel Uriel Metatron Sandalphon Barachiel |

## Stifled

When roadblocks come up in life, the feeling of being stifled often comes with them. This is usually a situational emotion, but if it is chronic for you, look at the other emotions and their roots to help shift the stifled feeling. Look at when this emotion comes up as a clue.

An inability to speak up for yourself or speak your truth, such as in having the same argument over and over again with your partner, can lead to feeling chronically stifled. This is due to your throat chakra being in an arrested state. Not being seen, heard, and understood can lead to feeling stifled. Consider working on related emotions of anger, depressed, frustration, hopeless, powerless, sad, stressed, unable to speak up, and unable speak your truth.

| Colors to Use | Organs | Essential Oils | Crystals/ Stones | Archangels |
|---|---|---|---|---|
| Green | Brain/Head Throat Lungs Intestines Liver/Gallbladder Pancreas Bladder/ Kidney/ Adrenals Feet | Peppermint Lavender Rom. chamomile Frankincense Patchouli Rose absolute | Rose quartz Amethyst Smoky quartz Tourmaline | Michael Gabriel Chamuel Jophiel Zadkiel Uriel Metatron Sandalphon Barachiel |

# Stressed

Most of us deal with chronic stress. It is typically the most carried emotion. Stress is meant to be a fleeting state. We should experience being relaxed most of the time, but for the majority of people, this is the opposite. When we are stressed, our energy system contracts. We unground ourselves and cut ourselves off from Source. Our blood pressure goes up and we don't absorb nutrients from the foods we eat. Chronic stress can create an addiction to the state of stress. When we are stressed, we release adrenaline, which fuels us further. However, this release of adrenaline can become an addiction. This can cause us to create more stress in our lives subconsciously or seek out dangerous activities to create an adrenaline release.

Breaking the habit of stress can take some lifestyle change as well as mindset change. Learning to stay grounded can help manage the things that you have to get done, which in itself can relieve some stress and create emotional stability. Delegating tasks can also help. Locating the source of stress is the first step. Next, look to your imprints to see if this is a learned behavior, as it is for most people. Was this modeled to you growing up?

Releasing stress along with related emotions, such as anger, anxious, fearful, frustration, hopeless, overwhelmed, overly independent, and resentful, can be helpful in shifting the stress pattern.

| Colors to Use | Organs | Essential Oils | Crystals/ Stones | Archangels |
|---|---|---|---|---|
| Green Orange | Brain/Head Heart Lungs Intestines Stomach Spleen Liver/Gall- bladder Pancreas Bladder/ Kidney/ Adrenals | Peppermint Lavender Ylang ylang Bergamot Frankincense Rom. chamo- mile Patchouli Rose absolute | Rose quartz Bloodstone Amethyst Smoky quartz Tourmaline | Michael Gabriel Jophiel Zadkiel Uriel Metatron Sandalphon Barachiel |

# Suicidal

Suicide is very serious, and if you are struggling with this emotion, get some help. Some people have suicidal thoughts from time to time, while others are consumed by them. Suicide is closely linked to depression, loneliness, neglect, and physical and emotional pain. Depression is the most common state that people are in when they commit suicide. Depression is a deep feeling of emptiness, like you are in a hole and there is no way out. It's a hopeless feeling, and that is often what leads people to suicide. Chemical imbalances in the brain are often pointed to as the cause, and while this is not untrue, it is important to address the energy system as well. People in this state of suicidal thought have very arrested energy systems and often have serious energy system leaks. They most often have holes in their aura and chakras, which cause their energy system to not be able to hold on to energy. One way to address this is by working on the traumatic and verbal inhibitory imprints. These are often the "infection" that causes these tears to occur in the first place. Working with an energy healer is also recommended. Related emotions can be abandoned, anger, depressed, detached, flawed, guilt, hopeless, lonely, overwhelmed, powerless, sad, tired, unloved, and unworthy.

| Colors to Use | Organs | Essential Oils | Crystals/ Stones | Archangels |
|---|---|---|---|---|
| White | Throat Heart Lungs Stomach Liver/Gall-bladder Pancreas Bladder/ Kidney/ Adrenals | Peppermint Lavender Eucalyptus Ylang ylang Bergamot Frankincense Rom. chamo-mile Patchouli Rose absolute | Rose quartz Bloodstone Amethyst Smoky quartz Tourmaline | Michael Zadkiel Uriel Metatron Sandalphon Barachiel |

# Temperamental

Being temperamental can be wired into someone from the beginning, but it can also be learned. People who are temperamental tend to pull their roots up when they get upset and throw all of the energy upward into their head. This is where grounding can add a great deal of emotional stability, allowing the person to have more control when they get upset. Staying grounded when you are triggered helps to prevent the impulsivity that comes with being temperamental. It can give you more time to think about your actions and to choose to react differently.

Not being seen, heard, and understood can be a trigger for most people and can cause a temperamental person to react. This is seen in young children, who do not have a full grasp on language to communicate their needs combined with no learned emotional control. It is also seen in adults that did not have their needs met as children. These adults learned to communicate with their temperament and often had parents that responded by giving them what they wanted. Or conversely, their parents did not give in, but their needs were disregarded. Either way, the pattern of expressing their temperament never changed, and when they get triggered, they pull their childhood behavior into their adult world and inappropriately express it. To heal this pattern, one has to go back to the emotional imprints and start releasing the emotions that are present there. Abandoned, anger, fearful, frustration, impulsive, manipulative, overstimulated, rage, stressed, ungrounded, and unloved are all related emotions that should be released when working with the emotion of temperamental.

| Colors to Use | Organs | Essential Oils | Crystals/ Stones | Archangels |
|---|---|---|---|---|
| Orange Blue Violet | Brain/Head Heart Lungs Stomach Intestines Liver/Gall- bladder Pancreas Knees | Peppermint Lavender Eucalyptus Ylang ylang Bergamot Frankincense Rom. chamo- mile Patchouli Rose absolute | Rose quartz Bloodstone Amethyst Smoky quartz Tourmaline | Michael Raphael Jophiel Zadkiel Uriel Metatron Sandalphon Barachiel |

# Tired

Being tired can be a product of not getting enough rest, eating the wrong foods, or lack of exercise. It can also be a product of emotional and mental stress. In the energy system, when someone is tired, there is not a lot of energy moving around. It is not necessarily restricted, but it is stagnant. The chakras are not really moving and pulling energy through. However, being tired can be the result of a high level of congestion in the chakras if it is the result of other emotions and energy being in the way of its movement. For example, if you have been working hard (mentally, emotionally, or physically) and you are in a good mood, moving around a lot, and really in the flow of things, you have been pushing a lot of energy through your system. This is a "good" kind of tired, where you feel accomplished and just need to rest. There is not much restriction, you are just tapped out. Replenishing yourself is your best bet.

If you are working hard (mentally, emotionally, or physically) but it is accompanied by high levels of stress and frustration and is not in alignment with you, this tiredness will have a good deal of congestion and restriction accompanying it. It's important to do emotional releasing so that your energy can flow again, in addition to getting much-needed rest. Accompanying emotions to clear are anger, fearful, frustration, overwhelmed, stifled, stressed, temperamental, uncreative, ungrounded, and unsuccessful. If you tend to put yourself in situations to overwork yourself, look at your imprints to see if this was modeled to you growing up. If so, work on releasing these imprint emotions to shift your belief that life has to be that way.

| Colors to Use | Organs | Essential Oils | Crystals/ Stones | Archangels |
|---|---|---|---|---|
| Red Yellow Orange | Brain/Head Lungs Stomach Bladder/ Kidney/ Adrenals Feet | Peppermint Eucalyptus Frankincense Rom. chamo-mile Patchouli Rose absolute | Amethyst Smoky quartz | Michael Gabriel Jophiel Zadkiel Uriel Metatron Sandalphon Barachiel |

## Unable to Express Self

Expressing ourselves is a big part of why we are here on this planet. Our unique being wants to share what it has with the world, and not being able to do that can lead to big problems in life. When we can't express ourselves, verbally or otherwise, it shuts our energy systems down. Depression can easily set in, and we become lost in life. If you are in a position where you can't express yourself, whether it be at your job, in your relationship, or in your culture, chances are this was modeled to you as a child. Sayings like "That's just the way it is" were probably repeated to you multiple times in various ways. Look at your traumatic and verbal inhibitory imprints to see if this was modeled to you. Releasing these patterns can dramatically open your life up, allowing you to see other pathways you can take to be happier. Other emotions to work on are abandoned, anger, depressed, frustration, fearful, guilt, overwhelmed, sad, shame, stifled, and unloved.

| Colors to Use | Organs | Essential Oils | Crystals/ Stones | Archangels |
|---|---|---|---|---|
| Blue Yellow Orange | Brain/Head Throat Lungs Spleen Bladder/ Kidney/ Adrenals | Tea tree Lavender Ylang ylang Bergamot Frankincense Rom. chamomile Patchouli Sandalwood Rose absolute | Rose quartz Amethyst Smoky quartz | Michael Zadkiel Uriel Metatron Sandalphon Barachiel |

## Unable to Speak Your Truth

This is similar to not being able to express yourself. In the case of speaking your truth, the throat chakra is specifically affected. When you cannot speak up, the throat chakra gets arrested and shuts down. People with this issue typically have a weak, quiet voice, or they sound sad. If they are not allowed to speak their truth for long periods of time, they can develop thyroid disorders or suffer repeated throat infections that may lead to having their tonsils taken out. This pattern is often modeled to them as children by their mother or father not being allowed to speak up for themselves. The person then subconsciously seeks out situations—jobs or relationships—that allow the pattern to continue. To break the pattern, look to the related imprints and release the emotions found there, such as anger, depressed, fearful, frustration, guilt, overwhelmed, sad, shame, stifled, and unable to express self.

| Colors to Use | Organs | Essential Oils | Crystals/ Stones | Archangels |
|---|---|---|---|---|
| Blue Yellow | Throat Heart Intestines | Tea tree Lavender Ylang ylang Bergamot Frankincense Rom. chamomile Patchouli Sandalwood Rose absolute | Rose quartz Amethyst Smoky quartz | Michael Jophiel Zadkiel Uriel Metatron Sandalphon Barachiel |

# Unclear

When one is unclear, they often have a lot going on in their minds, but really this is just a reflection of what is going on in their energy system. Being unclear is kind of like swimming in muddy water. Everything is stirred up and you can't get your hands around what to do in a situation or how you feel about it. This is an emotion that is particularly helped by journaling.

You really need to move the energy through you to get a handle on it. List out all of the emotions that you have about whatever it is you are unclear about. Go through the exercises in chapter 10 until you feel like things are clear. If you have imprints that reflect what you are unclear about, work on releasing the emotions in these imprints. Related emotions may be anxious, confusion, fearful, guilt, indecisive, insecure, overwhelmed, sad, stressed, unable to express self, unable to speak your truth, unsafe, and withdrawn.

| Colors to Use | Organs | Essential Oils | Crystals/ Stones | Archangels |
|---|---|---|---|---|
| Blue Yellow | Throat Heart Intestines | Tea tree Lavender Ylang ylang Bergamot Frankincense Rom. chamomile Patchouli Sandalwood Rose absolute | Rose quartz Amethyst Smoky quartz | Michael Jophiel Zadkiel Uriel Metatron Sandalphon Barachiel |

# Uncreative

We all have creative blocks from time to time, but some people just feel uncreative in general. Unique creative ideas are hard for them to come up with. Some of this is their wiring and some is from beliefs developed over time. Either way, creativity is mainly housed in the sacral chakra, and if creativity is lacking, it has to do with a weakness, congestion, or damage in that chakra.

If you feel as if you have never been that creative, look at your imprints to see when you have your first memory of feeling that way. Also think about whether this was modeled to you in some way by a parent or caregiver. Release the related emotions to this imprint such as confusion, fearful, frustration, overwhelmed, sad, shame, unable to express self, and unintelligent.

If you are normally creative and feel blocked, work on releasing the emotions above and breathe some white and orange light into the area. This will break up the congestion and replenish the chakra so that your creative juices can get flowing again.

| Colors to Use | Organs | Essential Oils | Crystals/Stones | Archangels |
|---|---|---|---|---|
| Violet Orange | Throat Bladder/ Kidney/ Adrenals Feet | Peppermint Tea tree Lavender Eucalyptus Frankincense Rom. chamomile Patchouli Sandalwood Rose absolute | Bloodstone Amethyst Smoky quartz Tourmaline | Michael Gabriel Chamuel Jophiel Zadkiel Uriel Metatron Sandalphon Barachiel |

# Underwhelmed

When nothing excites you anymore and everything seems hum drum, you may be carrying the feeling of underwhelm. This often happens when we need to make changes in our life. We are not in alignment with what we have been doing, but we keep doing it anyway. Underwhelm can also be a symptom of depression and tiredness. Ask yourself if being underwhelmed was modeled to you. If so, address this imprint.

To shift this state, work on releasing this emotion along with related emotions such as depressed, detached, frustration, sad, stifled, tired, unable to express self, and unmotivated.

| Colors to Use | Organs | Essential Oils | Crystals/ Stones | Archangels |
|---|---|---|---|---|
| Red Orange Yellow | Spleen Pancreas Bladder/ Kidney/ Adrenals | Peppermint Lavender Eucalyptus Ylang ylang Bergamot Frankincense Rom. chamomile Patchouli Sandalwood Rose absolute | Amethyst Smoky quartz Tourmaline | Michael Gabriel Jophiel Zadkiel Uriel Metatron Sandalphon Barachiel |

# Unforgiving

Forgiveness is not always easy, but it is necessary for our long-term health. Whether we are having trouble forgiving ourselves or someone else, it's important to release the energy you are holding on to. It can destroy you. People who have a habit of being unforgiving often feel as though they need to hold on to a grudge because the other person shouldn't "get away with" whatever they did. The problem is, this is not doing anything other than keeping the unforgiving person captive to the act and allowing the other person to have power over them. They are giving a lot of energy to someone who they feel wronged them and holding on to the toxic emotions that go with it. By forgiving that person, they are freeing themselves from the energy of it and allowing themselves to move on with their own life.

In the case of not forgiving yourself, this shuts down your entire energy system. You keep yourself captive to the event, freezing yourself in time. It's hard to do or think about anything else. Forgiving yourself sets you free to move on and just carry forward the wisdom you learned from having gone through it.

Think about the imprint of the event and work on releasing the emotions that are present there. Some may be abandoned, anger, betrayed, despair, fearful, grief, guilt, overwhelmed, rage, sad, and vulnerability.

| Colors to Use | Organs | Essential Oils | Crystals/ Stones | Archangels |
|---|---|---|---|---|
| Blue | Heart Lungs Pancreas Liver/Gall- bladder Knees | Lavender Eucalyptus Ylang ylang Bergamot Frankincense Rom. chamo- mile Patchouli Sandalwood Rose absolute | Rose quartz Smoky quartz Tourmaline | Michael Gabriel Chamuel Jophiel Zadkiel Uriel Metatron Sandalphon Barachiel |

# Ungrounded

Being ungrounded can be the way a person is inherently wired, or it can be a learned behavior. It is a contributing factor in a number of other emotional states and is of utmost importance to address. Ungrounded people tend to get stressed and frantic easily. They do things like leave their keys in the freezer or look for their cell phone while they are talking on it. Working on grounding can lead to greater emotional stability, better sleep, and less overwhelm. Releasing related emotions such as anger, anxious, fearful, impulsive, overwhelmed, and stressed can help, as well as addressing any ungrounding triggers in your emotional imprints.

| Colors to Use | Organs | Essential Oils | Crystals/ Stones | Archangels |
|---|---|---|---|---|
| Red | Stomach Bladder/ Kidney/ Adrenals Knees Feet | Peppermint Tea tree Lavender Eucalyptus Ylang ylang Bergamot Frankincense Rom. chamo- mile Patchouli Sandalwood Rose absolute | Rose quartz Amethyst Smoky quartz Tourmaline | Michael Jophiel Zadkiel Uriel Metatron Sandalphon Barachiel |

# Unintelligent

There is a quote that says, "Everybody is a genius. But if you judge a fish by its ability to climb a tree, it will live its whole life believing that it is stupid."

For people that struggle with the feeling of being unintelligent, this is often the case. They have not discovered their genius yet. On the way to discovery, they were compared to others and felt they did not measure up. This can keep them from exploring further to discover their purpose and passion. Look back to childhood to see if you can locate the first case of feeling unintelligent. It often occurs in elementary school. Work on releasing the emotions and events that led to that feeling, as well as related emotions. Then start exploring things until you find what you are good at. Related emotions to feeling unintelligent are angry, defensive, ineffective, insecure, lonely, sad, stifled, and unloved.

| Colors to Use | Organs | Essential Oils | Crystals/ Stones | Archangels |
|---|---|---|---|---|
| Violet Orange | Brain/Head Throat Spleen Intestines Liver/Gall- bladder Pancreas Bladder/ Kidney/ Adrenals | Peppermint Eucalyptus Ylang ylang Bergamot Frankincense Rom. chamo- mile Patchouli Sandalwood Rose absolute | Amethyst Smoky quartz Tourmaline | Michael Chamuel Jophiel Zadkiel Uriel Metatron Sandalphon Barachiel |

# Unloved

Feeling unloved often starts with our first experience of it from our parents. Strangely enough, we can actually equate the neglect and/or abuse that come with feeling unloved to what love is, since our parents are supposed to model that to us. This sets us up for relationships, romantic and otherwise, that mirror that experience. People who feel unloved or unlovable often have very weak boundaries and will bend over backward for everyone for love and acceptance. This often leads to them getting taken advantage of. They may be viewed as weak or naive by other people, but the truth is they just want to be loved and accepted. Energetically, they have several underdeveloped chakras: the heart, emotional, sacral, and root chakras are all in various stages of arrested development. They tend to pull at people they latch onto for acceptance, which can drain others and cause them to pull away, materializing the fear that the person has of being unloved and abandoned. Seeking love inside themselves is where they need to get to first to feel balance. In order to do that, they have to address the trauma of not being loved as a child. By addressing the traumatic and verbal inhibitory imprints that contain these events and related emotions, they can start to unravel this repeating pattern in their lives. Some emotions that might be related in the imprints are abandoned, anger, fearful, grief, guilt, rage, sad, shame, stifled, unintelligent, unsuccessful, and unworthy.

| Colors to Use | Organs | Essential Oils | Crystals/ Stones | Archangels |
|---|---|---|---|---|
| Green | Brain/Head Heart Lungs Liver/Gall- bladder Pancreas Knees | Lavender Ylang ylang Bergamot Frankincense Rom. chamo- mile Sandalwood Rose absolute | Bloodstone Amethyst Smoky quartz Tourmaline | Michael Gabriel Jophiel Zadkiel Uriel Metatron Sandalphon Barachiel |

# Unmotivated

All of us get bogged down from time to time and don't want to do things, but some people are chronically unmotivated. There can be many reasons for this. Sometimes they are just burned out. Another cause is that they are doing a job that is not in alignment with who they are. Their souls are unmotivating them in order to cause them to shift. In this case, it's important to listen and make a change. Not doing so can lead to physical ailments or accidents. Letting go can be difficult and can bring up emotions such as anxious, fearful, grief, unable to express self, unable to speak your truth, and unsafe. Explore your imprints and see if someone modeled this unmotivated behavior to you. Starting to work on releasing energy from these imprints can help you shift into a space to see options to get motivated again.

| Colors to Use | Organs | Essential Oils | Crystals/ Stones | Archangels |
|---|---|---|---|---|
| Red Green Indigo | Brain/Head Throat Heart Liver/Gall-bladder Spleen Feet | Peppermint Lavender Ylang ylang Bergamot Frankincense Rom. chamo-mile Patchouli Sandalwood Rose absolute | Bloodstone Amethyst Smoky quartz Tourmaline | Michael Gabriel Raphael Jophiel Zadkiel Uriel Metatron Sandalphon Barachiel |

## Unsafe

While this can be a temporary feeling for some, other people carry the feeling of being unsafe long-term. People that carry this emotion tend to have underdeveloped lower chakras and are inherently ungrounded. They tend to be hypervigilant and react to situations from a place of fear. This pattern most often starts early in life and is a product of an unstable or volatile environment. The feeling of being unsafe can fuel safety in the short term by being hyperaware of one's surroundings and reading the emotions of others diligently to gauge whether or not things are going to take a turn for the worse soon. People that feel unsafe tend to grow up quickly and may feel as though they didn't have a childhood. Throughout their life, they may attract people that keep this pattern in place because the pressure of being hypervigilant is a comfort zone. Keeping a high level of stress like this also peaks adrenaline often, which can become an addiction, causing the person to subconsciously seek out and create situations that are in some way unsafe.

This can be a hard habit to break, but it is possible. Working on the root imprints and diving into all aspects of them is key in changing this behavior. Releasing the accompanying emotions helps the energy system to mature so as to not have blind spots for stepping into unsafe situations as one moves forward in life. Related emotions to work on are abandoned, anger, fearful, frustration, sad, unable to express self, unable to speak your truth, unloved, unwanted, unworthy, vulnerable, weak, and withdrawn.

| Colors to Use | Organs | Essential Oils | Crystals/ Stones | Archangels |
|---|---|---|---|---|
| Green Yellow | Brain/Head Throat Heart Lungs Liver/Gall-bladder Stomach Intestines Pancreas Feet | Peppermint Lavender Ylang ylang Bergamot Frankincense Patchouli Sandalwood Rose absolute | Bloodstone Amethyst Smoky quartz Tourmaline | Michael Jophiel Zadkiel Uriel Metatron Sandalphon Barachiel |

# Unsuccessful

People with an underlying feeling of being unsuccessful often compare themselves to others. They try to make themselves fit in a box they weren't meant for and get frustrated that they aren't excelling. Societally, we are expected to follow certain tracks in life. Those that don't are often looked down on by peers and parents. It's important to remember that some of the most successful people did not follow the same course as everyone else. That is the very definition of extraordinary.

If you are feeling unsuccessful, look at where you are right now and ask yourself, do you like what you are doing? Is it a passion? Are you good at it? If it's a passion and you are still learning, you are in alignment with your path. If you hate it and are bad at it, do something else. If you have to, do a new thing part-time if what you are doing now is paying the bills. Break the mold of conformity and give yourself permission to explore.

Think about where your feeling of being unsuccessful is coming from. If it is from your family, start working on the traumatic and verbal inhibitory imprints that are related. If it is societal, think back to when you got the idea that you had to follow a set path (possibly elementary school) and work on the emotions in that imprint. Related emotions may be abandoned, fearful, overwhelmed, stressed, unable to speak your truth, unclear, unloved, unsafe, and unworthy.

| Colors to Use | Organs | Essential Oils | Crystals/Stones | Archangels |
|---|---|---|---|---|
| Indigo Orange | Brain/Head Heart Liver/Gall-bladder Stomach Bladder/Kidney/Adrenals | Peppermint Lavender Eucalyptus Ylang ylang Bergamot Frankincense Rom. chamomile Patchouli Sandalwood Rose absolute | Rose quartz Bloodstone Amethyst Smoky quartz Tourmaline | Michael Chamuel Jophiel Zadkiel Uriel Metatron Sandalphon Barachiel |

# Untruthful

People who have a strong habit of lying are uncomfortable with who they are at their core. They feel unlovable and are afraid of being abandoned. This core feeling of discomfort can grow into a pathological habit of lying about most things, even if whatever they are lying about doesn't matter at all. Sometimes it is for manipulation or to avoid confrontation, but oftentimes it is just to make others see them in a way that they think will be revered. Regardless of how often they are caught in their lies, their compulsiveness to keep lying never goes away. The only way to change this is to address the root cause, which is usually imprints that have to do with abandonment, being unloved, and sometimes survival. By working on releasing the energy from these deep wounds, they can start to speak their truth. Related emotions are abandoned, anger, fearful, ineffective, insecure, lonely, manipulative, unsafe, unsuccessful, unworthy, and vulnerable.

| Colors to Use | Organs | Essential Oils | Crystals/Stones | Archangels |
|---|---|---|---|---|
| Blue Green | Throat Heart Liver/Gall-bladder Stomach Intestines Knees | Lavender Ylang ylang Bergamot Rom. chamomile Patchouli Sandalwood Rose absolute | Rose quartz Bloodstone Amethyst Smoky quartz Tourmaline | Michael Gabriel Raphael Chamuel Jophiel Zadkiel Uriel Metatron Sandalphon Barachiel |

# Unworthy

This is an emotion that can start in the womb, and the pattern is repeated in one way or another throughout one's lifetime. It can be reinforced by parents or at school. The belief that one is unworthy helps to recreate circumstances that reinforce the belief. A person that feels unworthy acts in a similar way to one that feels weak or unloved. They have weak boundaries and will do things for others sometimes at the detriment of themselves.

Another aspect of unworthiness can manifest as anger or bullying. They project their feeling of unworthiness onto others in an attempt to make themselves feel better. This doesn't actually fix anything and can create bigger problems.

If you are struggling with the feeling of unworthiness, look to your childhood and remember the first instance that made you feel this way. Work on this imprint and any others that you remember in the process. Releasing related emotions such as abandoned, anger, flawed, insecure, sad, stifled, unintelligent, and unloved can help to move through the emotion of feeling unworthy.

| Colors to Use | Organs | Essential Oils | Crystals/ Stones | Archangels |
|---|---|---|---|---|
| Violet Orange Green | Brain/Head Throat Heart Lungs Stomach Intestines Pancreas | Peppermint Lavender Eucalyptus Ylang ylang Bergamot Rom. chamomile Patchouli Sandalwood Rose absolute | Rose quartz Bloodstone Amethyst Smoky quartz Tourmaline | Michael Gabriel Raphael Chamuel Jophiel Zadkiel Uriel Metatron Sandalphon Barachiel |

# Vulnerable

While vulnerability can actually be a strength in life, feeling vulnerable all the time is a different expression of the emotion. People that feel chronically vulnerable are typically missing part of their aura. At some point they had a great deal of damage to this part of their energy system, and quite possibly their physical body in the same area. The aura is the field around us. It helps us to feel safe. Without this shield, we can feel raw and exposed. It's hard to not take on a great deal of energy from outside sources, as there is no filter to keep it out. Since the rest of the energy system is exposed, it can become inflamed and very sensitive. This can make it difficult to control emotions, have clarity, or accomplish tasks.

Taking salt baths with baking soda, sandalwood, and frankincense oil can help rebuild the aura. Lighting candles while bathing can help to clear out energy that is impeding healing.

Working on the traumatic and verbal inhibitory imprints that are related to feeling vulnerable is also key. Related emotions are typically ones that affect the lower chakras, such as abandoned, fearful, insecure, powerless, unsafe, and unworthy.

| Colors to Use | Organs | Essential Oils | Crystals/ Stones | Archangels |
|---|---|---|---|---|
| Red Indigo | Throat Heart Lungs Spleen Pancreas Intestines Knees Feet | Peppermint Tea tree Lavender Eucalyptus Ylang ylang Bergamot Rom. chamomile Frankincense Patchouli Sandalwood Rose absolute | Rose quartz Bloodstone Amethyst Smoky quartz Tourmaline | Michael Gabriel Chamuel Jophiel Zadkiel Uriel Metatron Sandalphon Barachiel |

# Weak

When one feels weak, their boundaries are often not well-developed. They can't say no easily, and people walk all over them. They are generally people-pleasers and will do anything for others, even to the detriment of themselves. There is usually a high level of damage in their energy system from trauma that caused arrest in chakra and general energy system development. The outside world has no idea what they have been through, and they usually aren't ones to talk about it. To start the process of healing, gently breathing in white light is a good place to start. This will begin to break up the heavy congestion present and begin healing tears in the chakras and aura. After this is done for several days, begin addressing the traumatic and verbal inhibitory imprints. If there are many situations that come to mind, just start with the first and move on to the next, calling out and releasing the emotions that come up. Related emotions may be anger, fearful, guilt, overwhelmed, powerless, rage, sad, stress, unable to express self, unable to speak your truth, unsafe, unworthy, and withdrawn.

| Colors to Use | Organs | Essential Oils | Crystals/ Stones | Archangels |
|---|---|---|---|---|
| Red Blue | Brain/Head Heart Lungs Pancreas Bladder/ Kidney/ Adrenals Knees | Peppermint Tea tree Lavender Eucalyptus Ylang ylang Bergamot Rom. chamomile Frankincense Patchouli Sandalwood Rose absolute | Rose quartz Bloodstone Amethyst Smoky quartz Tourmaline | Michael Gabriel Chamuel Jophiel Zadkiel Uriel Metatron Sandalphon Barachiel |

# Withdrawn

Being withdrawn is a defense mechanism that is done for protection. When one is energetically sensitive, some environments can feel chaotic and overstimulate the person. They may feel vulnerable or raw, either emotionally or energetically, and withdrawing their energy from a situation may be the only way they know how to deal with it. People that have a habit of withdrawing have underdeveloped lower chakras. These are the physical reality chakras and make a person heartier both physically and energetically. Strengthening your energy system and working on grounding are ways to stay more included in your environment. There is typically trauma associated with this pattern, and it can start in the womb. If the child is rejected by the mother, this can create an arrest very early in life, preventing lower energy system development. Exploring the traumatic and verbal inhibitory imprints that occurred early in life and releasing related emotions can help to strengthen the person energetically, emotionally, and physically. Related emotions can be abandoned, anger, insecure, ungrounded, unloved, unsafe, unworthy, and weak.

| Colors to Use | Organs | Essential Oils | Crystals/ Stones | Archangels |
|---|---|---|---|---|
| Violet Orange | Throat Heart Intestines Stomach Liver/Gall- bladder Pancreas Bladder/ Kidney/ Adrenals Feet | Peppermint Tea tree Ylang ylang Bergamot Rom. chamo- mile Frankincense Patchouli Sandalwood Rose absolute | Rose quartz Bloodstone Amethyst Smoky quartz Tourmaline | Michael Gabriel Chamuel Jophiel Zadkiel Uriel Metatron Sandalphon Barachiel |

**Technique Index**

CPSIA information can be obtained
at www.ICGtesting.com
Printed in the USA
FSHW020107101121
86020FS